PRAISE FOR

'Suzanne's useful new book delves into the [...] competence are assessed and valued in the w[...] we accurately determine success in our teams; how we identify real expertise and how we reward genuine competence as opposed to perceived confidence – across all diversities in the workforce.'
Maggie Berry, OBE, Executive Director for Europe, **WEConnect International**

'Too often in today's society, we hang on to the perceived notion that a person's confidence should have a higher value than their actual ability. As ever, Suzanne cuts to the chase to tackle our tendencies head on, using her experience of coaching work with individuals and corporations to challenge, elucidate and educate.'
Annabel Bosman, Head of Relationship Management, **Royal Bank of Canada**

'Get ready to question what you thought you knew about confidence and come out with better answers about who has it and why than you did before.'
Professor Lynne Cadenhead, Chair, **Women's Enterprise Scotland**

'This brilliant book bust myths that affect who we hire and promote, as significant people with great skills and experience are too often being overlooked. It's time for change. This book challenges the status quo, reimagines a more just workplace and provides strategies for talent in all different forms to rise to the top.'
Emma Cashmore, Diversity and Inclusion Director International **Facebook**

'I have believed for quite some time that women, in particular, overrate confidence, and overestimate confidence they see in others. I'm delighted that this book studies this, researches the evidence, and articulates what we can all do about it with far more clarity than I ever could have done. I've learned a lot in reading this, and suspect you will too.'
Sharon Moore, MBE, Board Member, **CENSIS**

'By challenging our norms on confidence and indeed the definition of leadership itself, Suzanne Doyle-Morris has created a must-read for all those who are truly committed to creating more diverse and inclusive workplaces.'
Amanda Sourry, Former President, **Unilever North America**

'An expert analysis of the relationship between confidence and competence: essential reading for all those aiming to improve their progress in the workplace.'
Dame Veronica Sutherland, DBE, CMG (Former **UK Ambassador to the Republic of Ireland**)

'Suzanne Doyle-Morris draws on her practical experience in a wide range of organisations. The result is an insightful, engaging book that busts myths and challenges tired thinking.'
Jo Swinson, Former **Leader of the Liberal Democrats**

'Jam-packed with advice and real-life examples from leaders who have been there, done that.'
Vanessa Vallely, OBE, Founder, **WeAreTheCity**

Suzanne Doyle-Morris, PhD

The CON Job

Getting Ahead for COMPETENCE in World Obsessed with CONFIDENCE

WIT & WISDOM PRESS

The Con Job
Second edition 2021
Copyright © Suzanne Doyle-Morris, PhD
Published by Wit & Wisdom Press

ISBN 978-0-9562688-2-2

Typeset in Times New Roman and Trajan Pro
Cover design and layout by Wendy Rose
Printed and bound by Ingram Spark

LINKED IN
https://www.linkedin.com/in/suzannedoylemorris/

FOR WENDY, WHO'S OVERCOME THE CON JOB BETTER
THAN ANYONE I KNOW

ACKNOWLEDGEMENTS

There have been countless people who have helped at various stages of this book, from when the idea was just a 'twinkle in the eye' all the way through to final edits. I am grateful to have them in my life and the book is far better because of them.

In helping formulate my idea at various stages, I am grateful to both Erin Sines and Amy Cox as well as Lynne Cox and Leanne Sherry for being the sounding board I needed. Whilst having the normal crisis of confidences of my own, Danielle Krebs, Melody Pounsett, Nick Tsatsas and Sophie Taylor talked me down from my self-imposed ledge.

I am also grateful for honest feedback from Helen Sayles, Sally Penni and Kirsten Mackenzie. And I could never have proceeded without the support of my biggest fan and husband, Geoff Morris.

I must also thank my long-suffering editor Claire Bell, who no doubt looked at more drafts than she anticipated, Wendy Rose for her design work and Arlene MacKechnie, Jennifer MacFadyen and Mary-Jo Devlin for getting the message out there.

In terms of those I interviewed, I am hugely grateful for the contributions of Jenny Garrett, Amanda Jones, Sarah Burbedge, Georg Schmundt-Thomas, Neil Stevenson, Kate Atkin, Lindsay Porter, Toby Mildon, Kiera Tsenti, Reem Hayati, Maria Camilla Vargas, Alejandra Corona, Celine Jahn, Shoku Amirani, Rosemary McGinness, Nikki Slowey, Vanessa Vallely, Ben Capel, Silka Patel, Kainaz Gazder, Douglas Morrison, Lynne Cadenhead, Sarah Douglas, Martin Donnan, Elaine Eisenman, Barbara Ann King, Carol Stewart, Kiruba Sankar, Naomi Pryde, Elizabeth Uviebinené, Sam Friedman, Sandy Kennedy, Derek Watson. While she is not mentioned in the book, I also want to thank Martina Poulopati Gerhardt, whose advertising campaigns normalising the experience of menstruation and relatedly 'the c-word' were fantastically inspiring.

TABLE OF CONTENTS

ONE

HONESTY AND THE 'CON JOB'

*The greatest trick the Devil ever pulled was convincing
the world he didn't exist*
– Verbal' Kint in the 'Usual Suspects'

Before tackling the challenges of the workplace and how you can resolve them, let's set the scene for where confidence started. It's a big task, but worth exploring as it highlights how far off track we've become in what we now expect. This starts with understanding how much the meaning of confidence has skewed and become distorted over time. It's gone from a meaning that suggested *earning trust through your actions* to now being an almost showy sense of certainty and celebrated virtually above all other qualities.

Confidence does have a utility, but not as much as you think. First mentioned in early 15th-century writing, it was inspired from its Latin derivative 'con' and 'fidere' – which is about the *trust you have with* someone or something.[1] It started as something you earned; confidence was something *other people had in you*.

Indeed, we still have shades of that original expectation in our modern meaning. You still *confide* in people you think are ethical or would be responsible with your secrets. A *confidante* is someone who's proven, no doubt through a history of dependability, that they are reliable. However, we've moved too far away from these Latin roots, and not for the better.

Now most people do not equate confidence primarily with the trustworthiness *which was the linchpin of the whole definition*. Indeed, when we praise someone for confidence, it's largely about the show they are putting on. That's a million miles away from the synonyms for trustworthiness *on which the whole definition originally rested*: being principled, responsible, believable, credible, truthful, honest and upright. For the sake of all the institutions, businesses and hard-working individuals who'd benefit, we must get back to the original meaning.

---

1. https://www.etymonline.com/word/confidence

Over time, this original meaning cheapened and the eponymous 'con job' is now associated with everything from modern telemarketing frauds, illegal money transfer schemes, pyramid and Ponzi schemes. How exactly did this happen?

While the history of the con job goes back hundreds of years to fraudulent charities and quack medicines, it's only in the mid-19th century things start to get interesting in terms of 'confidence men' and their 'confidence jobs'. James Houston was the journalist who coined the term 'confidence man' in his reporting of the crimes of Samuel Thompson, a small-time swindler in the *New York Herald* in 1849. In his first article, Houston highlighted the *unearned trust* or confidence people placed in Thompson. The swindler, pretending to be a long-lost acquaintance, asked people to *place their confidence in him* by lending him a watch or money, a request with which they often complied.

The article described in detail the 'confidence process' that enabled Thompson to use his 'persuasive power' to influence 'sensible men' into giving their money and valuables to a stranger. Houston's editorial was a satire on the escapades of this small-time crook, particularly as Houston also was making a larger political point. He pointed out to readers how 'real' confidence men were those who operated on Wall Street. In his writing he pointed out they worked as financiers, who 'lived comfortably in palaces and made their scamming public'.[2]

While the paper initially put Houston's article in the inner sheets of the broadsheet, it became one of the most talked about pieces of the time. There followed a series of subsequent articles on Thompson's trials, and the way he subsequently duped prison guards, witnesses and legal authorities at every turn.

These articles and the term the 'confidence man' – the nickname Houston *gave* Thompson – captured the nation's imagination. The term had an immediate impact on journalism, literature, law and wider culture.[3] In later writing, the term 'confidence man' morphed into variations around a 'confidence trick' and 'confidence job'.

However, Houston's irony in the way he described Thompson as a 'genius operator' wasn't understood by all readers, who took his description of the criminal as a sign of Thompson's sophistication, boldness and genius. It was regarded as a genuine compliment.[4] The term 'confidence', which originally denoted *trust* devolved to become a trait to which we all aspire because of its impact – without any proof of credibility.

2. Houston, J. 1849 The Confidence Man on a Large Scale, *The Herald*, 11 July.

3. Bergmann, J. D. 1969 The Original Confidence Man, *American Quarterly*, (21)

4. Braucher, J. and Orbach, B. 2015 Scamming: The Misunderstood Confidence Man, *Yale Journal of Law and the Humanities* 249; Arizona Legal Studies Discussion Paper No. 13–37.

Indeed, in his 1940 book, *The Big Con*, Mauer explained the unique nature of confidence men when compared to theft: 'Although the confidence man is sometimes classed with professional thieves, pickpockets and gamblers, he is not really a thief at all as he does no actual stealing.'[5]

It's a point of pride a con man doesn't need to steal *as the victim literally hands over* the spoils. This resonates now in the way we give away power, opportunities and promotions to seemingly confident people – often by citing the confidence *they* have. We erroneously assume their competence matches their confidence.

MODERN CON JOBS

People now overuse confidence when talking about the traits they'd like to develop, even if they don't mean 'trustworthiness' as per its original meaning. Aspiring for confidence persists even as people theoretically appreciate confidence doesn't guarantee success *on its own*. Undoubtedly some of its appeal is in how confidence *hides* real skills deficits – something the 'con man' has known all along.

In truth, confidence is less of a zen-like umbrella under which good life experiences comfortably sit. Confidence actually depends on two things: your skill on the task at hand *and* the way the world has previously responded to you. However, this means certain people benefit more than others.

Let's look at how the *Oxford English Dictionary* now defines confidence: It's the 'feeling or belief that one can have *faith in or rely on* someone or something, the state of feeling certain about the *truth of something*'. While people recognise that definition, it's not how most people responded when I asked leaders about confidence.

Rather than focus on behaviours that suggest faith or reliance, people often described confidence via the self-promoting and showy qualities we've all come to recognise. As Houston could have told us nearly 200 years ago, this is ironic given confident people are often not the most trustworthy upon whom we should all rely.

For confidence to be truly meaningful and more valuable to us all, confidence as a concept needs a new definition. The new definition should start with the *sense that a situation will work out in your favour, most often based on previous experience*. This starting definition gives credence to the inner feeling we all experience. However, it *also* explains any differences in confidence we think we see between individuals, but also groups. It allows us to understand confidence in *context*.

---

5. Maurer, D. 1940 *The Big Con*, Random House, New York.

Suddenly, it makes more sense as to why certain people appear more confident than others. Once you understand *context*, confidence gets clearer as two things happen. First, confidence becomes much more achievable for a wider range of people, as we recognise a broader set of behaviours.

Additionally, we can then understand *why* certain people interact with others in a way suggesting optimism, again borne out of prior experiences. For example, if you contribute in meetings and others respond: 'Great point!', your confidence will cumulatively grow. However, if your points are routinely ignored and your ideas 'accidentally' credited to others, that too would have an impact. Unfortunately, as we'll see, this response happens far more frequently for those from historically disadvantaged groups compared to the group I'll call the 'status quo'.

CONFIDENCE IN CONTEXT

Understanding the status quo, and how people *respond* to confidence in different groups, is vital in developing a sustainable sense of confidence. A few years ago, I got a call from an international law firm asking for my help in getting more of their female employees onto their partnership track after a merger. This type of work had been my bread and butter based on my PhD work. As part of that project I conducted focus groups; some with men and others just with women, all of whom were identified as 'high-potential' by the firm.

These were the employees whom management wanted to progress up the career ladder, ideally to partnership. As part of these sessions, everyone was friendly, self-assured and articulate in their beliefs about what the firm did well – and what it didn't. I asked if people felt 'confident' they'd make Partner. The response from many of the women was: 'I'm confident I'll be a Partner somewhere, but maybe *not here*.'

As people shared their observations, one woman relayed her memory of an e-mail sent by the new senior leadership team made up of the senior and managing Partners and all the practice area heads of the two merging firms. This e-mail was a 'welcome to the new team' ostensibly sent to boost morale, saying all were valued by the 'new firm'. It came complete with a 'team photo' of the new leaders, highlighting the lack of diversity.

One Senior Associate pointed out all of the nine new leaders were men and mostly White, something she'd theoretically known. She said it hadn't 'sunk in' until she looked at the picture of their smiling faces. The women all laughed and shared their own reactions to also receiving that e-mail, sent nearly *two years beforehand yet still remembered* – long before I'd arrived.

16

In the subsequent sessions with the all-male groups, I again asked if people thought they'd make Partner. Certainly, not all men claimed they'd land, or even wanted the 'prize' of partnership. However, in their comments partnership seemed much more possible, if not *probable* for this group.

Interestingly, when I asked if anyone remembered receiving that company-wide e-mail, none of the men recalled it. They wrote off my query, explaining 'we get a lot of emails'. However, this group was optimistic that *if* they wanted to, they could achieve Partner status at *this* firm.

When I was hired, senior leadership reasoned the lack of women in their partnership was due to women's lack of confidence or the fact they all 'left to have babies'. In fact, I pushed to do exit interviews with four women who had left in the previous year. This was not something they'd originally asked me to do in the brief.

As I made those telephone calls, I discovered *none* of the women were at home full time. All were working for other organisations or in law firms where they had made partnership. This was where I first started to unpick the vital difference between confidence in oneself *versus* confidence in the system. As I was discovering, there was a vital relationship between your confidence and the belief you'll progress *in that environment.*

This is something we need to address, as too often these types of confidence are lumped together. This means outsiders to that system, or as I'll call them, the 'non-status quo' are blamed for their own 'lack of confidence'. Worryingly, too few people look at *why* these outsiders no longer have the confidence they did on the day they were first hired.

Getting to understand these issues is vital as it will save countless amounts in 'confidence-training' and the cycle of self-blame inherent in thinking confidence is always just out of reach. This particular project could have happened at *any* of my traditional clients; banks, technology firms, engineering consultancies, pharmaceutical companies – or indeed where it did start; law firms.

What's important is that it started my journey into realising our push for 'confidence' was ultimately a hoax, a fallacy and a convenient excuse. This con job contributes to the lack of progress amongst outsiders – the non-status quo. However, it's something we could all change if we questioned how we think about the value of confidence. We need to realise that all that glitters is far from gold.

ULTIMATE CON JOB

I'll be honest, this isn't a journey I wanted to take. I wasn't looking to redefine confidence. As it is, confidence is already probably one of the most commonly used, if not misunderstood, words in the English language. It's a sexy word – something we'd all like to be. And far more appealing than it's seemingly boring corollary: 'competence'.

However, competence *deserves to be the sexy word* when compared to confidence – but it just isn't. What would your reaction be if, before being introduced to a future mate, a friend tells you 'You two have got to meet, they'd make someone a very competent Partner!' It's not compelling or exciting; more akin to the 'I'm washing my hair' type of response it would likely get.

In my coaching work, I ask every new coaching client what they'd like to achieve from our sessions. They don't always mention a specific promotion or a new role. They rarely say they'd like a pay rise specifically. Instead, they say they'd like greater 'confidence'. Confidence, as we'll see, is a pretty easy sell. It's viewed as *the shortcut* to all of those things. It's short for 'I want to progress, for my comments to be heard and to be offered interesting opportunities'. Confidence, it seems, delivers the goods and makes everything better.

In fact, a lack of confidence is often why new clients are referred to me in the first place. Previous clients tell their friends that 'building confidence' is what I do. They left our sessions more confident about the way forward and acting more strategically about what it will take to get to their end goal. But the truth is, I *don't focus* on confidence with clients.

Instead I focus on building their *competence*, which then creates a compelling sense of direction, purpose and ultimately confidence. Let's be clear, my clients are most often technical experts in the areas in which they specialise: commercial law, cancer research, intellectual property, international taxation, cryptocurrencies, derivatives markets and auditing are amongst a few areas I'll never understand. I know virtually *nothing* about these things, nor could I ever pretend to.

Instead, I work with them on their competence in managing their stakeholders, their goals and the impact they have on others. For this, we work on their *competencies* in their communications, reading others, and standing up for themselves and their team. If you can get these competencies right, you'll be a heck of a lot closer to confidence. However, I'm still not convinced confidence should ever be the end goal.

For over two decades, I've worked on gender balance issues, my PhD topic at the University of Cambridge. Now, after all the subsequent speeches to audiences, advising organisations and coaching, I've come to believe that we need to challenge the pursuit of confidence as the final destination. It's a con job, a hoax, a fallacy to value what is both a fleeting feeling and a relatively worthless trait so highly.

What do we risk when we value confidence so highly? Our expectations of 'confidence' are far too binary: either you have it, or you don't. We all know confident people whose confidence isn't hindered by their lack of expertise. They use confidence to hide a hollow interior. Similarly, we also all know people whose apparent 'lack of confidence' hides just how accomplished and insightful they really are. We risk rewarding the very people of whom we need to be a bit warier and overlooking the people who could add real value.

I'm also concerned a perceived lack of confidence can turn into a convenient excuse for leaders to not invest in some of their best employees. It's easy to write off swathes of people as 'not high potential' simply because they don't exhibit confidence in the way leaders recognise from their *own* career trajectory. Worse yet, it means we don't get the leaders we need – the competent deliverers who know their stuff. Let's be clear: competence is how good you are at something, confidence is how good you *think* you are, but as we'll see, there's little overlap between the two.

The reality is most of us already have more confidence than we need and in areas where we can't all be top performers. Most of us think we give presentations and manage colleagues 'better than the average'. Similarly, most of us believe we are healthier, drink less, are smarter and weigh less than other people. Most of these are actual objective metrics where 'average' can and has already been calculated – which, if we all are 'better than average', renders the term average nonsensical.

We all know what it's like at times to feel like an outsider, someone who is not of the status quo. Most of my clients have felt like this, as they are most often women working in male-dominated fields. However, the more I looked at confidence – who has it, who doesn't and how it's judged – the more I saw how many more 'outsiders' were also affected, again simply because, like most of my clients, they are less likely to be part of the status quo.

Being non-status quo may mean that you work in a different country from which you are born, you have a disability, or you are one of just a few from your racial group in your organisation, just to name a few contextual differences. But just like the women with whom I've historically worked, for these groups, being the non-status quo also affects both how much confidence they have and *how well they are received* when they do display it.

It's easy to tell people to 'blag it', to 'big themselves up' or perhaps the most common, to 'fake it until you make it'. However, doing so will always leave you feeling a bit exposed and fearful of being found out. As we'll see, sustainable confidence truly only comes *after* you've developed competence.

Does it matter which comes first: competence or confidence? It matters indeed. Otherwise, we encourage people to develop 'confident' traits with little competency. That serves no one and undermines the wider good. It also means we risk overlooking people who don't identify with 'status quo' versions of confidence in the first place. Additionally, we penalise non-status quo people who demonstrate confidence – but in ways we're not accustomed or *comfortable* seeing in non-status quo members.

LACKING CONFIDENCE ISN'T THE ISSUE

In writing this book, my aim is to get under the skin of a self-limiting belief, created and supported by the experiences of hundreds of my clients either in training sessions, Board meetings or individual coaching sessions. It is a belief that one of the key things holding many people back is *their lack of confidence*. This rationale and 'self-inflicted problems' are laid at the feet of many outsiders or non-status quo people.

While my professional background is in gender, this issue is more profound and nuanced than 'men versus women'. Furthermore, if certain groups are truly less confident, we need to understand *why*. They did not become under-confident in a vacuum. As anyone who has watched a baby explore and toddle off in any direction knows, we are all born very confident! Instead, our confidence is reliant mainly on *how the world responds to us*.

I did not write this book alone. Instead, nearly 40 senior leaders – both men and women – gave me their insights on these topics. They helped me make sense of multiple issues surrounding confidence and competence and how our identity impacts them all. For example, as we'll see, women have long been the biggest consumers of self-help books, of seeking confidence.

If you further 'professionalise' confidence-building pursuits, you'll notice women also outpace men in terms of completing advanced qualifications. Similarly, as we'll discuss, proportionally, more Black, Asian and Minority Ethnic (BAME) students enrol in higher education than their White counterparts. In both cases, advanced degrees should hardly *diminish* confidence. Shouldn't those educational gains have led to *more progress* for these groups, both in their careers but also in building their confidence?

Additionally, if lack of confidence was truly holding employees back, wouldn't the amount of confidence training many companies have invested in *for decades* have fixed this issue by now? Most people take up advanced degrees and confidence courses on the assumption it will speed progression. However, 'getting ahead' isn't shared around the population evenly, even amongst those with most training.

Our expectations of the behaviours *that count* is what matters. The way we currently define confidence is outdated and inaccurate. 'Confidence', and the way we expect to see it displayed to move up the ladder, doesn't work for far too many people. Is 'table-thumping', 'blagging it' or interrupting others *actually a valuable skill*?

How beneficial to an organisation is self-promotion when you work in a team – as almost everyone does? These are all behaviours that appear to fall under the heading of demonstrating 'confidence'. Yet they serve no one. Instead, they hold back those who could contribute more, but for whom bravado doesn't resonate.

In my interviews with clients, I'm often left thinking: how does our tendency to reward outdated versions of 'confidence' overlap with rewarding younger versions of the people already in power? Furthermore, what's the cost and risk of overvaluing confidence? Why do we not spend more time looking at the *upsides of under-confidence*? What would it look like if we were to redefine confidence so that it worked for a broader range of people? This book answers those questions.

It's about how these profound, yet ill-defined words like confidence and competence operate. It's how to become more of one – confident – by first focusing on the other – competence. This approach is both authentic and maintains your integrity. This is something any leader should be aiming for – as should the companies that promote them. If not, you're 'faking it' without ever quite 'making it'.

Ignore these ideas and you will continue to focus on how you don't quite live up to increasingly outdated expectations of confidence. Plus, you'd miss the hidden way competence is the only *real way* to build a grounded and sustainable sense of confidence. Take these lessons on, and you'll set yourself apart as a grounded, self-aware and authentically confident leader.

STATUS QUO VS EVERYONE ELSE

The issues I will raise draw on the experiences of women, Black and minority ethnic groups, people from different socioeconomic backgrounds, introverts, the physically disabled and those who have worked across cultures. Along with looking more clearly at the status quo, they are a starting point for this discussion. While each of these groups is worth a book about how they relate to confidence on their own, I can merely scratch the surface.

'Surface scratched', we can also identify how confidence is displayed and reacted to among people with these identities. I seek to be a Partner in creating a fairer workplace, not a saviour. As someone who often sits too comfortably amidst the status quo myself as a White heterosexual woman, I merely want to draw the attention of others to the experiences of those with whom they might not immediately identify.

You'll see throughout I use terms such as 'outsiders' but also 'historically disadvantaged' and 'under-represented'. However, the most common way I'll refer to people revolves around whether they are part of the status quo or not. I use this term because I'm also calling out the power inherent in this status. For the purposes here, 'non-status quo' refers to those less likely to sit within the 'status quo' of senior people running organisations. The status quo are the people in charge of deciding what behaviours matter and what we *expect* from confidence.

For argument's sake, where you work the status quo (that is, people who hold the most seniority) may be Black, disabled women. However, if that is the case, you'd statistically be in a real minority amongst the types of clients I have in Europe and North America. In these settings, I have yet to come across any large organisation that is run *primarily* by non-status quo leaders in senior management. Even so, if this *is* where you work, the power of the status quo remains: those Black, disabled women would set the tone for what gets rewarded and what doesn't.

In the organisations where I consult and present, however, the status quo are overwhelmingly held by White men. These men are predominantly heterosexual, native speakers of the language in which they operate, often from privileged backgrounds, and able-bodied. Let's be clear, you don't have to fit all of these criteria to be part of the status quo.

However, the reality is that the more categories you do match, the more likely you are to at *least identify* with the status quo. Furthermore, I don't mean that all men who fit that description have an automatic pass to success. Instead, they are just statistically more likely to get to the top than people who have less in common with those in power.

You'll see I mention ethnic background where relevant. When interviewing, I asked people from historically under-represented groups how they preferred to be recognised. Aggregating identity is a challenge. I use language and identity as defined by the norms adopted in the country in which the research was conducted. This means there is not one single categorisation that encompasses all nations. Instead, when citing research, I'll use the term the authors did.

For example, in American research, 'Black people' often refers to African Americans. However, even in the US, not all Black people are African American, so not everyone identifies with that term. In the US, the term 'people of colour' is also frequently used and includes all non-White people inclusive of African, Latinx, Asian, Arab and Native American (ALAANA) communities. Unless otherwise specified, in most research, mixed-race people are also included in that category.

In Britain, BAME refers to all Black and Minority Ethnic people. For the people I talked with from this background in the UK, this is a phrase I've used. For most research I cite, people from BAME are categorised together, mainly because they are in a statistical minority compared to the White status quo, but as we'll see, that too is changing.

Let's be clear, I am not defining people by the challenges they face. Instead, I'm highlighting that particular challenges can affect the confidence we see in these groups. As we'll see, this sheds light on *how we react* when people from under-represented groups demonstrate confidence. I do this ultimately to highlight how more equitable definitions of confidence could serve a much broader population than simply a definition that favours a few.

AN IRONY

As an American by background who has lived in the UK for over 20 years, I recognise the irony of me asking you to lower the value you put on confidence. After all, it seems 'unbridled confidence' is one of America's chief exports. However, we need robust conversations about what we value. Is the choice between promoting people skilled at 'profile raising' or rewarding those great at their job? How much better off would we be if we rewarded less talk and more action?

People in Europe sometimes joke that my 'Americanness' makes me seem confident, as if it's a trait they hand out with the birth certificates. Like most people, I have days when I appear confident and others when I'm a lot less so. In those latter days, I focus on doing more of what got me this far – my competence. However, it's not enough simply to 'be better' if we don't also address our obsession with confidence.

Despite how this all sounds, I don't want you to be less confident. Instead, simply ask yourself if confidence should be the gold standard for determining progression. I believe we use it too frequently as an excuse for not promoting 'less confident' people who are always improving. It's a variation on the excuses I hear around: 'I'd like to promote her, but she's not that ready yet'.

Blaming a lack of confidence in others allows the speaker to evade personal responsibility for her development or even their judgements. We can continue to train people from under-represented backgrounds in all that they are perceived to be lacking. However, a better idea would be to help people see the far higher value in competence, not confidence.

This is something with which I personally identify. On the day I collected my PhD from the University of Cambridge, a neighbour denigrated my achievement with the perceived 'ultimate criticism'. She said to a friend of mine: 'I don't even think Suzanne's that smart. She's just a hard worker.' My friend assumed I'd rage against the slur, but I told her: 'She's right, I'm no genius – but I can work hard and keep going.' I'm far from brilliant, more just masochistically diligent.

But here's the beauty of it: if you can be the hard worker and own the confidence *that* gives you, you'll be ahead of the pack. When people tell me I'm 'productive', 'reliable' or even 'earnest', I take it as a compliment, just like I want you to. They are far from the sexiest terms, but I'll take them.

There are no superheroes in real life, just a daily choice between action and inaction. Most people won't put the advice we'll cover into practice. They'll search for a quick fix to a confidence that never truly delivers. There is no 'shortcut' to confidence any more than there is one to intelligence. But I can help you get to that confident feeling, *via* your competence, faster.

You may be thinking, 'I'm working. I have a decent life. Is worrying about my confidence just a first-world problem?' In some ways it may be. However, I'd argue *not* progressing is the far bigger problem than labelling this as an issue affecting only the privileged. Not progressing is a problem for *who you could become*, but also for the wider workforce. Ultimately, confidence problems will limit your impact in the world.

Certainly, we will delve into tactics to improve your confidence. Oddly enough though, *focusing on your competence is the single biggest thing you can do* to improve your confidence. It is what real experts do because they recognise the more you understand your field, the more there is to unpick and discover. Beware the person who says they have all the answers. If you know your stuff, you'll know that having 'answers' primarily leads to better questions and an appreciation for the nuances. That's real expertise.

Myth of meritocracy in a global pandemic

Much of what we call 'confidence' is based on the behaviours we expect from heterosexual, able-bodied, extroverted White males in the West as they hold the most power in most organisations. Let me start by saying I don't believe these men are all the same. I am humbled by female readers of my previous books who tell me: 'I loved 'Beyond the Boys' Club', but my husband needs it more than I do.' I recognise confidence troubles many who on face-value, appear to be part of the 'status-quo'. For me, a better goal for us would be to redefine confidence, so it engages a far wider range of people.

However, that doesn't diminish the historic power of the status quo. Collectively, they set the tone for terms like 'merit', 'commitment' or 'high-potential talent' – all of which look different based on who is doing the judging. They also determine, even if subconsciously, what 'confidence' looks like until it appears to be a virtually agreed-upon term, even in only modelled by a small subset of these workers. This historic definition might work if all the people who showed confidence were received equally well, but they aren't. We praise status quo members for being a 'take-charge, no-nonsense kind of guy' while rebuking others as 'aggressive', 'bossy' or 'angry' for the same behaviours.

Let me be clear, I'm also not presenting either research or the experiences of the people I spent time with to undermine the success of others. My goal is to highlight how different groups' ability to progress is affected by far more than what they can affect as individuals. Instead, it also rests on how the status quo defines 'confidence' and how much trust we put in the confidence they display.

As I readied the book for publication, that trust was being sorely tested as Covid was sweeping the globe in early 2019. I never expected to witness first-hand the inherent dangers in overvaluing confidence above competence so lethally on the world stage. Public warnings were issued by skilled professionals as early as January, yet we were reassured by leaders who felt a 'confidence-first' approach was a priority over well-distributed medical supplies, rigorous testing or consistent national policies. As a result, we are still counting the millions globally who paid for this approach with their lives.

Instead, who's left to actually wage war on this invisible killer? Not the hubristic leaders whose denial of the scale of the problem has cost countless lives. Instead, our lives literally depend on the genuinely competent; medical and research staff, transportation workers and delivery drivers, sanitation workers, shop keepers and carers. We can clap for them all day long, but these brave and competent people are routinely underpaid and largely invisible, mirroring the way competence has been undervalued to date.

SELF-DOUBT SERVES THE STATUS QUO

We too frequently assume confidence and competence are interchangeable. We mistakenly think demonstrating confidence means the person is competent and vice versa. This false assumption is helpful for the status quo, as it creates self-doubt in the non-status quo. In fact, your self-doubt is the greatest tool the status quo uses to remain in power.

The problem with saying women or other groups of people aren't as confident is that women have internalised this myth, as have men. Men feel they are supposed to be more confident than perhaps they are or are entitled to be. Equally, women can blame their lack of progression on 'low self-confidence' and not question the systems in which they work. Self-blame is very convenient for the modern workplace.

It is easy to reach for meritocratic explanations when talking about pay and progression gaps, particularly from leaders. It legitimises both the status quo and a leader's own career progression. Self-serving assumptions make inequality regrettable, but an ultimately fair result in a competitive job market. A 'lack' of confidence amongst the non-status quo shouldn't be surprising. It explains the punitive treatment they get when confident enough to demand better treatment.

By creating a system where certain people feel less confident, they become likely to challenge gaps at work. This self-blame and quiet acceptance of inequality affects everything from leadership teams that don't look like their consumers to gaps in pay packets between groups. This internalisation of blame runs deep as research shows female university students will pay themselves less than they will pay male students who are doing *the same job*.[6]

If you believe the idea women are less confident, you'll internalise that and act accordingly – 'stereotype threat' in action. These feelings about the supposed equity in pay gaps continue even after we've entered the workforce.[7] If you buy the myth your lack of progression is solely up to you and that you might not be worth more, the status quo doesn't need to lift a finger to change.

This challenge resonates for Lynne Cadenhead, the Chair of Women's Enterprise Scotland (WES). She has set up numerous companies in multiple sectors. WES promotes growth in female entrepreneurship across Scotland via advocacy and policy work. Has Cadenhead seen people overlooked because of their perceived lack of confidence? Exasperated, she says: 'Every single day. It's one of the most frustrating things I ever see.'

6. Major, B. 1992 Gender Differences in Comparisons and Entitlement: Implications for Comparable Worth, *Journal of Social Issues* 45(4): 99–115.

7. Desmarais, S. and Curtis, J. 1997 Gender and Perceived Pay Entitlement: Testing for Effects of Experience with Income, *Journal of Personality and Social Psychology* 72: 141–150.

Under-confident or Simple Realism

How would you feel if you entered a party where those making the most admired jokes, commanding the biggest audiences and eating the best food were all people who appeared to be nothing like you? Would you feel out of place? Would you honestly think: 'This looks great. I think I'll stay all night!' Probably not, as even subconsciously you'd recognise your chances of 'belonging' were pretty slim. Would you open up about yourself? If you left early, you'd no doubt make your excuses, but you'd unlikely talk about how unwelcome or 'different' you felt.

If anything, after your early departure people might blame your poor social skills, your lack of motivation in getting to know others, but they'll *also likely blame your lack of confidence*. So, if we think certain groups of people are less confident, it begs a simple question. Are they truly less confident, or just realistic about their relative chances of success, particularly amongst status quo groups?

Confidence is used as a catch-all phrase. As we've already discussed, blaming a *lack of* confidence is far easier than addressing what eroded their self-belief in the first place. It's worth asking, do non-status quo people adapt their aspiration levels based on what they'll *likely* achieve? When facing the reality of biased pay structures and promotion tracks how confident should you expect to be?

For example, in the UK, female managers have to work 14 years *past* the pensionable age of 65 to earn as much as their male counterparts over their career. This hardly fosters confidence or it's related cousin; optimism.[8]

By statistics alone, in many ways women should feel more confident than men: women are earning more degrees globally and better academic grades than men.[9] However, these accolades don't translate into how women rate themselves. Nor does it stop male boasting: in a survey of MBA students, 70% of female students rated their performance as *equal* to their co-workers, whereas 70% of men rated themselves *higher* than their co-workers.[10]

Tomas Chamorro-Premuzic, who has written on extensively on people analytics observed in his book:

8. Houghton, J. 2014 Most Female Managers Would Have to Work up to 80 to get Equal Pay, *Chartered Management Institute*, 19 August 2014.
9. Chamorro-Premuzic, T. and Furhnam, A. 2006 Intellectual Competence and the Intelligent Personality: A Third Way in Differential Psychology, *Review of General Psychology* 10(3): 251–267.
10. Eagly, A. H. 2003 More Women at the Top: The Impact of Gender Roles and Leadership Style, in *Gender: From Costs to Benefits*, ed. U. Pasero, Westdeutscher Verlag, Wiesbaden, pp. 151–169.

*Looking at the combined data for both sexes, we found
that males almost always exhibited more confidence
than females did, even though they were systematically
outperformed by them ... Women are less delusional than
men when it comes to assessing their academic career
potential, and that does pay off.*

Chamorro-Premuzic continues:

*In almost every country around the globe, women's
academic performance has been rising often to the point of
outperforming men (certainly the case in the US), yet men
remain more confident in their career success than women
do.*[11]

While I would argue that men's confidence has certainly benefited them far
more than women have benefited from their modesty, his point is fair. Women's
gains globally mean they should be *very* confident. However, they haven't yet
reaped the rewards we'd expect to see if we *really* valued a highly educated,
yet over-modest population.

LOW CONFIDENCE ISN'T AN EQUAL OPPORTUNITY FEELING

Let's be clear: not everyone needs to 'check' their confidence levels equally.
In leadership research, we see reams of evidence for sexist stereotypes about
leadership continuing to favour men.[12] Evidence shows time and again that
women are promoted on past performance, men on potential.[13] When asked
how leaders spot 'potential', they often depict stories related to taking risks, big
wins, killer presentations – all associated with our definitions of 'confidence'. If
you are part of a visible 'status quo' you'll be praised for displaying confidence.

The default for 'leader' is man, as much as it is 'able-bodied' and 'White'. As
such, it becomes easier for men who fit these categories to be viewed as high
potential and subsequently groomed for these roles. This trend makes it harder
for people from different backgrounds to break in or for others to see their
'potential'.

11. Chamorro-Premuzic, T. 2013 *Confidence: The Surprising Truth about How Much You Need and How to Get It*, Profile Books, London, p. 95.

12. Koenig, A. M. Eagly, A. H. Mitchell, A. A. and Ristikaria, T. 2001 Are Leader Stereotypes Masculine? A Metaanalysis of Three Research Paradigms, *Psychological Bulletin* 13(7): 616–642.

13. Corinne, A. et al. 2012 Science Faculty's Subtle Gender Biases Favor Male Students' Proceedings of the National Academy of Sciences of the USA, 109(41); Steinpreis, R. et al. 1999 The Impact of Gender on the Review of Curricula Vitae of Job Applicants and Tenure Candidates: A National Empirical Study, *Sex Roles* 41(7–8): 509–528; Hellman, M. and Hayes, M. 2005 No Credit Where Credit is Due: Attributional Rationalisation of Women's Success in Male-Female Teams, *Journal of Applied Psychology* 90(5): 905–926; Williams, J. and Dempsey, R. 2014 *What Works for Women at Work: Four Patterns Working Women Need to Know*, NYU Press, New York.

Unlike many of my clients, over their careers, you may not have had anyone explicitly say 'You need to be more confident to get ahead'. As we'll see, many interviewees received other advice *with the same intention*, if not the exact language. For Elizabeth Uviebinené, who co-wrote the bestseller *Slay in Your Lane* with Yomi Adegoke, this advice came from a former boss.

In our discussion, she reflects: 'He was a mentor, but told me I needed to trust myself more to share my ideas and thoughts.' While superficially sound advice, Uviebinené described herself as having a more quietly confident style. This former boss was an older White man, and while his advice was well-intentioned, it was based on how his own career progressed.

It ignores the reality of *how* 'speaking up and sharing ideas' can be heard by listeners when the speaker is not a White man. He's potentially less cognisant of Uviebinené's challenges as a Black British woman, as publicly 'trusting oneself' clearly worked for him. With good reason, he trusts the system. For him, this optimism makes complete sense. People like him have benefited from the system much more than those who are not part of the status quo.

The challenge is that in many organisations' gatekeepers are looking for the very behaviours *they* exhibited to get to the top. The assumption is 'If it worked for me, it should work for everyone'. However, even well-intentioned bosses fail to see that the expression and interpretation of different behaviours don't exist in a vacuum, which leads us back to confidence. As we've heard from others, you can have confidence in *yourself*, but less confidence in the *system or likelihood* people will appreciate your difference.

This difference between the types of confidence *in the system* versus confidence *in self*, is vital for us to understand. According to research with over 13 million American employees across 329 organisations, approximately two-thirds of employees believe they personally have equal opportunity to grow and advance, but they *aren't equally convinced the system is fair* for everyone.

Fewer than half of women and men think the best opportunities go to the most deserving employees, and fewer than a quarter say only the most qualified candidates are promoted to manager. On both fronts, women are *less optimistic* than men.[14]

So why exactly are the status quo more likely to be overconfident? In their world, flaws are more likely to be overlooked, mistakes forgiven, and strengths highlighted. Like the fairground mirror, this makes it tougher for them to see themselves or the situations of others accurately. Confidence is a by-product of privilege and building a career as part of a majority group; only a heavy dose of self-awareness prevents this veering into overconfidence.

14. Huang, J. et al.,McKinsey and Co. and LeanIn.Org, 2019 Women in the Workplace study

TWO

BATTLE BETWEEN COMPETENCE AND CONFIDENCE

> *The difference between genius and stupidity is that*
> *genius has its limits*
> – Albert Einstein

Let's set the stage as to why confidence versus competence matters. On a scale of 1–10, where 10 is ultra-compelling, how attractive and even sexy is the word 'confidence'? How about the word 'competence'? If you were offered a new hire for your team, but they could only be confident *or* competent, most people would select competence hands down.

Competence is indeed what we need more of in the world. However, it's rarely what people pick when asked what they want more of *themselves*, or indeed what they recognise we reward. Competence is a dull and much-maligned term – and undeservedly so. While everyone assumes themselves competent, it's not a word that sets the world alight.

When discussing competence, I think the tale of Heidi Roizen, who I interviewed as part of a panel discussion in Edinburgh a few years ago, is apt. Two identical case studies were presented to business school students about a successful technology entrepreneur. The only differing factor being their first name: Heidi or Howard.

The case described the true story of how the protagonist became a successful venture capitalist. As part of their entrepreneurial journey, this hero used their extroverted personality and network of influential business leaders in the technology sector. Half the students read the protagonist as 'Heidi', the other half as 'Howard'. Their lecturer then asked them for their impressions of both.

Heidi and Howard were deemed equally competent. Yet Howard was considered the colleague with whom they'd want to work. By contrast, Heidi was often seen as selfish and not the type of person you'd hire or want to work for. This research illustrates how the same data with a single difference – gender – create vastly different impressions.

The more Heidi's confidence and ambition shone, the more she delineated from what we expect to see. For this, she was disliked by both the male and female students.[15] This negative judgement feeds into our expectation that to retain social equilibrium and be 'likeable', women should temper their goals publicly or downplay their accomplishments. Such expectations don't exactly set anyone up for 'confidence'.

To this point, non-status quo employees know they are better off working on their competence than *outwardly* working on confidence. Kainaz Gazder is a Vice President at P&G, a company she's been with for over 23 years. She's now based in Singapore but got her first lessons about workplace confidence as a trainee in India, her country of origin. Like others, she first interpreted confidence as what you *say* about yourself. Only secondly was it about what you actually *knew*. Gazder jokes:

> *Most people spend a lot more time focused on that first element to the detriment of the second! When I first started working, all my fellow MBA graduates had grandiose plans for their future. Compared to them I felt I knew nothing and had no master plan. My only option was to build credibility through my work, and then talk about that.*

Building their skills, and not just how they talked about them, was vital. Gazder reflects:

> *When I'm hiring, I'm not looking at how well people present their own plans – that first element of confidence. That's actually the easy part of confidence! The far better question is 'Do they know their stuff?' That's in the recommendations they make and their ability to answer tough questions.*

While Gazder is talking about the qualities every leader should actually value, her brilliance is in that she actually gives those people credit. As linguist and researcher Deborah Tannen explains:

> *Individuals in positions of authority are judged by how they enact that authority. This poses a particular challenge for women ... Women are expected to hedge their beliefs as opinions, to seek opinions and advice from others, and to be 'polite' in their requests. If a woman talks this way, she is seen as lacking in authority.[16]*

15. Merchant, N. 2013 3 Reasons Men Should Read Lean In, *Harvard Business Review*, 11 March.
16. Tannen, D. 1995 *Talking from 9 to 5*, William Morrow & Co., London, p. 170.

A few years ago, a male colleague told me I was a 'very competent woman'. Hardly the most glowing of recommendations, but it turns out, statistically, he was likely right. In an effort to unpick assumptions we make about male and female leaders, a review of 95 separate leadership studies found *no difference* in the perceived *effectiveness* of male and female leaders.[17]

However, there was a stark gender difference when they looked at *who* was making the judgement. According to *self*-reports, men rated themselves more favourably than women rated themselves. However, when the verdict was from colleagues, female leaders were judged more competent by everyone around them. I wonder how much further the modern workplace would get if we valued 360° feedback more than self-reports, which are prone to unwarranted exaggeration.

If you're not excited about being described as 'competent' try:

- **Experienced**
- **Skilled**
- **Insightful**
- **Knowledgeable**

While women are often rated more competent on 360° assessments, the type of *constructive* feedback they get is usually not specific or helpful. As Correll and Simmard explained:

> *The developmental feedback for men was more likely to be linked to business outcomes (60% for men versus 40% for women) ... Clearly, these dynamics can disadvantage women at promotion time. Without specific, documented business accomplishments, it is difficult for a manager to make a case for advancement. Conversely, if a business objective was missed, a lack of frank feedback deprives women of the opportunity to hit the mark next time.*[18]

17. Paustian-Underdahl, S. C., Walker, L. S. and Woehr, D. J. 2014 Gender and Perceptions of Leadership Effectiveness: A Meta-analysis of Contextual Moderators, *Journal of Applied Psychology*, 99(6): 1129–1145.
18. Correll, S. and Simard, C. 2016 Vague Feedback is Holding Women Back, *Harvard Business Review*.

DAMNED BY FAINT PRAISE

Even when women did perform well, it was more likely to be attributed to luck or extra hours in the office, not through their skills or intelligence. In the context of confidence, all of this is clearly problematic, but perhaps not surprising. It is far easier to encourage a woman to be more confident than to identify *exactly* what needs improvement before a promotion. This tactic is particularly useful if your reasons for holding her back wouldn't bear scrutiny.

I struggle to think of a role where we'd be better off rewarding confidence over competence, though this is commonplace. This came up in discussion with Barbara-Ann King, a former MD at Barclays who now advises financial services clients. Who does King thinks gets overlooked? She answers:

> *Compliance and operational roles. These are the people who keep people like me on track. They contribute hugely, making sure everything the client sees from the code in your online banking to your paper bank statements is accurate. Plus, their competence is vital as they make sure the ever-changing landscape of risk and regulation is being followed so we're not at risk. They're hugely valuable, but not the sexy jobs that come to mind when we all think 'banker'.*

The financial rewarding of confident client-facing roles compared to competent operational roles is important to understand. It not only determines how bonuses are allocated, but how easily someone can access subsequent career tracks. While she never worked in compliance herself, King explains: 'The spoils of bonuses go to those closest to the clients. But people in operations are equally important. They ensure our financial system doesn't just work; it doesn't collapse!'

In the banking sector, someone's financial value is often influenced by the type of bonus they've *received in previous years*, creating a circular argument. As King points out:

> *It's like saying 'We've paid this person well before, so they must be valuable! They'll expect as much if not more this time!' It means we undervalue the risk and compliance people. They don't get a big share of profits from deals they've done, so we end up valuing them less! They get overlooked for promotion and senior roles, because they've never earned as much as the front office people. This perspective then suggests: 'I guess they're not worth it!'*

In fact, the mere words themselves can be weaponised in order to diminish someone. Equally, a 'I'm sure he's very competent' can sound like you are trying to find compliments about an otherwise bland employee. A surprised 'Well, she's very confident!' indicates someone was bolder than you expected!

WHAT CONFIDENCE LOOKS LIKE

So what do we expect confidence to *look like*? Elaine Eisenman is a Board member of multiple US-based companies and specialist in scaling and growing companies. She points out: 'People don't differentiate enough between what it's like to *feel* confident and what it's like to *look* confident.' In one leadership role, Eisenman had a stellar female direct report, Ana. However, Eisenman took Ana to task for the way she displayed confidence, or in this case, her lack thereof.

Ana grew up as the youngest in a large working-class Italian-American family. She spent her childhood being talked over and so retreated into academics rather than argue her way amidst the loving melee of noise. For Ana, school was a safe place, which meant she not only excelled at university, but she achieved a professional status far beyond any of her siblings. All from the introverted child whose parents didn't plan on sending to university, because it was a 'waste for girls'.

If Ana was highly competent, why did her confidence become an issue for Eisenman? She answers:

> *Ana managed a significant job, but she didn't act like a significant person. She always made fantastic points, but only if you could pry them out of her in a meeting. Anytime we sat in a group setting, she'd fold into herself.*

Not surprisingly, Ana's contributions were either ignored or her ideas credited to others. Eisenman continues:

> *Invisibility was a not an option; other teams assumed she was incompetent. Eventually I said she had to change her approach, or I'd have to let her go. This was tough talk as she was a fantastic contributor. But our work was often undermined, and I couldn't send her to represent the team to a wider audience.*

So how did she react? Eisenman sighs:

*Ana sobbed and asked if she was being fired. Again, not the
reaction I wanted. I told her how valuable she was, but that
she was on notice for 6 months over which I had to see real
progress. She went home hysterical and told her husband
she should quit. But he agreed I was right, saying it was
the best thing for her as he also believed in her. I got her a
coach, and that made a big difference.*

For Eisenman, she couldn't have made this edict without offering professional
support. This seemed like an obvious answer to Eisenman, who continues:

*If she'd known what to do before, Ana would have done
it. You need help on these challenges. It didn't make a
difference to the value I placed on her. But coaching helped
how others viewed her, reflecting well on our whole team.*

As Eisenman speaks, she highlights that coaching worked *because* it was
behavioural; it didn't focus on Ana's mindset. Only our behaviours, not our
confidence, are visible. Eisenman explains:

*No one can see your mindset; they can only see your
behaviours. She was completely competent, that was never
the problem. In fact, Ana's contributions in meetings
were no better than they had been before, they were just
delivered more skilfully. That's what people reacted well to.*

These myths are hard to shift and affect who we hire and promote. Indeed,
confidence doesn't affect corporate performance. Charisma, one of the words
I heard the most when asking what confidence looks like, isn't even a sure
sign of success. The CEOs of 128 companies who were deemed the most
charismatic had the largest salaries but did not provide any better corporate
performance.[19]

These assumptions about what confidence looks like are familiar to Rosemary
McGinness, the Chief People Officer at the Weir Group. In her 25 years
leading HR teams, she agrees leaders assume confidence should rule. Instead
of relying on confidence to make judgements, she wants leaders to rely on the
competence someone has *previously* demonstrated.

McGinness explains:

19. Agle, B. et al. 2006 Does CEO Charisma Matter? An Empirical Analysis of the Relationships Among
Organisational Performance, Environmental Certainty and Top Management Team Perceptions of CEO
Charisma, *Academy of Management* 49(1): 161–174.

> *If someone says to me: 'Well I can't imagine a certain candidate in front of customers' I have to then point out, 'Well, not all customers are the same!' If the person has done a job where they interacted with customers, and can prove their results, that alone should be enough – not your imaginings of what a fictional sales visit would look like.*

She recalls:

> *I once worked with a leader who answered this question by saying they needed someone 'strong enough to stand up to Board!' The truth was the Board was actually pretty friendly. The new hire would only have to present once, or maybe twice a year. So the leader's version of confidence wasn't relevant when we looked at what the job required.*

When it comes to defining confidence, most people say they 'can recognise it when they see it'. This is particularly true when people can't quite articulate the exact quality to which they are responding. McGinness says: 'Confidence is a term people use to cover a multitude of sins. It means everything from having coherent answers and a willingness to stand up for their ideas, to your tone of voice and body language.' It's a blanket term, and one that we use to judge not just ourselves but others.

We have a host of expectations about confidence, most of which reward what's gone before. They range from a sense of presence to public displays of almost theatrical leadership skills or even 'cultural fit'. What they don't do is challenge convention to address what we'll need going forward. Let's start by unpicking further what people mean when they describe confidence and the expectations they have around those behaviours. Let's begin with assertiveness.

PRAISE FOR THE SQUEAKY WHEEL

I was raised in the US where expressions like 'The squeaky wheel gets the oil' and 'Nothing ventured, nothing gained' were common parlance. 'Speaking up' is a behaviour we equate with confidence. It was only after moving to the UK that I even learned the phrase 'quiet confidence': until then, I didn't know confidence *could* be quiet! I assumed it was always assertive. This is the country for whom the term 'Often wrong, but never in doubt' originated.

People often used phrases like 'speaking with conviction' when I asked them to describe confidence. However, even those who describe themselves as lacking in confidence agree they have no problems amongst friends and family. Rather, they only lack confidence in the workplace, and even then, just in very specific settings, such as meetings of particular groups of people.

Again, this type of confidence is wrapped up in a familiarity with the way meetings unfold, often via shared yet unspoken assumptions. This version of confidence is contextual, subjective and primarily for *people experienced* at understanding these implicit assumptions.

Instead, perhaps we should be recognising 'cultural capital' instead of confidence as one of the key factors in determining who gets on in certain professions. If you live a life with economic security, it allows you the time, space and access to common cultural reference points. These then affect your choices, ranging from the way you dress to the way you speak. These choices can be 'cashed-in' on the job.

This 'cashing-in' goes wider than workplace advancement. It also signals to potential Partners your class background, facilitating mating choices that will only perpetuate this further. Because all of these tendencies feed into our ideas of 'merit', it would perhaps be more accurate to describe 'merit' as 'cultural capital'. It's this that allows those from privileged backgrounds to get on at the expense of others.

IF THE CULTURE FITS

Talk of 'cultural fit', and what we're *expecting* to see, has come to the fore recently. However, it goes back further than we think and has real implications today, and certainly in fields where many of my clients' work. 'Fit' largely means what it *feels* like to work someplace, primarily determined by who works there now and the behaviours they reward or penalise. Organisations, but even the teams within, all have their own nuanced cultures, which can change over time – even in surprising ways.

For example, in the 1940s and 1950s, women made up the vast majority of computer programmers.[20] IT was largely a female 'culture'. Even by the 1960s, women were still 30–50% of computer science students. Computing was initially deemed a clerical skill. Even the term 'debugging' comes from one of the earliest computer programmers, Grace Hopper, in the 1940s. She was initially referring to the task of repairing system glitches. Debugging simply meant removing moths and other foreign creatures from the back of heavy machinery; ideal for smaller, feminine fingers!

Information Technology (IT) only became more masculine as employers began to recognise how *profitable* these fields could become as computing became more mainstream. Increasingly new leaders designed assessment tests heavily biased towards male stereotypes. No surprise, these new tests resulted in men being deemed a better 'fit' than the women who'd actually held these roles much longer.[21]

---

20. Cohen, R. 2016 What Programmings Past Reveals about Today's Gender Pay Gap, *The Atlantic*.
21. Ensmenger, N. 2010 *The Computer Boys Take Over*. MIT Press, Massachussetts.

The idea of fit grows ever stronger today in determining how far someone progresses. Georg Schmundt-Thomas, who led the Swedish based FMCG (Fast Moving Consumer Goods) firm Essity, saw how intricately tied confidence was to what people are expecting or even want to see. He explained: 'Some people weasel through simply because they fit in so well. If you behave in a culturally familiar way, you signal the appearance of confidence.' Schmundt-Thomas, who pushed for greater diversity at Essity, points out how *perceptions* of confidence can become even more complicated. He explains:

> *If we identify someone who hasn't delivered, we blame a bit of bad timing, extenuating circumstances or hitting a rough patch. We'll reassure ourselves they have tremendous potential. We could uncover competence faster if we ask: 'Is their career primarily a series of rough patches?' No matter how much we like or even identify with them, perhaps they aren't as capable as we need.*

Hiring for cultural fit has nothing to do with the competency of the candidate. Instead, it has everything to do with the interviewer's comfort levels. Schmundt-Thomas points out:

> *We might overlook very qualified people, disqualifying them on the seemingly cautious basis that they won't get along with others. That's shorthand for 'they're not like me', or more positively, 'I trust them because I understand them'. It's highly emotive and subjective when you are deciding who to invest in and who to trust, but you've got to look at the objective results. It should boil down to 'what are the metrics around this person?'*

Schmundt-Thomas also spent time in Japan leading teams in an American multinational and explains:

> *People know about the benefits of diverse thinking, but bringing different people together is harder. You're going to have to use your social capital. You're going to have to listen better, and you're likely to be questioned more frequently. For most people, it's not worth the extra trouble. For managers, we still have to justify our hiring decisions so 'cultural fit' is an easy rationale. Someone different is going to be a lot harder to identify with – and therefore, potentially manage.*

For him, determining who is valued for their competence versus their confidence is straightforward. He advises:

> *Ask your managers: 'If your team halved tomorrow – who*
> *are the people you'd fight to keep?' If you push them why*
> *they made the choices they did – it's usually evidence-*
> *based. Only worry if they mention cultural fit as the primary*
> *reason, as that suggests it's more about their comfort levels.*

I talked about this issue over with Maria Camilla Vargas, a talent management expert who was Columbian by background but was now living in Chile. Educated in the US, she saw how the excuse of 'fit' differed in some cultures, but also remained consistent. Vargas smiled: 'People don't reject candidates for not being confident outright. Instead, they'll say that candidate doesn't "fit the profile" which most often means "they're not who I imagined".'
As Elizabeth Uviebinené says:

> *Fit is a sugar-coated way of opening the discussion about*
> *'will they fit in?' This term hides a lot of assumptions*
> *about who will and who won't work for a culture. If you go*
> *into an office where you are in a minority group, it can be*
> *intimidating. But while that seems like an accident, it's not*
> *by chance, far from it. To exist, any in-group needs an out-*
> *group to exclude and differentiate itself by.*

Neil Stevenson is the CEO of the Scottish Legal Complaints Commission. He sees 'fit' being used even by those who likely know the word 'fit' itself is now loaded with assumptions. He observes:

> *People say they want competence so create competency-*
> *based questions, but what I often see are people choosing*
> *'peace of mind'. They're looking for who they feel confident*
> *in; often code for who they understand or who 'exudes*
> *confidence'.*

In hiring or promotion discussions, ask:

- **What do we mean when we say someone's 'a good fit' or 'fits the profile'?**
- **What does it mean we say someone has 'presence' or 'gravitas'?**
- **What was missing from this candidate if we say 'they're not who we were looking for?'**

DARE-DEVILS WELCOME

Besides 'fit', another term people used when describing confidence was 'willing to take risks'. This definition superficially seems accurate. However, it also depends on how much there is to risk and the consequences if you lose. If you are the sole provider for your family, you'll be less likely to take a risk than someone who can rely on family money.

Being well-connected to friends in senior roles who could help you to get back on your feet if a venture fails means you may be more of an adventurous 'risk-taker'. This will be especially true when compared to someone who can't access those types of social resources. For example, if you routinely find work easily via your connections, you're more likely to 'call out' an employer on lousy behaviour than to quietly accept it as the 'price of admission'.

While seen as a sign of 'confidence', taking more risks depends on the assumption someone or the system will catch you if you fall. In the workplace, you'll need to believe someone will advocate on your behalf or help find you another role. You'll also need to feel someone else could even pay the bills if you get it wrong. This security gives the people we like to think of as 'creative risk-takers' or 'out-of-the-box thinkers' financial leeway.

This safety net buys freedom of choice and the time to network. It also buys an ability to reject dead-end or even exploitative jobs, in favour of waiting for better work. This 'breathing space' is particularly valuable if there are likely to be spells of no work in between rejected gigs. This is a situation more likely to benefit the status quo than anyone else.

Let's be clear, few will talk about who in their personal lives has helped them financially, either currently or in the past. Yet not discussing it means people fail to see how the resources and benevolence of others support their confidence. This is something we'll look at more closely when we discuss socioeconomic class differences.

Instead, these people refer to themselves as lucky or having a sense of adventure. Bystanders credit them as being 'confident'. However, what greases the wheels towards confidence is access to money. This allows everything from starting a business, to moving to a new city or taking a poorly paid internship in order to gain experience.

Some have pointed out to me that women in particular should be able to access extra resources via a male Partner, giving them an ability to take more risks. However, this belief assumes many things – most of which are false. There is an assumption that all women are heterosexual and attached to working men who earn as much if not more than they do. It also disregards the experiences of single women, mothers or the childfree, situations which preclude a higher male income. Similarly, most families *need* to have both Partners working so can't easily afford to take the risks we attribute to confidence.

UNWRAP YOUR GIFTS AND 'PRESENCE'

Presence is one of the most commonly used words when describing confidence. However, putting a finger on what it looks like exactly is a bit harder. Harvard Business School Professor Amy Cuddy noticed how differently the White men in her MBA programme behaved in class compared to other students. They spoke for longer, took up more space in class and generally had a more expansive physical 'presence'.

She conducted a now-famous experiment whereby she asked students to give a short five-minute interview presentation. In the few minutes *before* they went in for these presentations, certain people, notably the women, were instructed to take up a more significant physical stance à la 'Superman'. It was a pose with legs spread and hands on hips. Those who did the Superman pose before going into the mock interview had more positive feedback, even though they didn't display this pose while presenting.

Just two minutes in this position was enough to raise testosterone, a hormone associated with assertiveness. Similarly, it decreased cortisol, our stress hormone. Those who had taken these positions gave stronger, more credible and self-assured presentations. These are the type of behaviours we *expect* to see in 'confident' people – irrespective of the value of what they actually said. If confidence can be easily affected by simple stance choices and their corresponding chemical changes after just a few moments, it illustrates how performance or 'confidence', as it's often interpreted, is *not at all related* to actual competence.

Interestingly, the story doesn't stop there. Cuddy's research was met with backlash from her mostly White male peers after she gained acclaim for her related TED Talk on these 'power poses'.[22] As a woman with over 45 million online video views, her work attracted attention from other academics and cyberspace bullies – groups that in this case overlapped. Her most high-profile detractors in the academic realm were two tenured academics nearing retirement. These were both White men in very safe positions.

22. Elleser, K. 2018 Power Posing is Back: Amy Cuddy Refutes Criticism, *Forbes*, 3 April.

Cuddy then spent five subsequent years *defending* her research by comparing her findings to 55 other studies on the effects of physical stance on the hormones related to confidence.[23] The findings?

Despite the criticism, her research was statistically every bit as valid and credible as it had been at the start. Power poses do improve emotion and displays of confidence. However, I suspect if Cuddy was part of the status quo, her work would not have received the harsh critiques it did, something we'll look at more when discussing online harassment.

Cuddy is not the only one to notice differences in body language when defining confidence. Amanda Jones, a Partner at the global law firm Dentons, says confidence looks like someone 'Who presents well and is well dressed. They speak with authority and look you in the eye.' To her, those behaviours are vital. She explains: 'It takes longer to undo that first impression' but admits like most other interviewees, she's been fooled by those more confident than competent.

The risk is 'You'll give them more autonomy when you should be monitoring their work before that trust is allowed. But I won't be alone in making that mistake.' For many, their impressions of confidence focused on public performance, using words like 'bravado', 'loudness' and as we've discussed 'presence'– almost a sense of theatre when commanding an audience, as part of an 'unofficial' show. This again highlights the truism that confidence is only what others can *see*, not with how skilled you actually are.

BIRTH OF A SALESMAN

The final element people repeatedly used when describing confidence was 'salesmanship'. Amanda Jones was also circumspect about the value of confidence, but says it has a place. She explains:

> *You need rainmakers – people who can bring in the business. They don't need to be as technically competent in the law, but they must be able to communicate other people's competence to a client. In any selling industry, confidence is probably more relevant than capability. But even so, that still requires you to be competent in understanding your colleagues' abilities, in a way that they might not even describe themselves.*

Jones is herself a Partner who built a formidable legal career. She reflects:

23. Cuddy, A. J. C., Schultz, S. J. and Fosse, N. E. 2018 P-Curving a More Comprehensive Body of Research on Postural Feedback Reveals Clear Evidential Value for Power-Posing Effects: Reply to Simmons and Simonsohn (2017), *Psychological Science* 29(4): 656–666.

We probably don't have enough of those conversations about who our unsung heroes are – the competent people. It's a challenge. However, it's one we don't focus on. Our clients will refuse even the best lawyer if they don't think she'll bang the table in a legal argument on their behalf.

Other leaders also admitted their sectors sometimes over-rewarded confidence. Sarah Douglas is the CEO of AMV BBDO, a creative agency which works across all aspects of online and broadcast media for their clients. She's worked in the field for over 25 years. Douglas notes:

Because of the focus on sales and client-facing work, I think the creative industries perhaps see more than our fair share of noisy personalities. We tend to focus on the bewitching magnetism of personality, but that can mask incompetence. Essentially, their personality is writing cheques their skill level simply can't cash.

Douglas continues:

When I'm hiring, like anyone, I'm initially attracted to confidence. At that point, though, it becomes all the more important for me to dig deeper. I've got to find examples of what they've done, so I don't fall victim to their well-rehearsed spiel. Their competence has to be at least as good as the confidence they have no trouble displaying.

However, Douglas points out that confidence may serve *her* industry perhaps even better than most. She explains:

It's advantageous in selling creative concepts to clients. The ideas that work will be ideas the client won't have thought of before. After all, it's our creativity they're coming to us for. Plus, because it's so subjective, there is never one single right way to run a campaign. The client expects you to have confidence in what will work, rather than just a list of things that could work.

For Douglas, the hard but competent work is in getting to the *best right way* amongst many options. That's a more valuable skill than simply salesmanship. It is fundamentally more useful than confidence without having explored the options and understood the implications of each.

THREE

ALL THAT GLITTERS IS NOT GOLD

> *Champions keep playing until they get it right*
> – Billie Jean King

Confidence does have value, but not nearly as much as you think. We all know the phrases 'winging it', 'blagging' or 'all talk, no action'. They come from the recognition competence beats confidence, but that you can *fake* confidence when you need to. The trick is not in faking it, but in *remembering* when you've felt competent before.

As you progress in any organisation, you won't be able to do all the hands-on work yourself. If you're anything like my clients, this can be hard for people to accept as they progress. After all, it was the day to day practical work that drew you into your field. However, if you keep all practical work, you'll create bottlenecks for everyone else. Confidence is useful in remembering that you *knew* how to do the hands-on work and be able to make sound judgements as a result. That's valuable confidence as it's via *evidence-based* competence.

Martin Donnan is the Director of NATS Prestwick, a 700-strong, highly technical workforce that controls airspace in the northern half of the UK and over the North Atlantic. Donnan notes: 'We expect evidence of competence, but you are rarely expected to prove confidence the same way. It's either noticed by others or it isn't. We only notice confidence when it's *lacking* in someone.'

This perspective also came to the forefront when I spoke with Toby Mildon, a Diversity and Inclusion expert, who's worked for over 16 years in fields ranging from media to accounting. Mildon observes:

> *People in middle management complain people above them*
> *got there by confidence, but I also hear the same thing*
> *from junior people complaining about middle managers.*
> *Deep down, people want to value competence – but it's*
> *confidence that gets noticed.*

Derek Watson is the Quaestor and Factor at the University of St Andrews where he's worked for the last 17 years. This COO type role oversees all non-academic services employees and how the university works with the broader world. He says: 'I'd like to think I'm always looking for competence in people, but confidence is vital. It's easy to miss someone's valuable competence if they don't speak up.' He elaborates:

> At a senior level you are selling concepts to others – most
> of whom have no idea about your area. Because of their
> own overconfidence, they'll either ask detailed questions
> about your plans or trust you've made the right decision
> because of the confidence you display in that meeting and
> your advocates.

Interestingly for Watson, it's not just about the individual's confidence, but about the likely advocates an employee also has. Watson clarifies:

> I need people to speak up earlier in meetings, not just in the
> meeting, but also to have done their homework before that
> meeting. I accept you'll make some decisions that will end
> up better than others. But not speaking up because you fear
> being wrong is a real problem for me. I don't respond well
> to bravado, but it's equally a problem if someone's quiet in
> a group and only mentions their observations to me later.

In the interview, I can sense he's conflicted about this paradigm. He's clear he relies on the insights of the most competent. However, he doesn't have the time to 'grow' them all individually and points out:

> I don't have time to circle back to everyone in a one-to-one
> setting, and say 'You were a bit quiet there, is that really
> what you thought?' Essentially, you have to be patient,
> warm them up and ask them before meetings for their
> opinion. Even then, I have to implore them: 'Please open
> your mouth. You make sound judgements, and I trust you!'

For Watson, leading a large team, this takes more time than he and most leaders have explaining: 'I need them to influence others. That's not solely about what they say in a meeting, but the time they spend preparing for that meeting.' Like most the senior leaders I've worked with, for Watson that doesn't necessarily mean quiet work reading or perfecting slides. In fact, Watson is disparaging of slideshows. He shakes his head: 'If you need slides to do a 10-minute presentation, I don't want you in the room as you haven't done the *right* work.'

Kiruba Sankar is the Director of Corporate Social Responsibility and Global Lead for Supplier Diversity at Global Procurement at the Royal Bank of Canada. Sankar feels even the most technical roles still need a high level of confidence, particularly as they move towards more client-facing positions.

Sankar observes confidence as less about what you display and when you talk about your skills, and more about the confidence the people *on the other side of the negotiating table have in you*. For him, it's on your ability to deliver, often evidenced by the way you talk about your background and the work it took you to get there.

Similar to Watson's view, for Sankar, who has a long history in IT, it's also about the trust you instil. Sankar questions:

> *Does a client leave a pitch feeling like they trust you enough to give you a million-dollar contract? That's the confidence I'm interested in – the client's, not the employee who's pitching. For me, it's about demonstrating how you've done it before or showing them a proof of concept.*

Sankar's answer still puts the onus on the deliverables – competency. Sankar works with new suppliers in his role, increasing the diversity of suppliers to the bank. His role is about pushing *past* a confident pitch. He wants to see multiple proofs of concept and a track record of delivery for other clients. Only then will he onboard them to deliver smaller projects as he considers the supplier for larger-scale projects in the future.

Many of the leaders I spoke with felt that as you progress upwards through an organisation, your confidence becomes more critical. You won't be able to do all the hands-on work yourself. This makes it all the more important to derive confidence from growing past the technical skills, by relying on your hard-earned but ever-stretching competencies. Cumulatively, they create your better judgement.

How to highlight your background 'research':

- **'When I talked to (another person in the business, a client, a competitor) etc., they observed … How do we take that on Board?'**
- **'When I was reading up on the topic, I noticed …'**
- **'When I talked with (senior leader) about these issues, she mentioned …'**
- **'When looking at the history of this issue, you'll notice ...'**

OVERVALUING CONFIDENCE

Clearly, both confidence and competence are necessary. However, we must value and therefore reward competence far more. After all, the ability to believe in something patently untrue is often down to confident delivery alone. However, it may also be down to the judge's *lack* of competence.

In 1999, two researchers, Dunning and Kruger, studied relatively skilled versus unskilled individuals. They looked at how they evaluated complex information and *their confidence in having accurate evaluations.* Unskilled individuals 'overestimated their logical reasoning ability and the number of test items they got right' by a wide margin.[24] In fact, despite their actual low performance, their sense of superiority remained constant *even after seeing the evidence of their poor performance*. They simply could not accept they were wrong.

This research also had real implications for highly skilled individuals who instead recognised the complexity of certain issues, particularly the issues they knew the most about. Therefore, the most competent gave more respect to the poor performers who had no evidence for their beliefs *beyond the certainty they were right*. Additionally, the highest scorers on the cognitive test assumed everyone else had done just as well. Unwittingly, this undermined any belief the competent had in their own uniquely high skill set.

In the real world, this means highly skilled people *underestimate* their abilities while relatively unskilled individuals *overestimate* theirs. Simply put, the most confident were the least able and most susceptible to believing outlandish ideas – even after those ideas had been disproven. What happens when they saw the evidence that their belief is factually inaccurate? As the researchers observed:

> *The individual will frequently emerge not only unshaken,*
> *but even more convinced of the truth of his beliefs than*
> *ever before. Indeed, he may even show a new fervour about*
> *convincing and converting other people to his view.*

This reality has had far-reaching implications for everything from decreased vaccine rates and climate change to 'flat-earthers' and even national election results. When the media gives equal air-time to both sides of an argument as if they were similarly weighted by evidence, this creates a real disparity.

It gives the passionate, yet incompetent more credence than their knowledge deserves. Competence, skills and knowledge should always win out for its inherent value. However, perhaps the only downside to being competent is in recognising how much there is still to learn about any given topic.

---

24. Kruger, J. and Dunning, D. 2000 Unskilled and Unaware of It: How Difficulties in Recognizing One's Own Incompetence Lead to Inflated Self- Assessments, *Journal of Personality and Social Psychology* 77 (6):1121- 1134.

A few years ago, I launched a mentoring programme for a financial services client that was open to both men and women as mentees. I led a masterclass on setting up these relationships as part of a drive to encourage people to participate – either as a volunteer mentor or as a mentee. The event was a great success as many volunteered.

The status quo twist in the tale? It was mainly White men who volunteered to mentor. By contrast, women, almost without exception, signed up as mentees. This was despite the fact many of the would-be mentees were women who were actually senior to the junior men who volunteered to mentor.

There is value in peer mentoring, but that had never been advertised as the format or even purpose of the programme. Instead, this could be interpreted as that old chestnut: 'women's lack of confidence and men's overconfidence'. However, it begs a more important question: What do the mentees want and *need* from these relationships?

In my experience setting up these programmes, people often use mentoring to secure guidance in an environment *in which they feel uncertain about their next steps*. That organisation was by no means unique. Non-status quo people need advocacy in navigating. By comparison, in this case, even the most junior of men was sure enough of the path forward to feel they could mentor women in some cases up three or four rungs up the ladder above him.

> **Magpie mentoring: Write out five people you admire and list:**
>
> - **The traits you have in common.**
> - **Their skills you admire.**
> - **The experiences or training they've had you could seek.**

Sarah Burbedge, the Head of Change & Content Production Workflows in Design and Engineering at the BBC, was relieved to see competence and confidence not treated synonymously in our discussion. She remarked:

> *There's been a shift. People have started realising; they aren't the same things, which is valuable for someone in my role. I've historically seen lots of meetings driven by the louder voices getting heard – even a butting-in culture. The art is to make sure you spotted the tiny pause where someone takes a breath to make sure you get heard! That was brash confidence, but I think that's changing.*

Like in any organisation some teams accept this more readily. Burbedge says:

> *Some teams still value confidence as it's traditionally displayed. However, I do take great comfort in the fact that I see new leaders coming through who are focused more on competence, and less on posturing or play acting.*

So, what's behind this attitude shift? According to Burbedge, a great facilitator in this newfound 'meeting democracy' has been a happy by-product of increasing their usage of technology – particularly for remote workers attending meetings. She explains:

> *We've been doing a lot to encourage best practice around flexibility and remote working. Meeting Chairs are increasingly judged if they don't include the people who aren't in the room. Historically it may have been easy to defer to them at the end. While that may have been normal, there's more etiquette now. I hear more 'Any thoughts from those not in the room?' being asked throughout a meeting. Maybe it's a softer skill, but it's incredibly valuable.*

She notices:

> *Technology has been a significant disruptor of the status quo, perhaps not in ways we initially anticipated, but especially with the use of video calls which democratises the whole thing. You don't get away with hosting a bad meeting anymore.*

Burbedge contiunes:

> *If only 2 or 3 people are speaking – and all just saying the same thing – other participants are now challenging that. People hosting a meeting are increasingly challenged to think much more about which voices are missing in the meeting invite, and in the room itself, and seek them out.*

This push towards collaboration as displayed by a growing number of leaders is a pleasant surprise for many. Burbedge says: 'People stop and notice the meeting wasn't bolshy or combative, and we actually got a lot done!'

PRIORITISE 360° FEEDBACK OVER SELF-ASSESSMENTS

Simply put, the evidence suggests confidence isn't all it's cracked up to be. Relatedly we see how self-assessments have a couple of real flaws. People aren't great at analysing themselves and in any case, are usually more interested in what others think of them. However, they are continually used as standard practice in most organisations. Self-assessments have value if they truly encourage self-awareness. However, my concern is how they tend to disadvantage not just women, but also people from cultures where self-promotion is frowned upon and definitely not a cultural norm.

By comparison, understanding your 360° feedback, on the other hand, is vital. Even if a colleague's views seem inaccurate, they are still critical. We all get hired, promoted or fired based on what other people think about us. Others' opinions are more consequential than what we think of ourselves. We love to trot out that 'Believe in yourself!' mantra, but real power comes from understanding what others think.

A meta-analysis of hundreds of studies found that for every skill examined, *reputation* was a more accurate predictor of competence than self-reviews.[25] This is a finding that's been replicated time and time again.[26] This has significant implications for the future of self-reviews. If what you think about yourself isn't shared by others, it probably isn't true.

The trouble is, similar to the aforementioned Dunning-Kruger effect, we maintain our self-beliefs and they're very resistant to change. I'm reminded of the popularity of being a 'legend in your living room' because to a certain degree, this belief is adaptive. Believing no-one understands us as well as we know ourselves gives us a sense of control and reminds us 'I know best'.

Unfortunately, self-assessments also embed bias. A few years ago, I was advising a global energy company on improving its gender balance at senior leadership. I asked to see the average 360° feedback scores of both men and women. Women on average got a 3.9 but just one-third of all that year's promotions. Men, on the other hand, earned an average score of 3.4 yet received two-thirds of all promotions.

I asked the leadership team about this discrepancy. Their immediate reaction was they'd promoted the *right* people. Instead, they rationalised their employees had probably been *too easy* on the women in the 360° assessments they gave. In this case, 'right' was primarily code for those with whom this senior team was most familiar and with whom they identified.

25. Connolly, B. and Ones, D. 2010 Another Perspective on Personality: Meta Analytic Integration of Observers Accuracy and Predictive Validity, *Psychological Bulletin* 136(6): 1092–1122.
26. Oh, I. S. Wang, G. and Mount, M. K. 2011 Validity of Observer Ratings of the Five-factor Model of Personality Traits: A Meta-analysis, *Journal of Applied Psychology* 96 (4): 762–773.

Cumulatively, this is likely part of the reason we see so many more men sent for leadership development or receiving extra support. Confidence in self-assessments encourages them to 'anchor' their bosses by telling them they are worth a higher score. By comparison, it's feedback that shows gender gaps between *how we see ourselves* and *how others see us*.

Research shows that men's self-ratings are .3 of a standard deviation *higher* than women's ratings. Doesn't sound like much of a statistical difference. However, it means over half of men (62%) will rate themselves more positively than the average woman will.[27] We can continue to encourage women to be more confident when doing their self-assessments. However, dispensing with self-assessments altogether would have a fairer impact in focusing on competence.

Using the feedback you receive:

- **Prioritise 360° feedback – what's possible if you believed you were as good as the people around think you are?**
- **Ask friends, colleagues and clients to describe you in three words and compare it to your historic feedback.**
- **Look for changes in feedback over time, and for what holds true – your unique selling points (USP).**
- **If constructive criticism is hard to hear ask 'what's the grain of truth in what they're saying?'**

COMPETENCY FRAMEWORKS WON'T SAVE THE DAY

As forward-thinking and well-intentioned as they are, our reliance on competency frameworks doesn't prevent the overvaluation of confidence. But if we value measurable outcomes and metrics, how is that even possible? The response to this question is immediate from Kate Atkin, an executive coach whose PhD focuses on the imposter syndrome.

Atkin jokes: 'Because we are human, we weigh the behaviours we *see* versus what we *think* we can measure.' Atkin is right; measuring is both difficult and time-consuming. It's far quicker to reward based on our perceptions, rather than take the time to ensure we measure the right things in the first place.

---

27. Fletcher, C. 1999 The Implications of Research on Gender Differences in Self-Assessment and 360 Degree Appraisal, *Human Resource Management Journal* 9(1): 39–46.

But this also creates its own danger. An overreliance on metrics can reassure people that what they are measuring must be valuable and even unquestionable.

Atkin explains:

> *People think 'Great, I've got an external measure!' But it's much harder to determine if we're measuring the right things. For example, the number of sales calls someone makes is a metric.*

Atkin continues:

> *However, we all recognise you could make calls all day and get no sales. So instead, let's say you measure the number of sales. Well, that's an improvement, but not the whole story. Who gets the best list of people to call? Who gets first dibs on the best opportunities? What does 'best' even mean in these contexts?*

The answers to her questions are tricky to unpick. They have tended to favour majority group members, like most workplace processes. The far easiest option is to agree with our superficial, intuitive judgements. If someone displays confidence in the way the status quo defines it, we'll often overlook someone's shortcomings.

Looking for *evidence* of competence in selection is undoubtedly a big step forward. However, using such frameworks can falsely reassure us that interview bias couldn't have played a part in any decisions. As Neil Stevenson says:

> *We trick ourselves into thinking we're objective and this only gets worse as you go up the chain of command. By senior level, interviewers assume incompetent people wouldn't get through the door. It's then primarily about picking people who will let them sleep at night, which goes back to their emotional comfort.*

Maria Camila Vargas is a South American Talent Management expert. She notes: 'Everyone knows we need more competence in the hires we make, but we're human. Humans respond to the *x factor* which is confidence.' The move towards competency-based interviewing is great in theory. However, many interviewees saw that the danger is in how it falsely reassures people they're making decisions based solely on facts and that feeling couldn't have clouded their judgement.

Vargas now routinely advises companies on how to build teams, so I asked if she had seen this destructive tendency. Her frustrated response?

Absolutely! We've developed metrics to identify top talent. We use hard data which included everything from the size of budgets they've managed, to the size of teams they've overseen, to their 360° feedback and more. However, when our algorithms recommend who would be in their critical roles based on that data, we immediately get pushback.

She says managers complain:

'Why isn't his person on your list?' or 'I think your model missed something – can we skew it a little bit?' They're ultimately looking for the people they deem confident. It's frustrating. No matter how good your model is, the ultimate decision is still made by people.

Vargas continues:

People don't like being told an algorithm can spot competence better than they can. So then you're back to having three people up for promotion who look good on paper and the decision is once again made by people. So then again, it's all down to the x factor – confidence. It's usually something they can't define, but they'll assure me they can feel.

Is there a future for models generated by artificial intelligence where no one meets their new hire until the day they start? Vargas says: 'We're not ready yet. There's still too much to do with AI and perfecting algorithms. I've seen some progress – but it always boils down to a humans' decision.' But when I ask her if we'll ever be ready, she laughs and admits:

Probably not. We value ourselves too much to let go. It's all about our sense of ownership over the people hired and promoted. An algorithm means an individual manager can't take that credit for a good hire, plus it's also easier to blame the computer if someone doesn't work out.

This suggests if a manager doesn't actively choose and therefore invest in that person, they'll take less ownership over the success of that hire than if the new hire was selected by AI. After all, if the new hire was never your choice to begin with and only recommended by a computer, you have less skin in the game in helping the candidate succeed.

In preparing for appraisals with your boss, consider:

- How does your manager define confidence and competence? Double-check their answer by looking at who they've promoted in the past.
- In appraisals, share your self-assessment *after* your boss gave their assessment of you to avoid anchoring bias.
- Record your time spent mentoring, speaking or organising events beyond the day job or other types of business development and ask how those hours are counted in your annual review.

ROSE-TINTED GLASSES IN INTERVIEWING AND MEASURING COMPETENCE

Competency-based interviews are often rolled out to save us from ourselves as part of reducing bias. Even so, they may not go far enough. People with long-standing HR experience, like Rosemary McGinness, says:

> *People aren't often thinking far enough into the future for what they'll need. There's a fundamental difference between who you'll pick if you're guided by hiring for now versus hiring for someone who can do an evolving role. Similarly, do you need someone practical or someone who's more strategic? The answers to these questions are very different. Even within these interviews, there's often a category for 'personal impact' which is all about how they came across.*

She continues:

> *A candidate can do well on all the competency-based items, but that's where the most bias comes in. Plus, too frequently, people overlook that you need a balanced panel of decision-makers to make those judgements in the first place. If confidence is raised during an assessment, I find it useful to ask the question: 'What does confidence look like for you – and how does that relate to this job?' Once people unpack that, their assumptions often are laid bare.*

This approach favours the confident in situations where they have to make an initial impression – from which many judgements flow. This tactic is also familiar to Kiera Tsenti, a recruiter based in Wales who uses competency-based questions daily. She suggests:

> *In reality we hire based on what people say, not what they do. This means you'll rarely be considered for a job beyond what you can convincingly claim you've done before. That favours the confident, if they communicate that well. Most companies want to play it safe and hire someone who could not just do the job, but who's done it somewhere else and can convince them of that.*

Another person who notices the inverse relationship between confidence and competence in interviews is Sandy Kennedy. It's a challenge he, as the CEO of Entrepreneurial Scotland (ES), increasingly faces. Since its inception in 2007, ES has facilitated career development placements for nearly 1,400, mostly young, people.

As the main focus of its outreach, ES arranges internships for high-achieving undergraduates in their penultimate year at a Scottish university. Each year, they work on widening access and appear at a range of universities to talk about their summer-long placements with companies across the world. The chance to get such a placement is a rare opportunity for most undergraduates.

After the ES open days for nearly 3,000 students, as part of their scholarship programme, the organisation receives about 1,500 applications. Of those, they hold approximately 600 interviews, which whittles it down to around 450 deemed good enough to submit to 'host' companies in Scotland and beyond. Kennedy explains:

> *It's at this point their name gets passed on to employers who again interview them, which generates about 180 placements. That means that of the pool of 450 who we thought were good enough, we're disappointing nearly two-thirds because there's just no placement.*

For Kennedy, this is where it then becomes a competence vs confidence issue, as he explains:

> *When only 10% of applicants get a placement, the stakes are high. So I need to make sure the 180 who get placements are the most competent. We can't choose the ones who wowed the judges with their presentation skills or knew how to write a killer CV. Because it's a quick and easy judgement to make, I worry that confidence in an interview becomes a surrogate marker for competence.*

56

> **If you hear confidence being overvalued in a candidate, ask:**
>
> - **If we had one more person for this team, should we prioritise confidence or competence?**
> - **What do we risk when we promote confidence over competence?**
> - **Who has been someone we wouldn't think of as traditionally 'confident' but who consistently delivers?**
> - **But are they *ready enough*? What could we do to get them the confidence and support they need faster?**

Prioritising competency, while always the better option, also has some perhaps unexpected challenges as we've been starting to see. Douglas Morrison, the Director of the Scottish Institute of Innovation and Knowledge Exchange, sees a challenge in *how* we even measure competence.

He suggests:

> *Competence seems easy to judge for certain jobs, such as manufacturing. There it appears to be about volume – how much can one person produce in a set time. Sounds straightforward, but we can mistake quantity for quality. There's a tacit acceptance that if you hit the basic benchmark, you're competent.*

Morrison continues:

> *However, I don't think we have a common understanding as to what competence means for us, so we fall back on those basic metrics I just mentioned. Realistically though, people know they aren't the most important things.*

You can overcome biases with clear metrics to some extent, but Morrison points out competency-based judgements are still subjective so prone to bias. It's difficult to find metrics equally valued by *everyone*. What competencies are valued tends to be based on the preferences of one leader or what's gone before, which are often the same thing.

This affects workplaces that produce ideas just as much as factories making widgets. Morrison, who works in education observes:

A social scientist might publish ten papers, which is a clear and obvious metric. The better questions to ask are: 'What impact did those papers have?' 'Have they changed established thinking or an industry in some meaningful way?' Why are ten papers better than one, if that one challenges mindsets and leads to a new innovation? Because we've become so focused on creating metrics around competence, we've unintentionally accelerated our pace of output. Instead, we should focus on quality of output, but that's trickier.

As Morrison suggests, this is difficult and a risk. After all, getting people to agree on what competence looks like can be as fraught as deciding what confidence looks like. Plus, it's a lot more intellectual work than just counting output. Morrison sees these challenges and agrees: 'So we default to agreeing upon essentially meaningless metrics. Things like how many hours they worked, the number of papers published or how many conferences at which they spoke.'

In his role, Morrison spends time with employers discussing how they measure innovation. Not surprisingly, it's a complex topic on which they're eager to get metrics. Morrison points out:

Measuring innovation works to a certain extent, like the ideas generated or investment secured. However, it's best to measure the value created by that bright new idea and in many different ways: socially, environmentally, economically, culturally. But just getting them to see past the economic value is often the first lightbulb moment.

Simply put, being aware of other people's responses to you is critical. This is the strength of 360° feedback. Knowing yourself is fundamentally about knowing what *others* think of you. Others are better able to observe your behaviours than you can. Leaders who describe themselves more closely to how others describe them tend to be more productive than those without that self-awareness.[28]

To this point, 360°s are useful not just in seeing how other people view them, but also in measuring self-awareness. Research shows self-awareness translates into higher leadership performance.[29] Yet, when I talk to groups, very few people are asking for more 'self-awareness' – it's self-confidence they want. Clearly, we are not the best judges of the most important character traits we need to display.

28. Attwater, L. and Yammarino, F. 1992 Does Self-other Agreement on Leadership Perceptions Moderate the Validity of Leadership and Performance Predictions? *Personality Psychology* 45(1): 141–164.
29. Christian, M. S., Edwards, B. D. and Bradley, J. C. 2010 Situational Judgement Tests: Constructs Assessed and a Meta-analysis of Their Criterion-related Validities, *Personality Psychology* 63(1): 83–117.

Focusing on your 360° feedback alone should work no matter where you are on the career scale. It's particularly important the larger the gap between your self-ratings and the ratings your supervisors give you. Studies show that self-ratings of performance are only weakly related to supervisors' ratings for two main reasons. The first is that employees are too lenient in their self-evaluations (mainly when they perform poorly[30]). This is particularly prevalent in Western workplaces, where employees are less self-critical and less modest about their accomplishments and where rewards often go to those who brag or self-promote.

As we've already started to discuss, the second reason for the difference between a manager's ratings and self-ratings is because of the assumptions a manager makes on how a direct report *should act*. These are often informed by our expectations about *what leadership should look like* but unfortunately will also be informed by stereotypes regarding a person's background. For example, as we'll discuss, a confident Black man may be misinterpreted as 'aggressive', a confident disabled man as 'entitled', a confident Latina as 'fiery'.

THE IMPOSSIBILITY OF 'CONFIDENCE TRAINING'

Confidence training is based on the assumption people will have to present to more status quo groups as they advance their careers – a near certainty. After all, the status quo defines *what* confidence looks like.

Confidence training is popular, partially because it is considered a quick fix. It's a lucrative business and is only expanding. In the US alone, the self-help industry is worth $9.9B and is expected to grow to $13.2B by 2022.[31] However, while it's a goal of much training, it often distracts from where we should be putting our attention: rewarding competence.

When we look at business-driven confidence training more specifically, we see it's also booming. By 2018, US research amongst 28,000 business leaders found that 14% of organisations were spending at least $7,000 on average per person on leadership development. While this is high, it shows no signs of abating. Certainly, 94% of all organisations – even the majority which invest less money – said they either plan to increase or at least maintain those levels of leadership development spend.[32]

However, identifying and instilling the *right* skills and types of competencies isn't done in a social vacuum. Buried within the content of almost every leadership development initiative is the fundamental if not explicit remit of

30. Heidimeier, H. and Moser, K. 2009 Self-other Agreement in Job Performance Ratings: A Meta-analytic Test of a Process Model, *Journal of Applied Psychology* 94(2): 353–370.
31. Marketdata LLC 2017 The U.S. Market for Self-improvement Products and Services, August, Marketresearch.com
32. Prakopeak, M. 2018 Follow the Leader(ship) Spending, Corporate Learning Officer. March 21, 2018

confidence-building. When asked what attendees get from various leadership development activities, people often list confidence as one of their top-of-mind tangible benefits.

However, contrary to popular belief, interventions designed to enhance self-esteem or confidence are rarely effective and can be counterproductive.[33] A bigger factor than we like to acknowledge is in how much the audience relates to you. Studies show how *identifiable and similar* a speaker is to the listener will play a *major* factor in how persuasive that speaker is to their chosen audience.[34]

One visible measure of similarity is race. Since senior business audiences are often more from White than from BAME backgrounds, this type of similarity disadvantages BAME speakers.

This is the classic 'He reminds me of a younger version of myself' we think of when we look at who gets guided up the ranks by whom. It goes beyond race and gender to incorporate other factors, as we'll discuss later.

In her role, Lynne Cadenhead routinely sees this overreliance on confidence training to 'fix' deeper issues about how people are received – but have nothing to do with their confidence or at times even their competence. She often contributes to panel discussions on the role of women-led SMEs in the UK and European economy. She talked about her recent experience on a panel: 'One of the male panellists rarely spoke, but when he did, everyone listened to his succinct points, which often got applause or appreciative nods.' She notes:

> The women also spoke up, as we've implored them to do
> throughout our careers. But they received less glowing
> feedback or praise from the audience. If they'd taken the
> quieter approach as the first speaker did, we'd likely be told
> to speak up more and sent to confidence training. It's ironic
> and you can't win.

Others have noticed how ineffective it is to urge people to be more confident – as if the state existed in a vacuum. Barbara Ehrenreich, the award-winning social justice author, writes personally in *Smile or Die* about how she was advised to 'be confident' and 'think positive' when faced with her own breast cancer diagnosis. The assumption was almost that positivity itself could cure cancer. However, there is no evidence that optimism is curative. In fact, startlingly it's often the opposite.'[35]

33. Baumeister, R. F., Campbell, J. D., Krueger, J. I. and Vohs, K. D. 2003 Does High Self-esteem Cause Better Performance Interpersonal Success, Happiness Or Healthier Lifestyle? *Psychology Sciences Public Interest* 4(1): 1–44.
34. Berscheid, E. and Walster, E. 1974 Physical Attractiveness. In L. Berkowitz (ed.) *Advances in Experimental Social Psychology*. Vol. 7.
35. Ehrenreich, B. 2009 *Smile or Die: How Positive Thinking Fooled America and the World*, Granta, London.

THE PECULIARLY INVERSE RELATIONSHIP BETWEEN CONFIDENCE AND COMPETENCE

So now we're getting to the crux of the matter, the heart of why confidence is not nearly as important as competence. Confidence shouldn't matter largely because it actually *undermines* competence. While we think obvious confidence predicts leadership, *it's the complete opposite*. In a meta-analysis of 500 studies over the past 50 years, the most essential attributes in successful corporate managers noted for their *integrity* were surprising. The attributes the highest ranked leaders shared were trustworthiness, kindness and empathy. Confidence didn't even come close.[36]

The prioritisation of these three traits is simultaneously troubling and comforting. Troubling as they're not the qualities anyone seems to be chasing as the key to success. Comforting, however, as these are the qualities with which a wider part of the population *can* identify compared to showy demonstrations of confidence.

Interestingly while trustworthiness, kindness and empathy are sometimes considered more feminine, no one demographic has a monopoly on them. However, what's also troubling is how infrequently we reward people with those attributes with promotions. Boosting confidence would be a great goal if it helped us be more successful or increased our skills and competence.

However, this isn't how it works. Instead, evidence shows overconfidence *leads* to complacency and increased risk-taking. As an example, researchers manipulated participants' confidence levels by giving random feedback on their performances on a straightforward task. Surprisingly, they found lowering people's confidence motivated them to *work harder on their competence*.

By comparison, increasing their confidence by giving them positive feedback had the complete *opposite* effect. It made them complacent.[37] Simply put, higher confidence leads people to overestimate their abilities. This makes them less attentive and focused than their less confident counterparts who work harder at getting the task right.[38]

This is ground-breaking stuff and may feel counterintuitive. Yes, successful people do tend to be more confident. However, this happens because they are often initially the most *aware of their competence levels and therefore work to improve*.

36. Hogan, R. and Kaiser, R. 2010 How to Assess Integrity, *Consulting Psychology Journal* 62(4): 216–234.
37. Vancouver, J. B., Thompson, C. M., Tirschner, E. C. and Putka, D. J. 2002 Two studies Examining the Negative Effects of Self-Efficacy on Performance, *Journal of Applied Psychology* 87(3): 506–516.
38. Stone, D. N. 1994 Overconfidence in Initial Self-Efficacy Judgements: Effects on Decision Processes and Performance, *Organisational Behaviour and Human Decision Processes* 59(3): 452–474.

In reality, successful people don't differ much in confidence levels from less successful peers. As you no doubt know, there are far more unsuccessful people who maintain a high level of undeserved confidence. These are the ones to watch out for. Looking closer at successful people, we see confidence is usually a mere *by-product* of their success. Competence *leads* to confidence, not vice versa.

Tomas Chamorro-Premuzic saw this disparity when he noticed how research echoed what he saw in some of his graduate students:

> *While male students had higher confidence levels than women, their grades were actually lower. Furthermore, analysing the data for male students only, those who displayed higher levels of confidence were often performing worse academically than those men who displayed less confidence. This shows male confidence is delusional, that the more overconfident males are, the more incompetent they tend to be.*[39]

In many ways, your lack of confidence is *a gift* of two parts. First, it warns you *not to take unnecessary risks* until you're more skilled or better prepared. Second, it tells you *where* to put in a concerted effort to improve.

The gap between being competent compared to feeling confident can only be closed in one of two ways. First, you could have a realistic understanding of your abilities and stop there, careful not to 'punch above your weight'. Alternatively, you could increase your actual competence, which is the choice for most of my clients.

This deficit between the two shows up in the way confident people tend to reduce their preparation. You know, the people who 'blag it' or 'make it up as they go along' who spend less time keeping up to date on their subject areas. Avoiding preparation then hinders their actual competence from keeping pace with their confidence.

They can only maintain that pace until they're found out. It's the truism about being 'promoted to your highest state of incompetence'. That's when becoming confident without putting the time towards *becoming* more competent becomes a real risk.

Essentially, it makes your performance increasingly reliant on confidence and your reputation more dependent on faking competence. Faking competence is far harder than faking confidence, but developing competence and skills is far more valuable to both employees and the organisations in which they work. That's why we should *always* push to reward competence.

39. Chamorro-Premuzic, T. 2013 *Confidence: The Surprising Truth about How Much You Need and How to Get It*, Profile Books, London, p. 95.

> **Give your competence the credit it deserves, list out:**
>
> - **Skills you only improved because you first had low confidence in that area.**
> - **Times others' underestimations of you worked in your favour.**
> - **Lessons you're now working on, but that you weren't ready to learn earlier.**

SECRET WEAPON: LACK OF CONFIDENCE

Naomi Pryde, the Head of Commercial Litigation at the law firm DWF, illustrated the converse relationship between confidence and competence perfectly in a story from her early career. She spoke of her competence almost as a secret weapon in creating confidence, simply because she was so routinely underestimated.

Early in her career, one of her first cases was a trial against another firm's Partner. She knew it would be a steep learning curve so over-prepared for her day in court. She was so successful in out-debating this Partner, his client eventually came to *her* firm. The Partner, now a friend all these years later told her: 'You taught me one of the most important lessons of my life: never judge a book by its cover. I'd completely written you off.'

After that Pryde was used by her firm almost as a 'stealth opponent', particularly for lawyers on the other side they suspected would be overconfident. In many ways, her opponent's underestimation of her skill helped her. This was a notable asset for the firm as they sent her to often argue cases against men nearly twice her age. She remembers:

> *In those days, I was pretty under the radar. Each time I won, I'd think it was another fluke. Even the fact that my cases were covered in the news didn't seem to sink in. It took me years to even be able to say 'I'm kind of okay at this'. But I didn't feel anyone was watching me closely, so there were no high expectations.*

Pryde sees her lack of confidence as almost a secret weapon, saying:

> *I do well because I feel anxious or uncertain about how well I'm doing. It means I just work harder. It also makes me a good litigator because I go through a hundred different ways a situation could go wrong in my mind. I'm aware of the traps. In my line of work, it's no bad thing!*

This outlook is fascinating as it highlights how supreme confidence, even in what can be very theatrical outlets like litigation, isn't always necessary. She continues:

> *I'm constantly thinking about the worst-case scenario, so my team now has great processes in place. I don't want anything falling through the cracks or deadlines unmet. It's an old school assumption that litigators have to be uber-aggressive. It's more about adapting your style to the case itself. Some of the best litigators aren't big talkers.*

Pryde notes:

> *Because I'm nervous, I have to zone out everyone else in the courtroom. For me, it's about being confident for just the one person I have to impress in that one moment – a judge or a witness. Most people can handle a one-to-one conversation with confidence. That's far easier to face than commanding an audience of hundreds!*

This approach keeps Pryde feeling authentic as well. She laughs: 'Does anyone *really* love giving speeches to big audiences? I've never heard anyone say: 'I can't wait to give more big presentations!'

This is a point with which Sasha Mooney, a Barrister at Law also identifies. For her, striving for competence was solely as a means of *earning* confidence. She remembers: 'My confidence was initially so fragile, I had to focus on my competence. It was the only thing I could access. I love the law because it's a tool, and you can always get better at using tools!' For Mooney, she takes pride in wielding this tool to benefit her clients. Mooney continues:

> *I only developed my confidence, not by assuming I belonged or deserved to have it, but by doing the things I dreaded. I volunteered for speeches and client presentations, organised events and wrote articles for the press outside of my day job. I didn't have the luxury of 'winging it'.*

For Pryde and Mooney, as well as countless other leaders with whom I spoke, sustainable confidence *only* comes from the time and effort they put in at being competent.

Presenting on your own:

- Treat presentations like a one-to-one conversation. Focus on one friendly face at a time, convincing that individual, before moving on to others.
- Turn 'failures' into jokes with a message. The funniest stories often start with mishaps and what you learned. Success is in how you share the 'joke' and lesson with an audience.
- Ask a status quo member to introduce you to new audiences with your title, expertise and *why* they advocate for you.

FOUR

DOWNSIDES OF CONFIDENCE

> *The big secret in life is that there is no secret. Whatever your goal. You can get there if you are willing to work*
> – Oprah Winfrey

As we've seen, confidence *in the right amount* can be instrumental. It insulates you from taking rejection personally and it's easier to fool others about how remarkable you are if you've already fooled yourself. However, as we're discovering, it works best in small doses and is only sustainable if you earn it via your competence.

So what exactly does overconfidence in the workplace look like at a basic level? It's the colleague who thinks they are invaluable when almost anyone could do their job. It's the officemate who makes inappropriate jokes because they think they are too profitable for the company to lose. It's the person who demands a raise, regardless of the financial situation of the organisation. It's the colleague who threatens to quit if they don't get their way.

Confidence, for its own sake, shouldn't be an end goal for two critical reasons. First, it demotivates you from focusing on improving your competence as we've already discussed. Second, it's highly contextual. This means it will be affected by the type of life experiences you've had, many beyond your control.

That context includes what socioeconomic class you come from, the gender with which you identify, if you have a disability or even your ethnicity. These are all about how you fit in comparison to the status quo where you work. This context means the race towards what the status quo deems confidence is unbalanced from the start. You can make headway, but it's a race you'll struggle to win if you're different from who's gone before.

As Chamorro-Premuzic, an expert in how inversely related competence and confidence are, says:

*Elevating the standards of leadership should be the goal ...
The much bigger problem is the lack of career obstacles for
incompetent men ... People tend to equate leadership with
the very behaviours, overconfidence for example that often
signal bad leadership ... The result is a pathological system
that rewards men for their incompetence while punishing
women for their competence.*[40]

Risky business

World-renowned psychologist and author Daniel Kahneman says that of
all the challenges that can hinder sound decision-making, overconfidence
is the worst.[41] The *Thinking Fast and Slow* author explains how intuition-
led decisions tend to be tainted by overconfidence and ignore alternative
interpretations about a situation. However, let's be clear, few people *admit* to
being primarily intuition led.

I suspect the word itself would be more popular if not for the feminine
connotations of 'women's intuition'. Instead, people will defend their
decisions as a 'gut feeling'. This reliance on *a feeling* is compelling. We are
so overloaded with stimulation on any given day that simplicity must prevail.
You'll subconsciously work with the information you already have, even if that
information is incomplete, not relevant or even biased.

With the pace of global change, both politically and in the business world, this
will likely only increase. We increasingly operate in settings that are so *volatile,
uncertain, complex and ambiguous* that the term 'VUCA' has now become
commonplace. The media and business schools are now teaching employees
about being adaptable to the VUCA world around us.

The inherent danger, however, is that the considered decision-making processes
for which we should be aiming could be regarded as passé and too time-
consuming to warrant. Considered decisions are certainly harder to make.
People trust their guts to quickly make decisions. We react well to those
displaying confidence, even if it's false or ill-informed. This tendency means
confidence rules the day and often leads to risk at best and bad decisions at
worst.

The costs of risk go much further than the effects on any one team or even
organisation. In just the last two decades, we've seen sobering effects of
overconfidence on the global economy.

40. Chamorro-Premuzic, T. 2018 *Why Do So Many Incompetent Men Become Leaders?* Harvard Business Review Press,
Boston, p 5.
41. Shariatmadari, D. 2015 Interview with Daniel Kahneman: What Would I Eliminate if I Had a Magic Wand?
Overconfidence, *The Guardian*, 18 July.

Anne Sibert, an acclaimed economist, investigated the causes of the financial crash where the global crisis started – Iceland. She explained in *The Economist* overconfidence fostered the crash saying:

> *An investor may buy into a known bubble so long as he reckons it will continue into the next period. He counts on his ability to time the market and sell the asset before the bubble pops.*

The research suggests making money off a bubble in the early stages inflates male overconfidence, feeding the bubble's growth.[42] Seeing it from the Icelandic perspective is unique, and Sibert was likely aware of research showing that on successful trading days, traders had higher testosterone levels in their saliva.

This testosterone 'high' increased their confidence and willingness to take risks in subsequent investments. Women's lower testosterone levels may be part of what makes them more risk averse. This chemical difference may be part of the reason women have fewer traffic accidents and are much less likely than men to drive drunk.[43]

John Coates, one of the researchers involved, was inspired to explore the effect of these hormones during his time on a trading floor. His observations concur with Sibert, noting:

> *Male traders were delusional, euphoric, overconfident, had racing thoughts and a diminished need for sleep. The guys were ... desperate to get involved in what some genius was up to and the women just didn't buy into it.*

When his team tracked the chemical levels in traders, they found persistently high levels of testosterone. Testosterone is affiliated with an increased appetite for risk and fearlessness, which can enhance *short-term* profits. However, these chemical traits suggest having too many men on the trading floor increased the very risk men felt confident enough, to handle.

Testosterone also mediates sexual behaviour and competitive encounters. Demonstrating the proclivity towards risk, perhaps relatedly, other researchers have found the more confident people are, the more they report a willingness to cheat on their romantic partners.[44]

42. Male Traders are from Mars, *The Economist*, 18 May 2009.
43. Coates, J. M. and Herbert, J. 2008 Endogenous Steroids and Financial Risk Taking on a London Trading Floor, *Proceedings of the National Academy of Sciences in the USA* 105(16): 6167–6172.
44. Lammers, J., Stoker, J., Jordan, J., Pollman, M. and Stapel, D. 2011 Power Increases Infidelity among Men and Women, *Psychological Science* 22(9): 1191–1197.

Unearned confidence is far from a virtue in finance and isn't profitable in the long run. Other research analysed over 66,000 trades from discount broker accounts. They found the most confident traders performed the most trades, yet they *underperformed in the market overall*. Male investors were so overconfident in their ability, they traded 45% more than female investors making significantly less money than their female counterparts.[45]

Risk needn't be such a key component of confidence if we address what we value. In my experience working with financial services clients, I've noticed women are often high performers *because* they take more precautions and do more research before entering trades. If removed from its hyper-masculine environment, financial trading, in many ways, plays to non-status quo tendencies. Over the long term, trading rewards caution, thoroughness and the ability to admit you're wrong so you can quickly recover.

In the aftermath of the financial crisis, I spoke about the prevalence of female breadwinners, the topic of my second book, at a sizeable London-based event hosted by a large financial services provider. I was struck by comments made by Matthew Hancock, one of the co-presenters and an author of *Masters of Nothing*.

The book focused on what went wrong before the meltdown, and why no one had seen it coming. He admitted to the audience how he and the other male author, Nadhim Zahawi, hadn't looked at gender initially when trying to unpick how the financial crash happened.[46]

However, the shortage of women at crucial decision-making tables became increasingly apparent as they talked to the leading players in financial services. Via the teams they met and the interviews they conducted, they quickly realised 'there were no women in the room'. Hancock said that while a lack of diversity was widely critiqued *after the crash, little real progress has been made in changing this dynamic*.

The work of David Brooks, the journalist and expert on individual decision-making, informed Hancock and Zahawi. In his book, *The Social Animal*, Brooks explains how career progress is often made in institutions like banks. He says: 'Because men dominate the status quo, confidence and assertion are deemed normal and necessary to climb the ranks.'[47]

This comment reminds me of the former banker Barbara-Ann King's earlier comment about how people in compliance and risk can be viewed with disdain. They are often treated as if they were in post simply to 'spoil the fun'.

---

45. Barber, B. and O'Dean, T. 2000 Trading is Hazardous to Your Wealth: The Common Stock Investment Performance of Individual Investors, *Journal of Finance*, 2.
46. Hancock, M. and Zahawi, N. 2011 *Masters of Nothing*, Biteback Publishing, London.
47. Brooks, D. 2011 *The Social Animal*, London: Random House, p. 219.

Similarly, Douglas Morrison says:

> *My issue with staff confidence isn't that some are too under-confident to perform. It's that some are overconfident yet don't always understand what they are doing. That's a real problem because they're often not open to negotiation or compromise or even admitting they need help.*

Morrison, who has worked with hundreds of companies, also sees this with individual leaders:

> *We talk with them about improving innovation. It's what they called us for. But you can't tell them anything new. Plus, they've often hired employees who won't challenge their ego. Invariably those overconfident leaders don't embrace change or the new perspectives they need. It's ironic because that's where innovation comes from.*

Confident risk-taking goes way beyond ill-advised financial decisions and can be literally a matter of life and death. I talked about this with Martin Donnan, Director of NATS Prestwick. NATS control all UK airspace, so safety is their key priority. Starting his career, he trained as an aircrew in the Fleet Air Arm. In our conversation, he points out how military history affects our definitions of what confidence looks like now, even though examples go back generations.

This type of role-modelling happens more in fields reliant on recruitment from the armed forces, like aviation, as his industry does. However, each industry has its own 'heroes' and looking at them more closely is often enlightening when it comes to understanding what we're rewarding. Donnan says:

> *The aviation industry arose in the post-war mentality. That venerated certain types of leaders, often with a military background. That's still with us and in other industries today. But in truth, their confidence sometimes belied some pretty big character flaws which create real limitations.*

He explains that all of the great leaders were often emboldened by their confidence – sometimes to the point of arrogance. This also makes them 'unlikeable' at best and likely to make choices that we'd consider questionable or even unethical. He speaks of Douglas Bader, a Royal Air Force fighter pilot and hero in his time. Early in his career, Bader lost both legs in a crash after performing an aerial stunt he was forbidden to do. The stunt had already killed two other pilots. After recovering from his accident, Bader returned to fly in WWII and was instrumental in the Battle of Britain in 1940.

In 1956, *Reach for the Sky*, a biographical movie about Bader was released. However, as Donnan and I discuss the war hero, it becomes apparent Bader's overconfidence and the risks he was willing to take *contributed* to his original injury. Years later, his arrogant overconfidence meant the movie production team didn't even involve him as an adviser in his own biopic.[48]

Kenneth More, the actor playing the war hero, smoothed out Bader's 'edges' to make him more likeable. Bader may have become more confident over time, in light of his wartime successes. However, the seed of arrogance in flouting safety rules started early. Arrogance is another side effect of confidence gone awry, and something professionals would do well to avoid.

WHO ME? CONFIDENCE, ARROGANCE AND NARCISSISM

There's a fine line between confidence and arrogance. However, both are labels we more readily give to men rather than women. For some, ignoring or trying to work around arrogant colleagues may be business as usual, as it has been for many of my clients historically and non-status quo members more widely. However, for others, calling people out for arrogance is part of a changing tide. Vanessa Vallely, OBE and founder of the WeAreTheCity network, describes:

> *Our tolerance of 'arrogant' men is lower than it's ever been. Arrogance, and I've seen plenty in the city, is still not being called out as frequently as it needs to be. But I think the increase of attention we're publicly giving it is promising. Amongst my own teenagers, there seems to be zero tolerance towards any bad behaviour amongst their generation. We'll see what happens after they enter the workplace. They may have to conform more than they want to, even though as a generation, they certainly expect better.*

We should be concerned about the people who *aren't* humbled when their arrogance is called out. This disregard suggests the next step up; narcissism and the toxic overconfidence ultimately destructive to teams. As we discuss the need for confidence to be redefined, Vallely agrees: 'Let's throw away the word "confidence", it has too much emotion wrapped up in it. Besides which, you're chasing a utopia that doesn't, and probably *shouldn't*, exist.'

Between exploitative business practices, geopolitics shifting towards populism and climate change, the modern world is not in a better place for our global excess of confidence.

---

48. https://en.wikipedia.org/wiki/Reach_for_the_Sky

As Vallely's comments suggest, encouraging people to take on typically status quo behaviours of 'confidence' won't work any longer. It too frequently spills into arrogance, which features self-centred thinking, risk-taking and ultimately narcissism.

At its core, narcissism is the supersized version of overconfidence. It also features a virtually pathological lack of concern for others. It's a psychological diagnosis, but most narcissists have never been diagnosed. Why the need? They're the ones in the right after all!

Research shows the more powerful an overconfident person feels, the more likely they are also to be narcissistic. In four studies, researchers found narcissism was a robust predictor of overconfidence in one's abilities and most noticeable when asked to remember a time when they've had power over others.[49]

> **Keep narcissists in check by asking:**
> - **When a decision they've made didn't end well.**
> - **When someone else had power over them and actually knew *more* than they did.**
> - **When a subordinate (or someone they consider a subordinate!) had a better solution.**

All of these questions will be profoundly uncomfortable for them. However, they'll illuminate their appetite for risk and how they handle poor decisions. In my experience, it's these types of questions I sometimes use with senior leaders that stump them. Their self-narrative is so focused on what they've done well and achieved, that they've very often forgotten the things that went wrong, as they do for all of us.

The researchers explained: 'Past literature examining leaders has indicated that narcissists often emerge as leaders in organisations. A good example of this would be the situation that occurred at Enron.' Macenczak and colleagues continue: 'There, many leaders that were likely high in narcissism, made overly risky decisions in which they had high degrees of confidence. Organisations should have processes in place to monitor the decision-making of top managers to ensure that decisions are properly vetted.'

Good as this advice is, reliance on people, particularly narcissists, to consistently follow 'processes' is easier said than done. The very people who need vetting are those who would largely eschew such a safeguard.

---

49. Macenczak, L. A., Campbell, S., Henley, A. B. and Campbell, W. K. 2016 Direct and Interactive Effects of Narcissism and Power on Overconfidence, *Personality and Individual Differences* 91: 113–122.

After all, they 'know best' and anyone who questions them doesn't appreciate their genius. Because confidence and competence aren't correlated, office narcissists are like little 'naked emperors' running around wreaking havoc.

Self-centred and satisfied in their superiority to everyone else, narcissists pay scant attention to negative comments from others and dismiss negative feedback. Narcissists are also *manipulative* so don't mind exploiting people to attain power, fame or success.[50] These are certainly not characteristics most people want to adopt in their drive towards confidence. More importantly, nor are they traits that are good for business or society at large.

How to spot narcissists? They don't take constructive feedback, blame others for their mistakes and readily take credit for other's achievements. We all know someone at work, or maybe even at home, like that. Worryingly, while our image of narcissists stems from the movies, a higher than average number are leading organisations.

One study compared the psychopathy scores and 360° feedback scores for over 200 senior leaders at four different US companies. The researchers remark:

> *Perhaps the most dramatic results of this study had to do with how the corporation viewed individuals with many psychopathic traits. That is, high psychopathy total scores were associated with perceptions of good communication skills, strategic thinking, and creative/innovative ability and, at the same time, with poor management style, failure to act as a team player, poor performance appraisals and overall accomplishments – as rated by their bosses.*[51]

This is damning stuff. What sounds like pathology can be a short-term strategy for an individual. However, it undermines teams and wider business. The other issue is that most of the people you truly *need and want to succeed*, the competent, don't tend to take on these qualities. Doing so would threaten their sense of integrity.

In my coaching practice, integrity is one of the most significant issues non-status quo people have with aspiring for the top. It's that sense of *What exactly am I selling if I 'sell-out'?* And if they don't aspire to the top? We don't question the value of what's at the top and the compromises it takes to get there. Instead, we often blame their 'lack of confidence' and ambition as the problem.

50. R. Lubit 2002. The Long Term Organisational Impact of Destructively Narcissistic Managers, *Academy of Management Executive* 16(1): 127–138.
51. Babiak, P. et al. 2010 Corporate Psychopathy: Talking the Walk, *Behavioural Sciences and the Law* 28(2): 174–193.

Narcissism features unrealistic confidence but, under specific circumstances, narcissists maybe your top performers, at least initially. For example, they may succeed in sales jobs that require projecting positive short-term impressions. Where narcissists fail is in *maintaining and growing* relationships over the long haul. That takes cultivating a broader perspective and developing empathy – skills narcissists simply don't have.

In the sales functions of many of my corporate clients, sales teams are noticeably even unwittingly split. Extroverts and often men work in the initial sales function for 'new client acquisition'. Introverts and more women sit in the relationship management roles that generate *ongoing* sales from existing clients. They keep clients happy on a consistent basis via listening and ongoing negotiation. Both types of sales are necessary, but landing a new client is deemed far more exciting than getting an old client to renew. This again speaks to *which* types of confidence are valued, how and by whom.

'Influencers' and the Narcissism Epidemic

No doubt we have had narcissists since time immemorial, but they have been increasing in the years since we've been measuring this trait. The only increase comparable to the rise in narcissism levels (during the same period of time) is the rise in obesity levels, which increased more than 200% from 1950–2010. Unlike narcissism gains, however, obesity is widely viewed as an epidemic and something we need to curb.[52] Weight gain is one modern increase we are actively trying to combat, while gains in narcissism are widely ignored, despite the risks they also create.

Compare this with how we continue to 'feed' our need for heightened self-confidence, even when there is no evidence, like extra weight, it does anyone any good. In fact, much like obesity, promoting narcissists costs us dearly. What makes narcissism seem like less of an issue is that it's less visible than weight gain. Just like the obesity epidemic, however, the growth in narcissism is all around us, particularly in senior roles, as narcissists interview and can even sell very well.

They have no trouble taking credit for their own, and even other's work. Several interviewees observed how the most confident people they knew often relied on a very competent team *below* them. You'll recognise this in many industries where when senior people leave, they take their team with them to the next employer.

---

52. Kluger, J. 2008 How America's Children Packed on the Pounds, *Time*, 12 June.

The culture of 'winner takes all', 'eat or be eaten' and 'watch out for number 1' encourages narcissism. It also makes inflated self-views *seem reasonable or even aspirational*, which is well documented by others focused on the impact of social media on millennials, as we'll discuss. Ideally, delusions of grandeur could *encourage people to work harder to attain that expertise.* However, these delusions have a reverse effect, primarily because they are nearly unattainable.

I am a good executive coach and speaker, and my clients make huge progress in their careers and in the way they feel about their skills. Am I the best speaker in the world? Not by a long shot. Knowing that however, galvanises me. It keeps me attending conferences to learn new techniques. It encourages me to read the latest research to make my presentations all the more current. It also means I hire people far better than me for tasks where I need them – which are the majority of tasks when you are running a business.

Coinciding with this rise in narcissism is the hollow desire to 'be famous for being famous'. In the age of confidence over competence, this goal of 'influencers' surpasses the drive of being famous for having an actual skill, particularly compared to generations past. 'Influencers' are not known for a specific achievement or useful ability, other than attracting followers to a carefully cultivated, stylised and edited brand. Their appeal has rapidly gained, and even a decade ago, over half (54%) of more than 1,000 16-year-olds in the UK said 'becoming a celebrity' was their main career plan.[53]

To this point, the more narcissistic people are, the more unrealistic their expectations. The less realistic, the more depressed you end up when realising statistically, you'll unlikely ever be 'the best' at any one skill. This wake-up call can lead to a spiral of depression and a feeling of emptiness, as we'll be discussing.

When to ignore feedback:

- **Focus on the *themes* in any 360° feedback, not your self-assessments.**
- **If not part of a theme, individual bad reviews may stem more from a single person's bias as to who they *expect* you to be or what serves them better.**
- **De-programme from social media to unfollow 'mood hoovers' or those who remind you of the version of yourself you *don't* want to grow.**

---

53. Kershaw, A. 2010 Fame the Career Choice of Half of 16 Year Olds, *The Independent*, 17 February.

No Tariff Required: Exporting American Ideals

So what's driving this rise in the value of confidence *over* competence? I've spoken with successful people from different countries in my research, many of whom worked for multinational companies. Many already held traits or adopted, where necessary, to the unofficial culture of headquarters. This happened even if their head office was in a different country from where they'd been raised. Many struggled to identify *when exactly* their organisational culture developed a head office mentality. However, most felt it stemmed from Western, and in particular, American values – particularly in our era of mergers and acquisitions.

These values, such as confidence, have seeped into many global organisations. Often these values underpin the definition of 'a good worker'. This monotheistic way of looking at the world is far from healthy. It's infecting the world with the dangers inherent in overvaluing confidence instead of competence.

It's also time to realise that confident governments don't have as much to be confident about as they think they do. Some may see these issues in light of political wins by leaders such as Donald Trump. While his win and populism more widely are exacerbating a trend towards the overvaluation of confidence, the origins of this shift go back further.

Paul Krugman, the American economist and columnist for *The New York Times*, responded to what he saw in his nation's smugness more than 20 years ago, in an essay entitled 'American the Boastful'. He warned that 'if pride goeth before a fall, the US has one heck of a comeuppance in store'.[54]

We got that comeuppance in terms of Trump's election. This was the rise of an overconfident celebrity incompetent in geopolitics. This is before you set aside other traits needed in a competent national leader – empathy for people from different backgrounds, selflessness in favour of the country's needs and a willingness to compromise.

Adding fuel to the flames, he was buoyed by confident status quo supporters. Many felt entitled to their natural right to have a disproportionately large share of the proverbial pie, simply because their parents and grandparents did. Trump's battle cry of 'Make America Great Again' was an elixir to people who felt that America had been great *for people like them*. The reality is that for most non-status quo people in the US, who now make up the majority of Americans, it was never *equally 'great' for all*.

---

54. Krugman, P. 1998 America the Boastful, *Foreign Affairs Journal*, May.

As Barbara Ehrenreich, the acclaimed author and social justice advocate, saliently pointed out *years* before Trump's election:

> *But of course it takes the effort of positive thinking to imagine that America is the 'best' or the 'greatest'. Militarily, yes, we are the mightiest ... But on many other fronts, the American score is dismal and was dismal even before the economic downturn that began in 2007 ...*

Ehrenreich continues:

> *Worse, some of the measures by which we do lead the world should inspire embarrassment rather than pride. We have the highest percentage of our population incarcerated, and the greatest level of inequality in wealth and income. We are plagued by gun violence and racked by personal debt.*[55]

As a fellow American, I have to ask, surely we need to look at our overall competence in these troubling areas? Rectifying these real problems should be the priority. It is certainly more important than claiming the right to be so confident, almost as a birth right that comes with US citizenship?

Indeed, research by the Pew Centre found that confidence in the US *by other nations* has fallen to a record low since Trump took office. Some 70% of leaders in the 25 economic powerhouse nations surveyed said they had 'no confidence' in Trump 'to do the right thing regarding world affairs'.[56] As we've discussed, this is what matters: *the confidence others have in you* – not the show you put on.

THE RISE OF POLITICAL STRONGMEN ON THE WORLD STAGE

Undeniably, Trump's win comes with a rise nationalistic populism. We see this with other overconfident leaders, who are undermining democracy on the global stage. Populist leaders such as Boris Johnson in the UK, Viktor Orbán in Hungary, Vladimir Putin in Russia, Rodrigo Duterte in the Philippines, Jair Bolsonaro in Brazil and Recep Erdoğan in Turkey have all risen via this 'confidence first' bandwagon.

They have often strategically embraced Trump's appeals to racism and at times even violence to build their support. They do this while personally smoothing out Trump's roughest edges in their own delivery. Many of these leaders, like Trump, have been working to build yet more control over judicial and legislative powers to garner greater power.

---

55. Ehrenreich, B. 2009 *Smile or Die: How Positive Thinking Fooled America and the World*, Granta, London p. 7.
56. Pew Research Centre, 2018 Spring Global Attitudes Survey.

At best, these moves maintain the status quo, while disenfranchising everyone else. At worst, these moves hinder democracy via a demonisation of journalism and subject matter experts; science and evidence-based facts.

We have reached an age where how you *feel* about a topic is as important as what *facts you know* about a topic. The US Press Secretary Kelly Ann Conway's statement about Trump's preference for 'alternative facts' is only logical in this world where confidence is more valued than competence.

These leaders use unquestionable self-confidence to not only fake competence in areas where they have little, if any, experience, but also to undermine critics and legitimate experts. Authoritarian regimes have favoured this tactic throughout history. Challenge the accuracy of a critic's evidence-based knowledge, but also the method by which they are distributed.

This is the 'fake news' agenda in a nutshell. Given that challenging the media was a tactic of authoritarian leaders such as Hitler, concern about these leaders' overconfidence, and the way they undermine the competent, should be very real.

My coaching clients are not politicians but have talked with me about their confidence levels for years. We work through those issues, often getting them promotions. However, the overvaluation of confidence on the geopolitical stage was one of my motivations for exploring this topic further, as I do see overlap. When asked what confidence looks like, many people I meet in the corporate arena answer with variations of: 'Confident people take charge in a group. They put themselves forward and take risks. They speak their mind and don't care what others think.'

Superficially this sounds right. However, by this standard, Donald Trump should be our *ideal* in confidence, but I have yet to meet anyone who would like him as a colleague or thinks he'd be a good fit for their organisation. Donald Trump, and other leaders like him, are a natural extension of a culture that values 'confidence' far too much.

Naomi Klein, the social activist and acclaimed author, wrote about this in *No is Not Enough*. She explains:

> *Trump is ... the logical endpoint of a great many dangerous stories our culture has been telling for a very long time. That greed is good. That the market rules. That money is what matters in life. That White men are better than the rest ... Trump really shouldn't come as a shock.*[57]

57. Klein, N. 2017 *No is Not Enough: Defeating the New Shock Politics*, Penguin, New York, p. 258.

We brought his mix of commercialism at the cost of ethics upon ourselves, and worse yet, we are growing these types of leaders across the world. They are extreme. Even so, what we see in the workplace is that when we overvalue confidence and the short-term thinking that often accompanies it, sometimes the incompetent get hired, promoted or voted in.

WORKPLACE MISTAKES MADE BY YOUR 'INNER GENIUS'

Most leaders are not taking us down such globally dangerous paths. However, that mix of hubris with an unwillingness to believe you are wrong or could benefit from taking on advice affects the workplace. All of that is borne out of confidence, and, worryingly for industry, it's also the opposite of innovation.

Douglas Morrison, the Director of the Scottish Institute of Innovation and Knowledge Exchange, observes that while he's asked to advise organisations on increasing innovation, they often don't like aspects of his advice. So why do people who need help in innovation, seem to reject it at the same time? Morrison pauses for a while before replying: 'I'm torn. Sometimes I think it's based on their fear of being wrong. Other times I think they are just so narcissistic they don't see that other people can bring value. I've seen both.'

Interestingly, I think the two can go hand in hand. When I mention narcissism, he laughs: 'That word was going through my head, but it seemed so extreme, it's hard to believe they live amongst us!' However, Morrison can think of an immediate example, even beyond the clients he meets in his advisory settings. He recalls a former colleague:

> We were in similar roles, and he had common narcissistic traits. He benefited from above-average skills but rated himself as 'the best' in every category all the time – never deviating. That would be admitting he'd made mistakes or had more to learn. If he decided to explore a new field because of some God-given insight, he'd move into that area full of enthusiasm.

Morrison explains:

> Over time he'd not only annoy everyone who recognised he wasn't competent, but he'd also exhausted every resource at his disposal. These might be funding, extra staff, potential favours, other people's time, committee memberships, conference speaking slots. All of these were originally extended with a sense of goodwill to him.

80

Morrison continues how this routinely played out saying:

> *Eventually he'd be ostracised, and then he'd leap onto*
> *a new specialism. He'd repeated the cycle five times*
> *over a decade. Every couple of years he'd then take on*
> *a new specialism in which he again knew best, creating*
> *enemies and resentment on both sides. At no point did he*
> *acknowledge he could ever learn anything. He took the*
> *approach of 'I could teach these idiots a thing or two'.*
> *But he'd only be annoyed 18 months later because his new*
> *colleagues hadn't recognised his inner genius.*

Morrison's example is recognisable to many of us. However, this attitude of 'only I know best' is recognisable. It stems from how historical leaders have approached leadership, even in the face of huge mistakes they've made. Their views trickle down to those who reported to them. Years later, even, these create real consequences for how we define confidence.

FIVE

ORIGINS OF THE CONFIDENT IDEAL

> *Success is sweet, but the secret is sweat*
> – General Norman Schwarzkopf

So where do our ideals for confident *leadership* come from? By now, I've referred to the 'status quo' numerous times. They run our institutions, our political systems and influence our commonly held beliefs. I'll start by saying these issues aren't solely about White men though they make up a majority of leaders in the organisations where I have consulted. However, you may work in a very different organisation. Equally, when I say, 'very different', it's worth remembering that having a few people of colour as leaders and a token woman or two amongst all the top White men is not 'diversity'. If that's where you work, you aren't exempt from these issues.

Often people from under-represented backgrounds make it to the highest echelons simply because they adapt to the most status quo expectations and behaviours. Their trajectory happens in part for the same reason it happens for the status quo. Hard work in some measure, but often also via other demographic similarities they share with the status quo. These similarities might be socioeconomic background, race or sexual preference, to name just a few.

Even so, this is a conversation that must include the status quo. The smartest White men I know understand our definitions of confidence matter, and that all definitions evolve. In fact, we need the status quo to help create definitions that could better work for everyone. They know getting to grips with diversity, across employees and markets, will be the name of the game in the 21st century. We need a range of mindsets to tackle everything from climate change and income inequality, to the rise of increasingly populist regimes.

These smart men also know all of us are like fish swimming in our individual bowls. Our bowls only reflect our personal lifetime of experiences. But fish can't see the water in which they swim. We all swim in different bowls – some of us have cloudier water than others, and some have more obstacles to swim around. The critical thing to recognise is that it's our water, our experience.

You don't swim in someone else's water, but if you look *outside of your bowl*, you can get an idea how clean or cloudy the water is.

That's the way privilege works – it's only visible if you don't have it, or you've taken the time to swim in someone else's bowl. These behaviours, particularly around confidence, are expected as the norm, and anything else is deemed inferior. Redefining confidence and competence will take work, and it won't be popular – particularly with the groups it already favours. They will find such ideas ridiculous and unnecessary at best, and personally threatening and dangerous at worst.

I am reminded of the work of Alexis de Tocqueville, who wrote *Democracy in America*. He travelled to America in the 1830s after living through the French Revolution. He came to the new country to understand what made the young nation work after its own revolution and *why* revolutions happen in the first place. Notably, he wrote that revolts *don't start where the need is greatest*; that is amongst the most disadvantaged.[58] Instead, he explained, they happen where *expectations are most unmet*.

This observation remains true. It highlights why we see a backlash from the status quo when previously disenfranchised groups make progress. The vitriol we see against successful non-status quo members most often comes from those who expected more for themselves. The status quo anticipates a certain standard of living, often based on what their parents and grandparents enjoyed. When things don't work out that way, they get angry at those living the life they feel they deserve. In the 21st century, that increasingly means well-educated working women, ethnic minorities and other groups making headway in the workplace.

Hillary Clinton observed this angry sense of disconnect after her 2016 defeat:

> *It's about loss. It's about the sense that the future will be harder than the past ... Anger and resentment fill that void and can overwhelm everything else: tolerance, basic standards of decency, facts.*[59]

Set against that contentious backdrop, maintaining status quo ideals of confidence, and what it should be, will be one such battle. Yet to make progress, we must address how our definitions of confidence favour or disadvantage different groups of people. We've changed and expanded definitions of other 'common sense' words before. This is the time to do it again. For example, on face value, most people somehow accept the 'truism' that 'men are stronger than women'. However, the truth lies in how you *define* strength.

58. deTocqueville, A. 1835 *Democracy in America*, George Dearborn & Co., New York.
59. Clinton, H. R. 2017 *What Happened*, Simon & Schuster, New York, p. 442.

Women can survive longer in icy water and can go longer without food. They live longer overall and female new-borns are more likely to live until infancy. They are also more likely to create new fulfilling lives after the death of a beloved partner. If we accept these as signs of strength, we have to expand our definition of 'strength'. However, if we only primarily see strength as *muscle mass*, we'll see it clearly continues to favour men. We also see this when we later look further at what it means 'to be a man'. Without the ability to redefine words and phrases, we are all worse off.

The earliest psychological research on confidence was about, conducted and interpreted by White men so it's not surprising that others 'lacked confidence'. We've accepted their standard on what confidence is ever since. However, this isn't the whole truth. Hundreds of studies find that when looking at confidence levels, particularly of talented youth, there is no gender confidence gap. This is true for a wide range of topics and even includes that old chestnut about women lacking confidence in mathematics.[60]

'GREAT MEN' IN HISTORY

If you're unconvinced how much dominant groups get to dictate the definitions we use, let's look at a far earlier example. The phrase 'Great Man Leadership' has been used in shaping ideology amongst both private and public leadership for hundreds of years. Thomas Carlyle first advocated Great Man Theory in the late 19th century. Carlyle argued it was 'superior intellect, heroic courage or *divine inspiration*' that led certain people to a state of rare greatness.[61] The assumptions about *who* could be 'great' clearly start with the title 'Great Man'.

The term met with great acclaim and was used as a model for generations. However, when looking at the examples he cited, it was also obvious Carlyle and his supporters only saw European men as worthy of the title. The Great Man Theory had contemporary critics even at the time, who sound positively modern by the standards of the 1890s when he was writing. Herbert Spencer noted in his 1896 book, *The Study of Sociology*:

> *You must admit that the genesis of a great man depends on*
> *the long series of complex influences which has produced*
> *the race in which he appears, and the social state into*
> *which that race has slowly grown ... Before he can remake*
> *his society, his society must make him.*[62]

60. Eccles, J. 1994 Understanding Women's Educational and Occupational Choices: Applying the Eccles et al. Model of Achievement-related Choices, *Psychology of Women Quarterly* 18: 585–610.
61. https://en.wikipedia.org/wiki/Great_man_theory
62. Spencer, H. 1873 *The Study of Sociology*, Henry S. King, London p. 31.

This highlights the argument I'd like to extend. The way we've been raised and the *lives we lead determine our definitions*. This is particularly important when trying to understand where our definitions and expectations of 'confidence' come from, because they affect *everyone* in an organisation and the way those people progress. As proof of how malleable our definitions of such supposedly stable words are, look at how far removed 'divine inspiration' is from modern leadership ideals though it was imperative for Carlyle.

We no longer expect modern leaders to cite guidance from God. Whether this is positive or not depends on your point of view. However, it shows even our most popular terminology like 'great man' can evolve. Evolve it must as we'll look at how confidence is actually a dual-edged sword, depending on who demonstrates it. Women are judged aggressive when they show confidence, let alone any of the 'Great Man' qualities. Men are judged 'weak' if they don't.

So how does this play out in the world of work? Elizabeth Uviebinené, a columnist at the *Financial Times*, writes on workplace issues, and notably how race intersects with your experiences. She says: 'We *absolutely* give the benefit of the doubt to confident men. The challenge is that if a new hire doesn't fit the mould of who was in that role before, we don't give them the benefit of the doubt.' It takes more creativity to visualise someone in a role if their predecessors looked different from the current candidate – a particular challenge for those from the non-status quo.

CASE STUDIES IN MODERNITY

'Great Man Theory' may have been one of the earliest 'case studies' as to what made a leader ideal. But also set a precedent of how we use real-life examples for the traits to identify with and copy. Understanding which models of 'ideal leaders' we use has real implications for modern leaders.

Case studies have far-reaching implications for what we teach about leadership partly because of their utility in generating discussion. Their appeal lies in how they focus on what 'real people' did to overcome specific challenges. However, authors don't write equally about all types of leaders. Instead, the vast majority of business school case studies feature leaders that are overwhelmingly White, Western and male.

However, with a global marketplace for these training materials, this is increasingly being criticised. The way case studies traditionally overlooked specific sectors, countries, themes and the role of labour unions does bear scrutiny.[63]

---

63. Jack, A. 2018 Why Harvard's Case Studies are Under Fire, *Harvard Business Review*, 29 October.

Plus, because so much of the action in the classroom often centres around verbal debate, they can over-reward 'presentation skills' rather than content that would be more widely applicable. The focus on presentation and debate is entertaining and engaging. However, it primarily rewards extroverts and begs the question on the overall utility in mastering this type of 'show' for the teams these students are preparing to lead.

Increasingly, some business schools are challenging the traditional case study with its focus on the 'leader as celebrity' approach. For example, MIT is now using case studies in less than half of its business school classes, opting instead for simulations, mentoring and consultancy projects. These put students directly in the action, rather than sharing opinions about the choices of others. This is a great move to improve competence, rather than simply a test of debating skills.

Similarly, Yale's School of Management substituted 150 open-ended exercises using links to a wide range of online sources and articles in place of their traditional case studies. This format highlights how complex business decisions are via this 'multi-perspective' outlook. Professors find students more willing to entertain the possibility of many different 'right' answers, something we'll need in a VUCA world.

Clearly the way leaders have been celebrated historically for their unshakeable confidence is something we must address. They are like the stories that entertain at a child's bedtime in that they shape the way we see the world. In this case, the 'stories' in case studies inform some of the most senior people we're developing to lead our organisations.

OVER-PROMOTING UNDER-DELIVERY

We all love a good show, and no one gives a better show than the visibly confident. However, by now, you know these are not necessarily the first people to promote or even hire. Too frequently we hire the overconfident who can give a great presentation, but eventually under-deliver. Ultimately, this is a business issue, as progressing the wrong people leads to mistakes, risks and unfulfilled potential in truly competent people. Instead, we should be doing more to advance the careers of the under-confident, but wholly competent.

You can do this if you recognise this will likely lead to better delivery, with a confidence boost for the successful candidate as a *side benefit*. Even if someone is confident about the results they can achieve, those results don't often come to pass. MBA students did a series of maths problems and handed theses tests to researchers, but weren't given their results. Fifteen months later, they formed new groups to reconvene for a new task. They were asked to select a group leader *at their own discretion* based on their perceived maths skills.

Each person pitched why they would be the *best leader* for a new upcoming maths task. Men were more optimistic about their future performance, overestimating their past performance by 30%. Women also overestimated their score, but only by 14%. Pitching to their teammates using solely their self-assessments, the men were more convincing in their bids for team leadership.

However, this had real consequences for the groups. The leaders were selected based upon their 'gift of the gab' as witnessed in selling their future potential performance rather than what *the researchers knew to be their actual performance* from 15 months earlier. A leaders' past performance was a far better predictor of future performance than their memories of how well they did or how well they sold their accomplishments to others. This means those who overestimated their future performance were indeed chosen, but their teams *did no better* from that supposed expertise.

Other research looking at externally recruited executives compared to internally grown executives bears this out. It took three years for external hires to perform as well as the internal hires, and externals were more likely to leave during that time. However, it was seven years before the pay of the internal hires caught up with external hires who were initially paid around 18 per cent more, based on higher levels of experience and education. However, just as the previously mentioned research, they also likely 'sold' themselves well contributing to the way we all underestimate the 'on-boarding' period for any new hire.[64]

Several of the interviewees explained the difficulty in avoiding being drawn into confident 'sales pitch', no matter how experienced the listening audience. Neil Stevenson smiles when he says: 'Seniority or level of experience doesn't inoculate people against overvaluing confidence.' Another interviewee saw a particularly difficult employee judged as 'highly effective' by Non-Executive Board members because of their presentational skills. Ironically, that 'star' was simultaneously going through a formal performance management process because their day-to-day delivery was so poor, something the Board didn't know.

This reality is frustrating as often senior leaders lack the truth behind the situation. The interviewee continues:

> *A NED's interaction with team members is limited to 'show-pony' presentations. However, their opinions are important, so this can cause particular difficulty. Worse still, because Board members are usually so senior in their own careers, they often feel they are 'beyond bias'.*

---

64. Bidwell, M. 2011 Paying More to Get Less: The Effects of External Hiring versus Internal Mobility, *Administrative Science Quarterly*, 56(3).

PROMOTING POOR ETHICS

When people become too confident, it can also lead to a sense of entitlement at best and catastrophic ethical decisions at worst. As Marshal of the Royal Air Force, Sir Arthur Harris led bombing campaigns during the First World War after his formative teenage years in Rhodesia (modern-day Zimbabwe).

As a member of a racial group who held power at the time and were rarely questioned, this no doubt grew Harris' confidence. However, it also shaped his beliefs in how different communities could be violated or 'dealt with', informing his feelings about bombing Germany years later. These decisions no doubt helped earn him his Royal Air Force nickname 'Butcher Harris'.

During the Second World War, Harris fiercely advocated 'area-bombing' over precision targeting. This type of attack was controversial even then because it was considered both less effective and led to far more destruction and civilian casualties. Years later, he still defended those choices, despite the massive loss of civilian life it caused.

Over his career, he was characterised by confidence and described by a contemporary historian: 'Harris made a way of seeing only one side of a question and then of exaggerating it. He tended to confuse advice with interference, criticism with sabotage and evidence with propaganda.'[65] History has not been kind to Harris, and while his statue stands in London, he is now regarded by many as a war criminal for the mistakes he made.

No doubt many of the people (most often members of the status quo) we now venerate achieved great feats in their career. While these leaders may be viewed as artefacts, their overconfident 'shoot first, ask questions later' approach informs what later leaders were modelled and now think about confidence and leadership. These role models trickle down to directly, if not subconsciously to influence what behaviours get rewarded in modern organisations. As Martin Donnan of NATS Prestwick describes: 'Leadership training tells you *these* are the people to emulate!'

Fast forward to modern times, and stories abound about the dangers of overconfident leaders. No matter how you feel about Brexit, it's largely recognised the decision to hold a referendum arose from the overconfidence of the then British Prime Minister, David Cameron. He believed it an easy win for 'Remain' that would stop his critics once and for all. Therefore he called for a referendum few people were asking for, on EU membership in 2016. At the time, there was no real public demand for a referendum that wreaked economic havoc even before the UK has left, something even Cameron now admits.

---

65. Webster, Sir Charles and Frankland, N. 1961 *The Strategic Air Offensive against Germany, 1939–1945*. Volume 4. London, pp. 135–137.

Even before then, Cameron's overconfidence was routinely noted in the press. One parliamentary correspondent wrote of his blasé attitude towards the harrowing, but weekly Prime Minister's Questions:

> *Harold Macmillan used to vomit after facing the Commons. Pitt the Younger used to fortify himself with a (whole) bottle of port. Tony Blair found the ordeal nerve-wracking. So why does David Cameron seem so supremely confident, even blasé, at Prime Minister's Questions, these days?*[66]

WHEN CONFIDENCE BECOMES SINISTER

However, the overconfident and narcissistic operate in all industries, beyond the military, politics or even big business. Harvey Weinstein, the poster boy for the #MeToo movement, was unlikely to have been a predator from childhood. However, his eventual overconfidence means his career is culminating with over 80 separate allegations of sexual abuse and rape to date from co-workers and aspiring actresses. His overconfidence came from a long career of publicity and box-office wins which grew into a sense of entitlement.

This overconfidence and willingness to be a bully showed itself even years before the accusations came to light. One example was when 23-year-old journalist Rebecca Traister questioned Weinstein on a fairly mundane matter at a party to get a quote. He repeatedly screamed 'fucking cunt' and 'fucking bitch' in a crowded Manhattan restaurant at her, before being confronted by the male journalist she was travelling with, Andrew Goldman. When Goldman dared to request an apology on Traister's behalf, Weinstein exploded with: 'I'm glad I'm the fucking sheriff of this shit-ass fucking town!'

Within seconds Weinstein realised he'd unknowingly been recorded by Goldman in that exchange. To get the tape-recorder back, Weinstein physically attacked the journalist, pushing him down a set of stairs. While dozens of photographers snapped away, no photograph was ever published – because just as Weinstein had confidently told everyone, he *was* the sheriff at the time.[67] This incident was still years before later allegations came to light, but highlights how confidence can grow into narcissism and entitlement, a sense of being 'above the rules'.

Clearly, not every problematic co-worker becomes a Weinstein. However, we often let people's confidence grow beyond their competence; in this case, Weinstein's lack of skill in dealing with other people, including colleagues.

66. D'Arcy, M. 2015 Why is David Cameron so Confident at PMQ's, BBC News, 15 November.
67. Bruney, G. 2019 Hulu's Untouchable Illustrates Just How Harvey Weinstein Operated in Plain Sight, *Esquire*, 3 September.

As Reem Hayati, a Cairo-based FMCG marketing consultant, explains: 'Credible confidence comes from knowing your area inside and out – your competence.' However, there is another type of competence in dealing with others – a skill he didn't have.

Weinstein was a very competent producer of films. However, his confidence in that one skill and the access to others it afforded him, made his behaviour grow out of bounds. Indeed, some allegations went back to mid-1970s, early in Weinstein's career, but a culture had already been fostered of protecting him and looking the other way. As Hayati continues: 'It's tricky. The only people who truly know you are competent and know the details are members of your own team. They're *not likely to call you out.*'

Similarly, Jeffrey Epstein died an ignominious death at his own hand in jail after being charged with sex-trafficking crimes against minors. *The New York Times* broke the news about how his overconfidence spilt into his work life, reporting:

> *Mr. Epstein, who was charged in July with the sexual trafficking of girls as young as 14, was a serial illusionist: He lied about the identities of his clients, his wealth, his financial prowess, his personal achievements. But he managed to use connections and charisma to cultivate valuable relationships with business and political leaders.*[68]

Epstein was well-connected with influencers such as Donald Trump and Prince Andrew – relationships from which both are keen to distance themselves. However, as further evidence of his grandiose overconfidence, he will likely also be remembered for not just those charges, but also his plans to impregnate up to 20 women at a time to *improve the human population*. He planned to have both his head and penis cryogenically frozen upon his own death, so he could re-join humanity later. Even if you never get to such bizarre heights, overconfidence and the way it spills into narcissism is deeply problematic. It fosters both questionable leadership and poor ethical choices.

What's equally worrying is that at different times, Harris, Weinstein and Epstein would have been seen as *role models among leaders* for their confidence. Yet their version of confidence has no respect for people *not of the status quo*; people of colour or the opposing side in a war in the case of Harris, or women in the case of Epstein and Weinstein. It may seem a stretch to talk about such globally now infamous people when discussing overconfidence in the workplace. However, all of these people had co-workers and led teams for years, likely with a great deal of confidence. Nor is it likely any of them *started* this way.

---

68. Stewart, J. et al. 2019 Jeffrey Epstein Hoped to Seed Human Race with His DNA, *New York Times*, 31 July.

Aspects of this behaviour can also be seen in the offices where we mere mortals work. It was only in 2018 that over 300 male business leaders were shamed publicly for sexual harassment at the 'President's Club' charity dinner in London. The organisers encouraged the hostesses to wear no underwear as they served dinner and drinks at this annual 'respectable corporate' evening. The scandal eventually closed the 33-year-old club, and initially shamed many of the business leaders and financiers who were regular attendees.

However, in the subsequent year, the *Financial Times*, which originally broke the story, reported not much has changed. Responses from the attendees were largely unapologetic: 'This happens everywhere, it's no big deal.' However, as Sam Smethers, the CEO of the Fawcett Society who campaigns against workplace sexual harassment, says: 'The FT investigation was hugely significant … It sent the clear message that if something like this was possible, then casual sexual harassment at work is normalised and just something women put up with.'[69] Just to be clear, this type of disproportional overconfidence extends beyond older White men to cross age and gender divides.

Elizabeth Holmes at just 20 years old, started Theranos, a healthcare company poised to revolutionise blood testing. Holmes was successful in getting investment from high profile investors and even other scientists which eventually helped lead to a $9B company valuation in 2015. All this, and the technology in her product did not actually exist, which came to light barely a year later when she was charged with fraud by the US Securities and Exchange Commission. In 2016, barely a year after that valuation, Fortune magazine named her one of the 'World's Most Disappointing Leaders'.[70]

Bill McFarland, barely in his twenties, founded the Fyre Festival, the ultimately fraudulent luxury music festival that was due to happen in the Bahamas in 2017. Concert goers had paid thousands to attend, and showed up to a woefully unprepared makeshift site. The event experienced insurmountable problems related to security, food, accommodation, medical services and artist relations which shut it down.

The ensuing chaos attendees found upon their arrival, inspired analogies in the press to the popular novels *Lord of the Flies* and *The Hunger Games* and eventually inspired two different, yet highly rated documentaries on Hulu and Netflix. This fiasco led to a class action lawsuit against McFarland and his co-founder Ja Rule for $100M on behalf of the attendees.

69. Marriage, M. and Wood, P. 2019 The President's Club Investigation: One Year On, *Financial Times*, 25 January.
70. https://en.wikipedia.org/wiki/Elizabeth_Holmes

McFarland was eventually imprisoned after the Assistant US Attorney who worked on his case said that his short, but eventful career showed a 'pattern of deception'[71] a hallmark of those who become too confident.

The commonalities in both of these? Both Holmes and McFarland were most often noted for their confidence with investors, social media influencers and future clients. It's what attracted people to them – yet also led to their downfall. The warning is that no one is born overconfident, or indeed narcissistic. Instead, we are rewarded for confidence until it grows out of proportion, compared to the effects on people around us.

Too often poor behaviour is overlooked or even praised until it sinks teams or even the companies in which these people work. That should be a warning for us all on what confidence – if allowed to grow into narcissism – can ultimately cost. Instead, we need more competence in our own skills, but also in how we bring others with us, for everyone's benefit.

Unpicking the thread of confidence

Competent people will tell you who they've consulted, what steps they took, what changes they've made, what reading or experiences led them to their opinions. A potential follow-up would be: 'And what do we still not know about this topic?' because they'll likely be able to explain even more. Remember, in our volatile and uncertain world, there will always be things that can't be predicted.

People rarely have all the information they need to make a perfect decision. It's normal to have to make some assumptions. What's *not* healthy is when someone brushes away any assumptions they had to make. It's only a concern if someone acts as if their assumptions don't matter or, more importantly, weren't considered at all.

This concern is a crucial point for Derek Watson, the Quaestor and Factor of St. Andrew's University, a role that is fundamentally a Chief Operational Officer. Part of Watson's role is to unpick overconfidence where necessary. He needs to identify why a decision was made and what were the assumptions. Watson explains:

> *I'm not questioning their competence, just whether their level of confidence is actually appropriate. If not, that's where bravado comes in. If I see their Superman shirt peeking out, I have to tell them 'calm down' and tell me how they've come to this decision.*

So how does this work? Watson explains:

---

71. https://en.wikipedia.org/wiki/Fyre_Festival

*They'll know I'm trying to get us from A to Z on a long-term
project, but all I need is their guidance from A to B. They
often put the cart before the horse based on assumptions.
The truth is that these are dynamic situations, and I do
recognise not everything will unfold the way we expect. I
point out that I can't get to Z without first going through
B, so I'll rein them in to focus on B. Reining in their
confidence could be taken as a criticism. It isn't – it's just
about me understanding their thinking.*

Occasionally Watson will find they've made a mistake, so needs to correct that
before it becomes an issue. But a perceived slight is hard to take, as Watson
points out:

*Most people can take it, but no one likes to be wrong, so
they'll sometimes put up a fight. It's the most confident who
often do 'the fight element' better than anyone. But they're
no more right than they were before we first argued!*

Watson's point is valid. It is hard to let go of an argument, particularly if you
feel you are in the right – which the most confident people often do. But it is
the taking on of the feedback and compromise that ultimately makes the idea
better – something the most competent realise.

Watson's observation reminds me of entrepreneurs I have worked with, who
are often initially wed to their original idea or beloved first prototype. Instead,
many successful entrepreneurs who have been through this pain advise: 'Listen
to your customers – what they think is far more important than your opinion.'

Yet it is often the most competent who will give ground on these issues.
Problematically, the competent also mistake the confidence in others for *factual
certainty* in that person's knowledge. As we've discussed earlier in the book,
the risks of this 'belief in groundless confidence' go far beyond the workplace.

However, it's not enough simply to seek evidence of the achievements a person
is claiming. It's also fundamental to understand what *drives* the assumptions
they are making too. Martin Donnan explains he finds it most useful when
asking for evidence about something that person supposedly *hasn't* displayed.

Donnan clarifies:

For example, if I suspect someone is being written off for being 'too angry' or 'too aggressive', I'll ask for the evidence. If they say something vague like 'I don't know, I just don't think they'd be good', alarm bells go off. Instead, I'd drive towards 'Where's the evidence that that confident woman is actually angry or aggressive? Has it held her back and who sees her that way'?

As Donnan knows, those comments are often limited to their critic's expectations as to how this person *should* be – rather than how the person *is in reality*. This is particularly difficult if the person has already built a reputation amongst colleagues. Perceptions build over time, making it hard to change people's original ideas of them.

Encourage humility by asking overconfident people:

- **When they made a poor decision and its ramifications?**
- **The effect it had on them?**
- **On other people?**
- **How did they fix it?**

DON'T BELIEVE THE HYPE

Suspect you work with someone more confident than perhaps they've earned the right to be? The best way to recognise them is to question their knowledge or experience to see their response. People with the highest confidence are the *most likely to dismiss or disqualify sources of constructive feedback*. They are also the most likely to praise those who think favourably of them. This creates the classic feedback loop.

Tell overconfident people they haven't quite hit the mark and they will respond in one of two ways: they will either confront or diminish you.[72] They often do this angrily, as we saw with Weinstein's reaction to a simple journalist question. While it's rarely comfortable for anyone to be questioned directly, narcissists respond with rash anger and vitriol. In fact, the more self-obsessed and deluded they are, the angrier any questioning makes them.

---

72. Baumgardner, A. H. et al. 1989 Regulating Affect Interpersonally: When Low self-esteem leads to Greater enhancement, *Journal of Personality and Social Psychology* 6: 907–921.

To be questioned about their qualifications or specific knowledge, for example, threatens the foundation of grandiose self-regard on which they rely. Often their reaction is completely different from those who are truly competent. Competent people are much more likely to recognise themselves as we all truly are.

We are all mostly people who have tried to live an interesting life, learned about a few topics, made a few mistakes and aimed to make an impact where we could. The competent can talk easily about the hard lessons they've learned and take acknowledgement when things have gone well. However, they'll prove that competence by owning their mistakes when things haven't gone well.

Rosemary McGinness has spent over 25 years leading HR teams. McGinness agrees the difference between 'bluster' and experience can be hard to detect, and often only after the person has been hired. She smiles: 'I'm always nervous interviewing salespeople because they can tell a great story. It's what they do, which makes them easier to believe.' After being part of the C-suite herself within several companies, McGinness admits she's become better at this, but it takes time and a few hard lessons. She advises:

> *Dig deeper when an interviewee mostly uses 'I' when talking about their wins. It's easy to take a face value but it means we overlook people who speak in the 'we'. That person could probably go into much more detail about their individual part.*

So why is this step so frequently overlooked? McGinness reflects:

> *It's simply harder work for the interviewer to dig deeper. I can lead them by asking: 'What did you do?' But if they still aren't getting it or responding to my guidance, it makes me worry about their listening skills. If they can't read the moment, another essential skill set, particularly at the higher levels where I'm hiring, that would give me caution. But by that point, the under-confident have possibly self-selected out, as the less confident people may never apply for a senior role. This self-selection makes it all the more critical to ensure senior people, in particular, are very competent. You can't let their confidence sway you.*

Plus, the overconfident will often dodge questions for which they don't know the answer. They may deflect to answer a different question instead, one on which they are on safer ground. However, a competent person is more likely to recognise they don't know the answer, but that there would be ways to find out. If someone tells you they 'don't know', believe them. They are being honest, which means they are more *worthy of having confidence in.*

A genuinely competent person will be curious about a question they perhaps haven't considered before. Remember, the competent *want* to improve and so knowing more will only motivate them.

Similarly, the overconfident will often advise a single course of action, giving a definitive answer to questions. While this may make them *seem* experienced, the competent know there are usually several ways to tackle a problem and can talk you through the factors that would affect their decisions. If you think you're dealing with an overconfident blagger, ask them 'And how did you get to that answer?'

'WHAT DID SHE SAY?' OWNING FEEDBACK

We like to think we are the best judge of our own character. Counterintuitively, the reality is that we are all only the person *most people think we are*. In reality, what others think of us is far more consequential than what we think of ourselves. Even if their views seem inaccurate, they are still vital to understand. Our career progression is largely based on what others think and say about us.

How well executive coaching will work for someone often relies on how well they take feedback. It's not that the coach necessarily gives feedback, rather it's a coach's job to help the client interpret feedback they've received from others in order to improve. That's about self-awareness. In the 15 years I've been working as an executive coach, I've seen this factor make a huge difference.

Simply put, some people are 'more coachable' than others. People who are less arrogant, more empathetic, and more self-aware respond more favourably to coaching interventions. This is largely because they're accustomed to seeking feedback[73] and genuinely want to improve.

So why is honest feedback so vital? Because it's rare. Georg Schmundt-Thomas, who consults in FMCG after leaving Swedish based Essity, also spent time in Japan leading teams in an American multinational company. He explains:

> *Unsolicited feedback only happens 2% of the time so most people hear nothing. It's only when something's broken others will complain. That means statistically it's the outliers who get that kind of unsolicited feedback – the absolutely amazing or those close to being fired. If you hear nothing, that doesn't mean you're doing well, just that you're doing enough to get by.*

73. Anseel, F. et al. 2015 How Are We Doing After 30 Years? A Meta-analytic Review of the Antecedents and Outcomes of Feedback-seeking Behaviour, *Journal of Management* 41: 318–348.

Sandy Kennedy, CEO of Entrepreneurial Scotland, sees the way a feedback loop in the way confidence is rewarded by investors when deciding which start-ups to support with their funds. He says: 'Investors will often go for the most confident pitches, even if that doesn't match the reality of what's really going on for the fledgling company.' He says this bias for confidence advantages White men, the type of leaders with whom most investors readily identify.

Kennedy sees projecting this almost theatrical confidence is an issue that affects people from non-status quo groups. He recognises it, however, as a lack of *experience in presentations or pitching* for funding in his world. This lack of experience also means the non-status quo get less feedback on how to improve.

He clarifies:

> *It's pretty simple, the more exposure you have to stressful situations like pitching, the better off you'll be. You'll be better practised, but you'll also have benefited from the feedback you'll get along the way. You'll get confidence if the feedback is good, but even negative feedback is useful. It helps you hone your pitch. It also builds your confidence in delivering what investors want to hear.*

In my experience, people who unpick mistakes to own their faults, and then improve, are the best placed for competence. They'll have learned something about their process, and, as we've seen, expertise and skill are an ongoing process. This is something also remarked upon by Derek Watson who observes:

> *Without generalising too much, I notice men are more likely to want to achieve as quickly as possible. When mistakes happen, that's unfortunate, but largely collateral damage. Women also want to achieve, but they'll take more time to ensure something's done well or that it was even the right goal to have.*

BLAME GAME

While they don't require shin guards or knee pads, some workplace meetings could be considered a contact sport. The onus is on 'players' to handle the 'field' of a meeting table well and sometimes attack or blame others to make themselves look better. The good news for you? In that meeting, you won't be the only one questioning your skills or confidence levels. Most people do at some point. However, hiding that doesn't make them any more *competent at the actual task at hand.*

So to return to the question: What are they trying to prove or hide? Everyone has a facade to maintain to others, and often to themselves. Realising it makes it easier to both listen but also relax. At that moment, you're neither the dumbest nor the least confident person in the room. You may simply be the most self-reflective; a key skill for anyone wants to handle a meeting well by understanding other's emotions.

Interviewees noted colleagues could hide a lack of competence, *behind a confident exterior.* Barbara-Ann King, who has a long history in financial services, shared a story about a senior colleague: a senior manager who routinely stole credit for other's work or blamed others when his work wasn't up to scratch. Sound familiar? She explains:

> *He's happy to do a 'good-enough' job until he realises his own numbers won't cut it in a few months. So, he'll instead look for junior people he can tie himself to, the ones who are actually delivering. He'll stake a claim on their project, annoyingly, by suggesting they need him.*

She continues:

> *He'll say with mock concern: 'Let me help you through this next part' or 'This is a bit beyond we'd expect you to do at your level; I'll speak to someone on your behalf.' Six months later his own numbers aren't great, which he'd likely predicted. But now he blames the time he had to give to an office junior during their 'difficult' project. He'd talk about how instrumental he'd been in their success. It's annoying to witness and undermines the subordinate.*

King said she interpreted these approaches as a lack of confidence. However, as we talked, she suggested it might be more a *lack of competence in meeting his own deliverables.* This approach allowed him to ride the coattails of someone he claimed to be mentoring, complete with an excuse for why he missed his own targets. Power differentials matter in these relationships. If the junior person is questioned, they'll unlikely admit the senior person had little to do with the project, so the secret is maintained.

> **Giving and getting credit publicly:**
>
> - Be the *first* to credit people with their work.
> - Publicly credit others for their role in *inspiring your ideas*. Everyone likes credit!
> - If someone shows vulnerability, praise their bravery and willingness to take a risk.
> - Credit where ideas started, with 'I think X first mentioned this?' to avoid crediting the loudest voice.

You can even determine a likely willingness to blame others early on when meeting someone. Rosemary McGinness, who routinely interviews candidates for top positions, notes this is vital to understand how people handle past mistakes. She advises: 'One of my favourite questions is "What did you learn?" If they struggle or say they'd make the same choices again or *blame someone else*, that's a red flag to me.'

Others also talked about a person's desire to claim credit for achievements they *could not have managed single-handedly*. Remember, most people operate in a team. Saying you did it all is a sign of overconfidence, not competence.

To this point, McGinness notices those who struggle most in using 'I' are often in support functions because everything they do in the organisation is collaborative. Interestingly, women and others from under-represented backgrounds often fill these support roles. Comparatively, those who use 'I' most often sit in loftier positions. This use of 'I' is ironic, given they are the least likely to 'do it all' on their own, relying on the team below them.

A TALE OF TWO QUESTIONS: ADAPTIVE REALISM

To me, confidence is made up of two aspects. The first is 'Can I do this?' which is about your skills and experience. The second is 'Can I do this *here*?' This latter question is the one we most often overlook. However, it's vital to unpick as it relies on role models with whom you identify, your access to sponsors and whether progression depends on expectations you actually want to fulfil.

Let's be very clear, nothing from this second question is ever covered in a job description, but it's important to recognise. The truth is the first question is about qualifications with high-level skills. However, the second question addresses the reality of your chances of success, once you get there.

We spend far too much time worrying: 'How can I be more confident?' The better question for a couple of reasons is 'How can I get people to recognise my competence instead?'

First, we worry under-represented groups don't have enough confidence. However, perhaps we should also recognise that frame of mind is a state to which we've all adapted – it's a type of 'adaptive realism'.

For example, in getting through an average workday, people from non-status quo groups become accustomed to being ignored, credit for their ideas given elsewhere, talked over or actively criticised, something we'll explore in more depth as we go on.

Conversely, people who are from status quo backgrounds are more likely to be taught the 'secrets', understand unspoken expectations and are more likely to have people extend a helping hand – even if all done subconsciously. It's like giving everyone a game to win – but only teaching the rules to certain players. Adaptive realism means we pick our goals based on what we believe is attainable for us based on what *people like us normally achieve* in that environment.

What role models can 'achieve' is slanted from the start. For example, data contradicts the convenient myths we like to tell ourselves about the lack of under-represented groups, particularly women, 'not applying or staying in jobs' once they have them. According to McKinsey & LeanIn, who looked at US employee data between 2015–2019, attrition has *never* been the issue in the lack of women in senior roles. Women and men leave at the same rates and are roughly as committed at staying with their current companies for the next five years.[74]

Instead, the gender disparity comes when people *first move from entry-level* into management. For every 100 men who get promoted to management, just 79 women do. However, because of the gender gaps that started as early as recruitment, this means men hold 62% of all managerial positions overall, and women, the remaining 38%.

Interestingly, while promotion rates for women slightly improve after managerial level, from senior manager/director level onwards, this means that women can never catch up. Instead, the damage started at early career development.

If women aren't winning leadership roles, perhaps it's not surprising that they are not more confident about their chances of success. Maybe they are more realistic about what it will take to get there and their chances of doing so. Instead, they may decide to use their talents differently.

---

74. Huang, J. et al. McKinsey and Co. and LeanIn.Org, 2019 Women in the Workplace study.

Americans like to hold onto the idea of being a world leader in terms of equality. However, American women's paid labour force participation has been decreasing in real terms since the 1999.[75] When compared to the educational potential of its women and the way other industrialised nations have improved participation rates, the US is actually falling behind.

While highly successful and ambitious, Sasha Mooney, a Barrister at Law of Nigerian descent, explains: 'The reason I'm not flying my flag to join the Supreme Court or the Court of Appeals isn't because I'm not confident. It's because there is no one sitting at the top jobs who represent ethnic minorities like me.' Mooney is confident, but circumspect or 'adaptively realistic' about her chances of being accepted there.

When people struggle with confidence, why don't we ask more frequently: '*Why* do they lack confidence?' We ignore how confidence is directly related to how successful the person perceives they would be in any given challenge. This is based on *how successful they've historically been and how rewarded they've been by others*.

Confidence is a self-fulfilling prophecy. As a person's confidence grows and opportunities to demonstrate them expand, they are given more high-profile opportunities. They are safe in the knowledge they've delivered publicly before, and it's been well-received. This experience provides the strength and support to experiment with new behaviours and new ways of exercising leadership.

An *absence* of validation, however, diminishes self-confidence and discourages the non-status quo from seeking developmental opportunities or experimenting. Leadership identity, which begins tentatively, eventually decreases, along with opportunities to grow through new assignments and real achievements. Over time, an aspiring leader acquires a reputation as having – or not having – 'high potential'.

Let's look at how this plays out. Doubt is contagious. This is particularly true if there are few role models around with whom you identify. 'Will I succeed *here*?' is the more fundamental question, which if not asked, starts to bleed into an even more undermining question: 'Will *I* succeed anywhere?'

This to the external world can look like a lack of confidence, which it isn't. It's not that the person doesn't think they can be successful (confidence in yourself). Instead it's uncertainty they can be successful in *that environment* (confidence in the system). Too frequently these two versions of confidence get lumped together as if they were the same.

75. Toosi, M. and Morisi, T. 2017 Women in the Workforce Before, During and After the Great Recession, US Bureau of Labor Statistics.

Kate Atkin, an expert in the imposter syndrome, understands adaptive realism very well. She said: 'Perception is a reality until proven otherwise. Are minorities barred from senior roles? No. But is it a relatively accurate perception? Yes. This means until we see enough people from under-represented backgrounds, we'll still be affected by adaptive realism.' As we've already seen, the presence of identifiable role models, or lack thereof, in your workspace directly affects confidence.

MIT in the US experimented with quotas as they promoted people to faculty positions in the years after 2000. Their skill was not the question; the women promoted were as academically qualified as their male counterparts in terms of achieving tenure and election to the highly esteemed National Academy of Sciences.[76] What's interesting is not their promotion, but that as the number of women hired to those faculty positions increased in the STEM subjects, so too did the number of women *electing to study* to PhD level at MIT.

This shift is notable for two reasons. First, the impact of improving the numbers of senior women, *even via quotas*, didn't diminish the quality on their teams in the least. Second, it wasn't solely a benefit to the promoted women as individuals. It was felt by all the women looking up the ladder to see how 'feasible' success could be. It drove recruitment of students who didn't as easily identify with staff at other universities.

Conversely, let's imagine you are an extroverted, able-bodied, White male who is a native speaker in the country in which you work. Looking around, you'll see many leaders ahead of you with whom you can at least superficially identify. That is hugely reassuring, even if primarily subconsciously. As we saw with my first story about the high-potential law firm employees, this creates confidence. It 'seeps' into your identity creating security and certainty. It suggests *you are on the right path* – confidence in a nutshell.

WHY WON'T SHE APPLY?

Illustrating this, my male consultancy clients often share their frustration when women they rate highly don't put themselves forward quickly for opportunities. They lament: 'If I ask her to consider a role, she says she'd love the job. But if I *wait for* her to apply, she won't.' Smart leaders dig deeper if a non-status quo member says they don't want to be promoted, particularly as we'll see status quo men haven't cornered the market on ambition. For argument's sake, let's set aside the fact a woman is statistically less likely than a man to be promoted. This is particularly true the further away she is from the status quo.

---

76. Hopkins, N. 2006 MIT 'Diversification of a University Faculty: Observations on Hiring Women Faculty in the Schools of Science and Engineering at MIT.' 16 (4) March/April.

Let's start with the fact she'll be very aware of her difference from the 'usual suspects'. There are a few additional things in her way. First, she may not want to be promoted into a job *as it exists now*. It may not be a good fit for how she wants to live her life with her other responsibilities. For example, she may perceive she'll have to compromise on her sense of authenticity. Second, she may be more aware of being viewed by others as too ambitious or vain enough to think she'd get a promotion. Instead, she may opt to save face by not applying at all, given her chances of success are lower.

Celine Jahn is a Global Brand Director at Essity in Europe. She agrees that confidence is not static, nor should it be. She observes: 'My own confidence has grown over time as I've had more wins and more promotions. However, I also learned that confidence is not at a set point and may go down.' This became clearer to her on maternity leave. She reflects:

> *I'm at a turning point. For the first time, I'm making career*
> *compromises that my pre-children self wouldn't have*
> *made. Then I was more confident about getting to the top.*
> *I've reached the level I aimed for. Now I'm not sure I can*
> *maintain it.*

Interestingly, she said this after her *second* child, rather than her first, when many women experience a dip in confidence levels. What maintained her confidence after her first child?

> *I was given a promotion almost immediately after I returned*
> *to work from my first maternity leave. My previous boss*
> *was keen to keep me and true to his word he promoted*
> *'the recently returned mother' – a rarity, I know. Equally*
> *important, they accepted my request to go to 80%, a*
> *schedule no one else at my level had.*

Whichever way you look at it, there's a fix – whether she has confidence or not, which, as Jahn points out, is in flux most of the time anyway. If she truly isn't going to apply because of lack of confidence, she'd likely benefit from more sponsorship and visible recognition of her competence to build that confidence.

To keep track of your growing competence, every week list:

- **What's the best thing you've learned?**
- **What went better than you expected?**
- **What you did *to* get better at a skill you want to improve?**

Similarly, several years later, Jahn's next boss also said he'd like to find her a new role after her second child. This was vital as too frequently employers don't appreciate how motivating interesting roles are for returners. By contrast, returning women are often side-lined or demoted – and then later blamed for their own 'low confidence' as a rationale for why they're not getting further.

Even when people do have the confidence to ask for what they want from their employers, they are often turned down. For example, while nearly 90% of UK workers want flexible working, just 11% of 6 million roles advertised online earning at least £20K cite flexible working as even a possibility.[77] So, a lack of trust and *confidence in modern employers* is perhaps not surprising.

Getting more flexibility than Jahn expected was what improved not just her confidence, but also how she felt about her employer. Based in Germany, she maintains: 'If my employer can be at the forefront of great reduced hours roles, not for mothers, but also for men and younger people everywhere who want to work this way, we'll easily be able to pick from the best people.'

To Jahn, her employer's only mistake was not publicising her first post-maternity leave promotion widely enough. She says: 'I don't think they made a big enough deal about my promotion to a senior role or the fact I was now working 80% after it happened.' Her point isn't because Jahn seeks personal publicity, but for the influence it may have had on the women below her. She says: 'They'd also reach higher because they see the evidence it could be done.'

This goes to *how* we define confidence. Even asking for reduced hours with no precedent is in itself evidence of confidence. It's a willingness to go against the grain. Jahn says: It's ridiculous now but I was afraid even to claim I was ambitious when I needed reduced hours.' Jahn felt ashamed, the opposite of confidence in asking for this 'favour'. However, her rationale went beyond benefiting herself. She says: 'I didn't want anyone to assume having children is a burden. I needed people to understand you could be a great worker *because* you have children – not in spite of them.'

77. Gartner & Timewise, Timewise Flexible Jobs Index 2018 https://timewise.co.uk/article/flexible-jobs-index-2018/

'DEPRESSIVELY REALISTIC' VS 'UNREALISTICALLY OPTIMISTIC'

Both self-doubt and confidence, based on how the world responds to you, start young, and creates your sense of adaptive realism. Maccoby and Jacklin, ground-breakers in looking at sexual socialisation of children, conducted many studies of 2–3-year-olds. Children are thinking early about who they'll change their behaviour for, and who they won't. They found:

> *When children played in pairs, they frequently object to something the other one does. However ... when girls told boys to stop doing something, the boys just kept right on doing it. However, the boys did respond to the verbal protests of other boys. Girls, however, responded to verbal protests of both girls and boys. When girls and boys played together in pairs, girls often stood aside while boys played with the toys.*[78]

Children learn how much they can affect the environment, *and the people within it*, from the start. These trends have been seen over and over again by other researchers, as described in Sadkers' book, *Failing at Fairness* which covered 20 years of research in American schools.[79] Essentially, in co-ed classrooms, girls often become bystanders and observers, while boys the active participants.

Ultimately, as a form of self-defence many non- status quo members won't express interest in roles they haven't been offered. There may even be evolutionary benefits to adaptive realism. As we saw in Chapter 3, confidence and competence are inversely related,[80] which means the more your confidence increases, the less concerned you are about your competence. This should concern any employer. There is actually an abundant body of research showing that those who have 'depressive realism' actually have a higher accuracy of judgement and self-views.

The 'depressively realistic' are more likely to accurately judge others' perception of their reputation, competence and social status than non-depressed individuals.[81] In many ways, a 'glass-half-empty' perspective helps them. Certainly, the under-confident spend more time building their expertise which benefits us all. The non-depressed individuals instead were called by the researchers the 'unrealistically optimistic'. In the wider world, we'd no doubt call them 'confident'.

---

78. Maccoby, E. and Jacklin, C. 1974 *The Psychology of Sex Differences*, Stanford University Press, Stanford, CA.

79. Sadker, M. and Sadker, D. 1994 *Failing at Fairness*, MacMillan, New York.

80. Chamorro-Premuzic, T. 2013 *Confidence: The Surprising Truth About How Much You Need and How to Get It*, Profile Books, London, p. 9.

81. Alloy, L. B. and Abramson, L. Y. 1979 Judgement of Contingency in Depressed and Nondepressed students: Sadder by Wiser? *Journal of Experimental Psychology: General* 108(4): 441–485 in Dobson, K. and Franche, R. 1989 A Conceptual and Empirical Review of the Depressive Realism Hypothesis, *Canadian Journal of Behavioural Science* 21(4): 419–433.

INTRODUCING THE IMPOSTER

One of the most commonly cited feelings I hear, particularly from female clients, is about their imposter syndrome. This is not to say men, and even status quo men, don't experience, at times, the sense of being a fraud or that they will be 'found out'.

However, non-status quo people, in particular, are in a more precarious role when surrounded by the status quo. With good reason, as non-status quo members are much more likely to have their expertise challenged, something we'll delve into further as we look into different identity groups.

However, it's vital to recognise the Imposter Phenomenon is situational. It happens in specific settings and isn't an overall trait that occurs across all settings. The crux is that people who most experience imposter syndrome often haven't had the same level of exposure to new challenges. With repeated exposure, your *courage in these tasks* and, relatedly, confidence levels will improve. It's the exposure that makes the difference.

Rosemary McGinness is like most other interviewees in having a low patch in their confidence in a new role. She, like others, focused on growing her competence to get through it. She recalls:

> When I first joined Weir, I was confident I could ultimately do the job, but realised quickly I was out of my comfort zone. At the time, remuneration policy was my weakest skill, but it became our key area of focus. So I worked on getting up to speed on all the new aspects to the role. This was like learning a new language – new industry, new company structure, focusing on policies I had little experience of. I also had no internal relationships, and I hadn't yet made an impact on anything else since I was so new in the role. I wasn't just in the deep end. I was worried about drowning.

She remembers:

> My confidence was low until I shared how I felt with my boss. It was uncomfortable, but he supported me. He knew I was skilled in other areas they'd also want to focus on eventually. He encouraged me to rely on my team to get up to speed. I picked a few easy and quick wins. Those reminded me why they'd selected me for the job, beyond my detailed knowledge of remuneration policy!

McGinness rolled out initiatives she'd led successfully multiple times before but were new to Weir. That gave her the breathing room she needed, and gave her new employer added value *beyond* what they were expecting. Her story is an excellent example of how confidence is not a one-size-fits-all blanket.

McGinness agreed that confidence ebbed and flowed. She turned up the volume on the parts of the job in which she had significant experience while improving the aspects in those which she knew less. Taking on the challenge to do both in many ways was itself an act of courage.

Kate Atkin, who has made a career of studying imposter syndrome, explained how courage plays a big part in what we expect from confidence. She explains:

> *Physical courage is about jumping into a river to save someone or even running a marathon. Moral courage is about doing the right thing even when you know it won't be easy. Psychological courage is that sense of 'I feel a bit wobbly on this, but I'm going to do it anyway.' We certainly credit physical and psychological courage both as 'confidence'. However, I don't know if we as readily credit moral courage as confidence in the same way.*

When we look at moving past imposter syndrome, there are just a few ways confidence can grow. The first, and I'd argue most credible way, is via mastery. Mastery is where the vast majority of us get our confidence. It's about trying out new behaviours and improving via feedback. You do that until you've mastered it, knowing you'll never arrive at perfection. It's all about competence and recognising you've done something well.

The second way Atkin describes how to grow confidence is via 'vicarious experience'. In other words, watching role models and realising 'If they can do it, so can I'. However, that can be a challenge if there aren't a variety of role models with whom you identify, something we've talked about via adaptive realism.

The third way to build confidence is via 'social support'. This is about receiving encouragement from others who say, 'Go on, you'd be great at that.' An approach like this sounds straightforward enough, and no doubt we all draw upon supportive friends and family. But again, in the workplace, this type of social support may be patchier for some than for others. As we'll see, non-status quo members are again less likely to receive unsolicited positive feedback about their performance, even when their actual performance equals or surpasses that of their peers.

The fourth and final way to improve confidence is by reframing your physiological responses. This means reframing the butterflies in your stomach

108

to 'this is just the excitement I feel when I'm about to share my ideas with a big audience'. No doubt this is easier said than done, but it's at least an option open equally to all.

However, that still leaves the first option, competence, as the one most likely to work well for non-status quo members. Undoubtedly, your capability at work is within your control. Getting this right is vital if you're surrounded by people who won't readily identify with you.

CONTEXT IS KING

Nikki Slowey, a Programme Director at Family Friendly Working Scotland, also pointed out how contextual confidence is and *should* be. Like all parents, she would much prefer a competent doctor working on her children than one just brimming with confidence. Her organisation, Flexible Working Families Scotland, is about encouraging more organisations to adapt to flexible working, something most employees want.

She agreed that if you can't access flexible arrangements, it's nigh on impossible to believe you will get far, let alone be confident. How confident can you be if you return, after a period of absence, to a job that doesn't exist anymore? Or where no one before you has ever asked for flexible working? Or where every one of your peers has someone at home full time? Then to turn around and say 'You need to be more confident' adds insult to injury and is woefully dismissive of context.

To her, it's miraculous that so many working mothers, in particular, have the confidence they do. Slowey observes: 'After having a rough morning getting three children to school and then managing to get to an inflexible workplace, how can that *not* affect your confidence? You are carrying a huge mental load before your workday has even started.' This is cognitive load in action.

She describes:

> As a mum to three kids, every day starts with a form that needs signing and lunches that need packing. Plus, there are house keys that need finding and a young heart that's been broken because of some social slight. The list goes on! So, if you come into work at 9.15, criticised for your timekeeping, your confidence isn't going to be at its best in the next meeting. It's even worse if no one around is going through the same challenges. It's the difference between someone crediting you with a great presentation or pointing out the baby sick on your jacket.

In upcoming chapters, we're going to dig deeper on context, as it's vital in helping us understand confidence better. For example, people from more politically unstable countries also have a more external locus of control, that is, a sense things are often 'beyond their control'.[82] Political unrest grows a sense that chance, fate and accident have a bigger influence on our lives than those from relatively stable nations. Unfairly, that could be viewed as a lack of confidence, but again I'd argue it's adaptive realism.

Understanding context is crucial. Historically, African Americans were described at best as 'less motivated' and 'lazy' according to inaccurate stereotypes. By contrast, a meta-analysis of 140 pieces of research showed African Americans were as motivated and as likely to feel in control of the outcomes for their life as their White counterparts.[83]

Sandra Graham who conducted the research, noted her findings could be interpreted by cynics as evidence that 'African Americans have unrealistically high expectations, unusually positive self-regard and exaggerated sense of control', given the economic outcomes for many African Americans, on average, are not as positive as for White people. However, Graham interprets this lack of ethnic difference in motivation levels much more positively by looking at context. She explains:

> *Everyone at some point adopts illusions of well-being to*
> *cope with the vagaries of life's successes and failures ...*
> *these illusions may simply be enlisted more often or used*
> *more systematically by African Americans who carry the*
> *added burden of social and economic disadvantage.*

For Graham, confidence is also contextual. Perhaps, then, confidence shouldn't be questioned in historically marginalised groups but seen as a mechanism that focuses them on a more positive future. Adaptive realism, it seems, becomes more prevalent as people age. As time passes, one's realistic chances of success become clearer, based on both the positives and negatives of what you've experienced before.

Among the 400 members of Scotland Women in Technology network, the founder Silka Patel notices age differences around confidence. She observes: 'The younger women are more confident than I certainly was at that age. What I recognise is how they're still trying to find the perfect line between confident and cocky – a big no-no for women.'

Patel pauses and laughs:

---

82. Schneedwind, K.A. 1995 Impact of Family Processes on Control Beliefs, in A. Bandura (ed.) *Self-efficacy in Changing Societies*, Cambridge University Press, Cambridge, pp. 114-118.
83. Graham, S. 1994 Motivation in African Americans, *Review of Educational Research*, 64(1): 55–117; JSTOR, www.jstor.org/stable/1170746

*The older women also have confidence. But given what
many have endured in their careers, some of that confidence
has been beaten out of them! When my male counterparts
say 'women lack confidence' it winds me up. They just have
different ways of showing it.*

Patel's referring to the enthusiasm of youth versus the reliability of experience.
Both are types of confidence but from various sources. Patel's comment
reminded me of a coaching client of mine, Sonia.

Sonia was a project manager in an IT firm struggling to find her way after
transferring to a different department. Competence didn't seem to be the issue,
compared to her peers. She'd worked for five years in a competing bank and
had earned her spurs. Her previous boss, Simon, loved her – her projects
always came in on time and budget. She got one piece of constructive feedback
from Simon. She needed to own her knowledge, speak up for herself, defend
her ideas – or as he put it: 'share more of the opinions for which you're getting
paid'.

When she switched roles, Sonia decided to reinvent herself. She spoke up in
every meeting, gave critiques on both her own and others work, based on her
previous experience, and used stronger body language. Sonia felt great – like
she was coming into herself. However, this time, Sonia was working for Scott
and her 'newfound confidence' didn't go down well with him. Within a few
months, Scott told Sonia she was too pushy, too vocal and too critical.

Sonia came to coaching with a fundamental yet troubling question faced by
many: 'How do I be authentic and stand up for myself without alienating my
boss?' Sonia's tale highlights the fine line leaders, and in particular non-status
quo members, must tread. If you give people what they expect, you could
be criticised for lacking confidence. However, if you manage to overcome
these typical 'frailties' to demonstrate confidence, you're quickly deemed too
aggressive, assertive or as Sonia's boss initially chastened her, for being 'too
confident'. When people get such differing feedback, it does beg the question –
is it any surprise so many people develop imposter syndrome?

SIX

IMPOSTOR SYNDROME AND THE UPSIDES TO LOW CONFIDENCE

> *Success consists of going from failure to failure without*
> *loss of enthusiasm*
> – Winston Churchill

So we've taken a peek at imposter syndrome, but let's look deeper, particularly as it's one of the most common issues my coaching clients face. Most of us know imposter syndrome as that feeling of always being just two steps away from being found out as a fraud. It affects us all, but to differing degrees in different settings – again why understanding context is so vital.

Derek Watson leads big teams of senior people and has seen his fair share of imposter syndrome in others, but also in himself. Watson recalled hiring not one but two confident senior managers in the space of as many years for the same job. Before making those hires, he'd initially wanted to fill the role with a very competent internal woman whom he originally approached. She turned him down both times as 'not being ready'.

It was only on the departure of the second hire that she was convinced she could step into the role. Watson recalls: 'We spent a lot of time talking about where we saw the job going. I also asked what she needed around her, to either remove or get through the aspects she didn't like.' In my experience advising organisations on gender balance, I'd speculate it was this *second* question that made the bigger difference to her. In asking it, Watson became her sponsor. He showed a willingness to give her the support she needed to succeed, rather than just say 'get on with it' and hope for the best, something that undermines even the best-intentioned promotions. He continues:

> She was doing well, but after three months in, I could see
> she didn't fully own the role. I sat her down and quietly
> said: 'You've got imposter syndrome, don't you? Don't
> worry. I've got it too.' She was so relieved. Four years in,
> she continues to be a star performer I'm lucky to have.

113

This admission of his own imposter syndrome wasn't something I expected. However, it made sense as while Watson is one of the most senior leaders at a prestigious university, he doesn't have a university degree himself. He built his career via stellar accounting qualifications instead. As we've seen with others, this sense of imposter syndrome actually makes many good people *great*.

They focus on delivery alone, assuming they'll get no favours. For Watson, there is a delicate balance to be had so manages this self-doubt well publicly. He must convince people of his decisions when he knows, as each leader does, that he's working with imperfect and ever-changing information.

Imposter syndrome is an equal opportunity feeling that cuts across all groups, though some admit to it more frequently than others. The doctoral work of Kate Atkin focuses on the Imposter Phenomenon. She explains: 'We need to accept imposter syndrome is situational. You never feel like an imposter in all settings, so you really shouldn't expect to feel confident in *all* settings.'

Instead, part of our confidence comes down to *what* we attribute our success. Atkin explains: 'If I see my success as a by-product of luck, circumstance, or someone being kind to me, that's all external. It will only foster my imposter syndrome. It's when someone disregards praise by explaining it away as: "Right place, right time" or "If I managed it, anyone could do it".' Atkin continues:

> *That person will go from one project to another, always hoping for another fluke. They'll never wholly own confidence. However, if you attribute success to your own choices, your behaviour, your skills, your own agency, that's where you start to see confidence emerge. Even if you work in a team, own your involvement.*

THE UGLY SIDE OF AUTHENTICITY

When I was writing my first book *Beyond the Boys' Club: Strategies for Achieving Career Success as a Woman Working in a Male-Dominated Field*, I noted how many accomplished women struggle with imposter syndrome. They led large teams, had a slew of qualifications behind their name, and were considered leaders in their field. They are the kind of people most of us aspire to be. In many ways, this book wouldn't have been complete without tackling imposter syndrome.

We think of successful people as a breed apart, but often they are often experts, perhaps not in delivery alone, but in *reputation management*. As someone who coaches very successful people, I can tell you they are as riddled with self-doubt as the rest of us, just *better at working around it*.

Furthermore, self-doubt is productive for two key reasons. First, it keeps you trying harder. Second, it prevents you from taking risky liberties as if you were entitled to them, like we've seen in the infamous cases we've already discussed. These people are bad for morale at best and an organisational risk at worst.

Imposter syndrome gets a bad rap but look at how much destruction can happen when we encourage people to 'just be yourself'. Even at a basic level, most people understand that's not an invitation to take off their shoes in the office. However, others will go far further and tell everyone what they think. They cocoon themselves in that supposed failsafe phrase of 'just saying' while making inappropriate observations under a faultless guise of 'banter'.

The trick in the workplace is actually *not to show your complete* and true self. This is the version of you that binge watches box sets all weekend in your stained pyjamas and opens that second bottle of wine after a long day. The person who puts the dishes in the sink hoping someone else will clean them up. We've all been there but we don't need more of that type of 'authenticity' in the office.

Authenticity sounds great. It can seem like it's about accepting yourself, 'warts and all'. I know this warts version of you exists; it's how social media and even the dark web makes money. However, this version is just a small piece of you. It's not the piece that's going to make you more competent or confident. In fact, if recruiters and employers were granted full access to Facebook or Twitter accounts, many people would be unemployed.

The world doesn't need more 'warts' version of you – and certainly not one wrapped up in a confident package. Instead, the world needs the best version of you. Be the version of yourself you'd admire. We're not talking about faking it. Instead, it's about making your 'best self' choices in handling difficult people, prioritising issues and the way you'd like to be remembered by others.

Others also saw the utility in how the imposter syndrome and self-doubt contribute to this best version of you. Vanessa Vallely points out:

> *I can get caught up with a good idea. Sometimes that demon helps me slow down and think through other eventualities. It allows me to answer: 'But what if this happened?' It reminds me to do a bit more research before charging ahead. My imposter is so useful; I don't even think we should call her a demon!*

This approach isn't about projecting a false image or being an imposter. It's solely about drawing attention to the capability you'd be proud of, and which already lives inside of you. It's the version that keeps you working to show others you *deserve to be in that room*.

Paradoxically, this also isn't about perfection, which just isn't attainable. Feminist campaigner Gloria Steinem said it best when she admonished the perfectionist goal: 'You can't do it all. No one can have two full-time jobs, have perfect children and cook three meals and be multi-orgasmic 'til dawn … Superwoman is the adversary of the women's movement.' It's about being honest about *how* you work, your skills and your weaknesses and how you are working to improve.

THE SYNDROME IS PART OF 'LIVING YOUR BEST LIFE'

For me, 'being yourself' or 'just saying' in the office can highlight the worst of your traits. This isn't cool even if everyone now works in an 'informal' office, complete with bean bags. For me, real authenticity is recognising you shouldn't have to project confidence or even a lifestyle like the status quo to get ahead. Instead, use your evidence of what you've learned, achieved and who you've brought with you. In reality, imposter syndrome keeps most of us on our A-game and 'living your best life' whether we shout about it on social media or not.

Imposter syndrome isn't a personal failing. It's a springboard for us to address what's potentially hindering your progress. As we've seen, it's *easy* to blame imposter syndrome and lack of confidence for why someone's not getting ahead. It's far simpler than asking 'what is it in *our system* that means they feel like an outsider, a fraud, an imposter?'

If we don't address *those* questions, we revert to the danger of the 'individualised explanation'. That's an excuse centred around the individual, rather than understanding a bigger trend for a group. If you can't see the trend and how it affects some people more than others, you won't fix anything. To this point, self-doubt does seem to affect women, no matter how skilled they are, more than status quo men.

The status quo are less likely to doubt their inclusion at decision-making tables or feel a pressure to over-deliver to 'earn' their place. The greater the 'status-distance', the more likely you are to feel imposter syndrome. On book tours for her bestseller *Becoming*, Michelle Obama exposed this frailty when admitting to feeling like an imposter most of the time. Similarly, the acclaimed novelist Maya Angelou admitted: 'I have written 11 books, but each time I think, 'Uh oh. I've run a game on everybody, and they're going to find me out now.' Naomi Pryde, a senior leader at the law firm DWF, suffers from imposter syndrome, but routinely gets compliments from both senior but also junior members of staff. They will surprise her with comments that she can't wholly believe, like 'I want to have a career just like yours'. They don't *see* her lack of self-confidence.

She clarifies: 'I do, however, believe in my competence, so I move past the self-doubt to lead meetings, to give talks at networking events, to do client pitches.' Pryde is an excellent example of how we too often erroneously judge confidence mainly based on what we can see, *not on what is hidden within* and how focusing on getting the experiences you need, can eradicate it.

The first step towards embracing imposter syndrome is accepting it is part of most people's day-to-day working experience. If you think you'll only be successful once you are entirely sure of yourself, you will be waiting for ever. Successful people with imposter syndrome have moments, even days of self-doubt.

The trick is not in kicking the syndrome but in developing your skills around that challenge. It keeps you on your mettle and improving. Doing so will remind you how to make the most of any situation and that you can *overcome* mistakes made along the way. I have yet to meet a professional non-status quo member from any field who has wholly dispensed with self-doubt: no matter how old, no matter how accomplished. The goal is not to overcome it; it's merely to work *around it*.

The people you admire certainly didn't go with the first thing they ever created. Much like you, successful people know they have to hone their craft and increase their skill level. Just like them, it's likely to take you a lifetime. The only way to 'get over self-doubt' is to learn instead to 'coexist with doubt'.

GROWTH MINDSET GAINS

I've certainly had my share of failed business projects. Personally, I know nothing is harder than saying, 'I gave it my all, and it wasn't good enough.' The key is to recognise it will happen - and often if you want to grow. However, the power is ensuring that doesn't stop you from trying, tinkering and honing – all before you may still ultimately decide to shelve the effort. With coaching clients, I remind them: If you can tick every box on the job description, you're not stretching yourself enough.

Carol Dweck, who has written extensively on the growth mindset, explains why the *effort* of trying something new is so terrifying. She explains:

There are two reasons. One is that in the fixed mindset,
great geniuses are not supposed to need it (effort). So just
needing it casts a shadow on your ability. The second is that
... it robs you of all your excuses. Without effort, you can
always say, 'I could have been (fill in the blank)'. But once
you try, you can't say that anymore.[84]

Dweck's fixed versus growth mindset is deeply related to our competence versus confidence question. Confident people, *satisfied where they are*, may not aim for something better. Failure would dent their confidence. However, if you focus on improving, you recognise the only way to getting better at a skill is by reaching higher – regardless of the recognition you expect.

As Dweck elaborates:

The top is where the fixed-mindset people hunger to be,
but it's where many growth-minded people arrive as a by-
product of their enthusiasm for what they do. This point
is also crucial. In a fixed mindset, everything is about the
outcome. If you fail or if you're not the best, it's all been
wasted. The growth mindset allows people to value what
they're doing regardless of the outcome.[85]

She also clearly sees this tension between confidence and competence, relaying a letter from a reader who wrote to Dweck admitting:

I've always had a problem with confidence. My coaches
always told me to believe in myself 100% ... I'm always
so aware of my defects and the mistakes I make in every
meeting. Trying to think I was perfect made it even worse.
Then I read your work and how it's so important to focus on
learning and improving. It turned me around. My defects
are things I can work on![86]

When reflecting upon the letter, Dweck admits: 'The remarkable thing I've learned from my research is that in the growth mindset, you don't always *need* confidence.' That is a fundamental shift from our 'confidence at all costs' culture – the culture by which we judge and reward people.

---

84. Dweck, C. 2006 *Mindset: How You Can Fulfil Your Potential*, Random House, New York, p. 43.
85. Dweck, C. 2006 *Mindset: How You Can Fulfil Your Potential*, Random House, New York, p. 48.
86. Dweck, C. 2006 *Mindset: How You Can Fulfil Your Potential*, Random House, New York, p. 52.

As a teen, I learned to drive cars with automatic transmissions. By age 27, I never thought I'd need to drive a manual until we rented a cottage in the grounds of a much bigger house. I now had to drive even to take our rubbish out, let alone anything else. Set in my old ways, learning to drive a manual transmission at the time was humbling in how difficult it was for me. I had to learn this new skill in the final year of doing my PhD. For my academic work, I was also attempting to master quantitative research methods – the ostensibly bigger challenge.

Yet, in the middle of the night, I'd wake from a nightmare. It was always about my impending driving test, never my upcoming viva where I'd have to defend my dissertation. I'm not one you would call co-ordinated or even graceful. Similarly, as anyone who's helped me move furniture knows, my spatial judgements are abysmal.

As a result, the driving instructor gave me twice as many lessons as what he charmingly called a 'normal' student. Upon seeing my frustration, he once remarked: 'You're not the type who normally struggles to learn new things, are you?'

He had my number. The written test was a doddle – few people can study as I can. But in manual driving, I'd found something I didn't just struggle with, but at which I was hopeless. My one saving grace? I had a growth mindset. I knew I could always do more practice, get more lessons and drive more with my fiancé. It's incredible we actually made it to the altar!

On the day I eventually passed – with the maximum number of mistakes one can make and *still pass* – I burst into tears with relief. My response shocked the examiner. He'd never seen someone so delighted with such a low – but just sufficient score! I'm still not what you'd call a confident driver, but 20 years later, touch wood, I've never had an accident.

Skills are essentially like muscles. With exercise, they grow until you have just as much confidence as you need. As importantly, these muscles will also help you accept setbacks as they happen – because you know you can get better. As anyone who has lifted weights knows, you can always develop stronger muscles. Focusing on competence grows those muscles. Confidence is just the body-oil you use to highlight them!

THE GIFT OF SELF-DOUBT

Most clients I speak with initially want more confidence. This isn't a bad goal. However, they'll often see that in the bigger picture, under-confidence also has some real benefits. I'd invite you to accept your self-doubt as a gift instead of a limitation. Clearly, this is the ill-fitting 'gift' you didn't want, the one in the terrible colour where you'd like to say to the giver: 'Really, you shouldn't have!' But imposter syndrome and even low confidence can *still be a gift – if you use it*.

That feeling is the crucial motivation which keeps people listening to others, motivates them to improve and encourages them to be empathetic – all of which move challenges on. In fact, as we've seen, research shows us competence and confidence are actually inversely correlated. That is, the more confident you become, the *less you try to improve your competence*. This is worrying stuff. No doubt you'd rather have a highly skilled team rather than one that just thinks they're the best.

By contrast, there is *no evidence* that how you see yourself affects how others perceive you – people can only *see* your behaviour. People aren't mind-readers and so don't know how you feel. That's fantastic news for competent, yet under-confident people because what people *think they* see is what they believe is the truth. That's key since we've already identified that *it's their* impressions that matter far more than your own.

The reality that people only see the confidence you project, rather than your inner self-doubt, resonates for Lynne Cadenhead. She is the Chair of WES and founder of multiple successful businesses. She admits: 'I'm under-confident daily! That's not the image I project, but it's the reality check more of us actually need. My "under-confidence" stops me from reacting too quickly and helps me think through how to approach a challenge.'

People can't determine when others lie versus when they tell the truth. More worryingly, the people who think they are the best at spotting liars are the worst.[87] This matters even if they are right or wrong. At its core, 'reputation' is just your competence *according to others*. And as you've seen, people are wrong a lot of the time. So to minimise the gap between your confidence and competence, you have to understand how others see you, and the values *they think* you bring. There are plenty of benefits for individuals and their organisations when people focus on competence instead of confidence.

---

87. Bond Jr., C. F. and DePaulo, B. M. 2006 Accuracy of Deception Judgements, *Personality and Social Psychology Review* 10(3): 214–234.

LIFE SHOULDN'T BE A POPULARITY CONTEST

The truth is, under-confidence can have real benefits. The person who is always slightly uncertain of themselves is often your hardest worker, most willing to explore alternative options and foresee potential problems. They also are the most cautious about thinking a particular idea, even one of their own, is bullet-proof.

There's a joke about how you don't want high school to be the best years of your life. In reality, this is true as the evidence suggests confidence and popularity have real downsides a decade later, namely anxiety and depression. Researchers who began tracking high-schoolers at age 15 found students who prioritised forging close friendships over being seen as 'popular' by a much wider group, were much happier by age 25.[88] It was better to be well-liked for how good a friend you are than it was to be thought of as confident and popular amongst a larger group.

Interestingly, the adverse effects of chasing popularity didn't manifest during high school, but *during early adulthood*. If you focus on popularity in your teenage years, you've likely hit most of your 'peak moments' of happiness. Others, by contrast, will be working to attain those moments they hope will come later in life. This finding makes sense. If you've already felt 'peak happiness', where do you go from there, when things get hard, as they invariably do?

It's actually the less confident kids who go on to be more successful because they don't expect anything to come easily to them. Many of the most successful people we see today were inherently under-confident, particularly as teens. They often seek out continuous self-improvement and show greater empathy. The last benefit of under-confidence? The under-confident know they're always learning and don't have all the right answers. This mindset means they are often great listeners – a vital skill for a modern workforce.

Similarly, it's far better to be your own worst critic. Even if you are feeling like you're doing well, it doesn't hurt to be humble. If you're succeeding, most people will point out your competence. This happens because humility is far more attractive to people than overconfidence. This is excellent news for those smart enough to focus on improving their competence.

This type of humility and even vulnerability resonated with many. Rosemary McGinness laughs: 'Confidence isn't the brash salesperson. It's the courageous leader who can show vulnerability publicly and still maintain certainty in themselves and the people around them.'

---

88. Narr, R. K., Allen, J. P., Tan, J. S. and Loeb, E. L. 2019 Close Friendship Strength and Broader Peer Group Desirability as Differential Predictors of Adult Mental Health, *Child Development* 90: 298–313.

HUMILITY IS A GREAT REALITY CHECK

The truth is the confident just don't have the same level of drive to improve. Competence only comes with lower self-confidence. The purpose of low confidence is to help you recognise what skills you need to improve and get more experience.

When low confidence triggers anxiety, it is only your mind's attempt to prevent disaster and protect you by reminding you where you could be stronger. Low self-confidence doesn't stop your efforts at getting better, it actually makes that more *likely*. Performance is only a single and tiny part of a result.

For example, because I speak to audiences'people sometimes assume the confidence I aim to project is natural (which it isn't) and never fails me (it does). What's important to me is getting people to understand the message. I don't want them distracted by poorly laid out examples or a disjointed and rambling talk.

That means I've spent years focused on understanding my specialism, months writing speeches and getting feedback from the types of people likely to be in my audiences. It also means I have to spend time creating the right visuals and engagement questions for a particular audience.

After all this, I still do several hours of rehearsal for each speech I give. Practice, practice, practice. This is my 90% effort to make the 10% I actually deliver look 'easy'. The work I put in is my competence. You likely do something similar in your career; read up on research, listen to feedback, observe other's objections.

Your confidence is only the *by-product* of all that time and effort. If you have colleagues you respect, have lunch with them to ask them about their 90%.

Take colleagues you respect to lunch and ask:

- **What were some of their hardest moments?**
- **What do they wish they'd done differently?**
- **What they've got better at?**

Developing a *realistic* sense of your competence is a secret weapon. It encourages you to develop more expertise and reduces your chances of appearing pompous or unprepared, something colleagues may already be trying to sniff out. Faking confidence will only help you hide any incompetence for a *limited time*. It will only work with people *who don't know better anyway*. Conversely, if your competence is paired with a touch of modesty and even a bit of open insecurity, you'll likely develop allies. They know how you feel because *they've felt it too*. You'll also probably gain their sympathy and support.

In developing the competent creatives on her team, Sarah Douglas advocates executive coaching to help people get through these challenges. She credits coaching with not just growing her confidence, but also helping her very competent team members. She suggests: 'I've always believed you can teach confidence, but you can't as easily teach competence.' Douglas explains where her version of confidence originated.
She reflects:

> *Early in my career I didn't see versions of confidence that*
> *I identified around me. But when I read about author Jim*
> *Collins' 'fierce humility', it completely resonated. I knew it*
> *wasn't all about the 'jazz hands' versions I saw around me.*
> *I wanted integrity and honesty, confidence to go deeper for*
> *me before I identified with it.*

CAREER COCKTAIL: MIX OF HUMILITY AND WILL

The workplace is tired of superficial and transactional 'shallow confidence'. People actually **respond** better to empathy, humility and competency. Douglas' reference to Collins' work in *Good to Great* is apt. Trying to identify what created great companies, Jim Collins and his research team looked at the records of 1,435 Fortune 500 companies over two decades. They delved into everything from financial records to press releases.

Collins' team identified elite companies that made the leap to great results and sustained those results for at least 15 years.[89] How great? After the jump, they generated cumulative stock returns far greater than any competitors over the same period. These results were better than twice the results delivered by a composite index of some of the world's most recognisable companies, including Coca-Cola, Intel, General Electric, and Merck. In the end, Collins found that only 11 of the original 1,435 companies qualified because of the strict success measures to which he held them.

---

89. Collins, J. 2001 *Good to Great*, Random House Business Books, London.

The main reason these 11 companies succeeded so dramatically compared to their peers, was their *focus on their critical field of competence*. This focus was by leaders Collins eventually called 'Level 5 Leaders', and it's very relevant for confidence. When Collins' team looked at the characteristics of the leaders of those companies, their traits went *against* our popular assumptions of leadership. There were no larger-than-life confident saviours transforming companies to this level. As individual leaders they weren't flashy and didn't seek press coverage.

Despite their remarkable results, those leaders got very little media atttention. In fact, they most often gave credit to those around them for making great things happen. They were seemingly ordinary people quietly producing extraordinary results. However, beyond humility and modesty it's equally about ferocious resolve. That is the almost stoic determination to do whatever needs to be done to make the company great. Clearly if you want to go from good to great yourself, the people to emulate aren't the overconfident, but actually the competent.

Humility comes from knowing there is always more work to do – and you'll need to have the will to do it. It's easy to focus on the end result of our goals or perhaps more accurately; the way *we believe things will be* when we finally achieve our goal. In reality, being successful doesn't mean that the work disappears — it merely changes, as do your next goals. Achieving your version of 'enlightenment' is not an endpoint in and of itself. You'll need to keep up the hard work, to keep moving forward. I meet very few executives who feel they're 'done'.

Level 5 leaders weren't huge personalities, but they were very well respected by their internal teams and created enviable results. Your social skills are going to be hugely important. It's a myth that confident people *don't care what other people think*. It's a Hollywood legend; celebrating the loner who ignores the doubters – but a falsehood all the same. The only people who get ahead are those who care a great deal about what others think *and* listen in order to act on feedback.

These people care about how they are regarded by others and will make adjustments as they need. For Derek Watson, taking feedback is one of the most critical competencies those who want to be 'promotion-worthy' must demonstrate.

As Watson says:

The right work is about thinking through who their supporters and critics will be in the room, getting insight from both before the meeting. It's about thinking through the implications of an idea from timing and logistics. It's an awareness of finance and the external bodies who might be involved as well as all the potential challenges.

Watson continues:

I want to see people who have tested out their hypothesis. People who have gone to every potential stakeholder and asked: 'Can you give me some thoughts on this? What am I missing?'

These stages are vital for two reasons. Watson smiles:

First, they don't just highlight who may support you in a meeting. They'll also get to think through how to address the challenges any naysayers raise. This step is important if you weren't initially able to get them on board. Addressing their concerns publicly will allow you to say you've them taken on board.

Watson continues:

Plus, it gives naysayers further evidence you want to collaborate with them. Second, it's useful for understanding how an idea might land and a set of steps to take if you think someone is going to raise an idea or plan of action you don't want to go ahead. It enables you to identify what it would take for you to support an idea. It makes you create your own list of go/no-gos for someone else's idea.

As Watson says: 'Don't come and tell me every interesting thought you have. Spend time beforehand validating that idea, and then come and tell me what you found.'

No doubt those steps make his job a little easier. Plus, Watson knows who else supports you, but also *who doesn't*, so he's also prepared. For Watson, this isn't an exercise in increasing your confidence in 'selling' an idea, but one aimed at increasing your competence. He knows you'll leave those conversations better versed in the unforeseen implications of 'your great idea' before you bring them to him as a leader.

Remember, the smartest person in the room isn't the smartest, just the best prepared. Pre-think about your goals, likely objections to your ideas and the impact on stakeholders and other decision makers.

The fly in this ointment is that in validating an idea, confident people will often be more convincing their ideas are worth pursuing, whether they actually have merit or not. 'Confidence-bias' happens even if the evidence indicates otherwise. However, it's the competent who make better judges of the evidence. They ask the right questions changing the direction of an idea for the better.

In preparation for meetings:

- **Ask leaders: 'One thing I've noticed is X, have you seen this too?' It shows you notice trends, gives them a chance to reflect and be primed if they hear related issues beforehand.**
- **Speak to stakeholders ahead of time to gauge their priorities and likely objections so you can address them.**
- **Before walking in, take up a 'power pose' – hands on hips with legs wide apart for a minute or two, to moderate both your 'feel-good' and stress hormones.**

THE OVERLAP BETWEEN TRUST AND LIKEABILITY

Watson also understood the upsides of under-confidence. They are the people he most readily solicits for advice. He explains:

> *They're the ones I can approach when I need the detail on something I don't quite understand. I'll ask: 'I'm getting some figures that don't make sense to me. Can we have a quick chat?' Alternatively, I might say: 'A mistake was made that I can't get my head around. Can you help me understand how this could have happened?'*

He continues on their value:

> *These people, while often in the lower rungs, are like gold dust to me. They know their stuff so bloom when I ask their opinion. They can spot if a process wasn't followed or an error was made much better than I can. It can be intimidating as what I'm asking may be 'above their paygrade', as I've been told. But they want to make a difference; often because they'll be the ones who either take the blame or who have to clean up a mess if it all goes wrong!*

In our discussion, Reem Hayati pointed out another upside to under-confidence replying: 'You can get more done because people don't notice you, and you're not considered threatening to anyone.' To that point, understanding how others see you is a stealth move for using people's misconceptions to your advantage.

Similarly, being unwarranted in your optimism and 'confidence' does backfire, even before you enter the workplace. At 18 years old, students were asked to rate their charm and intelligence. Those who overrated themselves, compared to how others viewed them at 18, were more likely to be described negatively by others five years later. At 23 they were more likely to be judged as arrogant, narcisstic, deceitful and not trustworthy. This criticism came from *people other* than the critics who'd initially rated them negatively when they were just 18.

By comparison, men who *did not self-enhance* and were accurate in how others saw them at 18 were the most likely to be seen as smart, straightforward and trustworthy at 23. Likewise, women who didn't self-enhance at 18 were later viewed as interesting, smart and introspective.[90] Contrary to popular belief it seems; *overconfidence is more detrimental than under-confidence*.

Interestingly, other research bears this out as well. People who think they have strong interpersonal skills were rated as *less likeable* by independent observers, not more.[91] Essentially, people with inflated egos aren't just deluded. Their lack of self-awareness stunts their relationships. For many, demonstrating confidence revolved around handling meetings well.

As I spoke with interviewees, I was reminded of how similar meetings are to a childhood game I loved: Skipping rope. There was a pace and timing, most often set by someone else. Other players are waiting to jump in as well. If you wait too long, you miss your turn and people may wonder if you *want* to jump at all. Similarly, in the office if you're quiet in meetings, people may question why you're even there or if you're not going to add anything.

However, you can't jump forever. You have to jump out to also give others a go. On the playground that might look like complaints from waiting others. In the office, that may be rolled eyes as others want to also get a word in.

Be the best skipper, who knows you have to jump in, but you also have *to get out* to facilitate the rest of the meeting well. You also have to be considerate of others, because you can't start afresh with your own timing – the whole rope will fall, ending the game and annoying everyone.

90. Colvin, C, Block, J. and Funder, D. C. 1995 Overly Positive Self-evaluations of Personality: Negative Implications for Mental Health, *Journal of Personality and Social Psychology* 68(6): 1152–1162.
91. Paulhus, D. 1998 Interpersonal and Intrapsychic Adaptiveness of Trait Self-Enhancement: A Mixed Blessing? *Journal of Personality and Social Psychology* 74(5): 1197–1208.

'IT'S NOT ALL ABOUT YOU' AND THE NEED FOR EMPATHY

Another reason to focus on your competence is that it's just *more interesting* to everyone around you; the very people you'll need. It's self-centred to spend time worrying about your confidence as the attention is focused on you. If you turn that around to work at getting better at an actual skill, you'll *have to focus on the others* because you'll need their skills and feedback.

Plus, if you can focus on others, and not your confidence levels, it allows you to connect with others far better. People feel on edge when talking to the most self-confident person in the room. It heightens their own fears about being 'found out'. People don't let their guard down, preventing you from ever truly knowing them or being known yourself.

However, if you know you aren't the 'best', you'll listen better, be more vulnerable and make more honest connections. It takes courage to show you don't have all the answers. But it's a more relaxing, not to mention authentic place than living in fear of being found out for your imperfections.

For the years before deciding to write this book, I'd simply ask people about their opinions on the topic. I certainly didn't have any answers, and these conversations were invaluable to me in setting my direction. This insight gathering also worked in reverse.

Nikki Slowey, Programme Director at Family Friendly Working Scotland, and I had talked about this topic before I wrote the book. She noted how the earliest discussions we'd had led her to new observations. She says:

> *Before our conversations, I would have said confidence is*
> *the person who speaks up. Now I can see it as someone who*
> *can show their vulnerability and trust others. The type of*
> *person who is more ready to say: 'I've hired you, I don't*
> *have all the answers, but I trust you to help me find the*
> *answers.' Don't get me wrong, you have to be in the room*
> *and share your opinion, but confidence doesn't need to look*
> *as brash as we have been conditioned to think.*

In the subsequent months, Slowey said she'd been more mindful of her role as a leader. She is now more likely to take a step back and let quieter members of staff speak up first. She smiles:

I was probably overprotective of who I may have thought of
as 'less confident' people on my team. I'd sometimes handle
questions they could have answered. Now I realise 'jumping
in' to save people doesn't always help. They may need a few
prompts, but they certainly don't need me to speak for them.
So now, I'm more likely to say: 'Emma, no one knows more
about this than you, can you tell us what you're thinking?'
Or 'Simon, 'I liked what you were saying about this a few
days ago, can you explain your reactions to this issue?'

SHOWING VULNERABILITY AND ADMITTING MISTAKES

We don't think of apologies as confident leadership behaviour. However, our
willingness to extend apologies is often informed by our background, and how
it relates to the status quo. As eminent linguist Deborah Tannen noted when it
came to the ways people use apology:

For many women and a fair number of men, saying
'I'm sorry' isn't literally an apology, it is a ritual way of
restoring balance to the conversation ... It's more akin to
'I'm sorry that happened.'

Tannen continued:

To understand the ritual nature of apologies, think of
a funeral at which you might say, 'I'm so sorry about
Reginald's death.' When you say that, you are not pleading
guilty to a murder charge. You are expressing regret
that something happened without taking or accepting
blame. In other words, 'I'm sorry' can be an expression
of understanding – and caring – about the other person's
feelings rather than an apology.[92]

Tannen's point is valid, and something I often see in my coaching practice
when women contribute or even disagree with others in a meeting. This
tendency may stem from women feeling responsible for the feelings of others.
Saying 'I'm sorry, but I just don't agree' may come out of a need to buffer any
possible repercussions of speaking their mind.

If you find yourself in this situation, it helps to name the elephant in the room.
Explain 'I know I may have a different perspective, but I also know the best
teams I've worked with have had a range of viewpoints.'

---

92. Tannen, D. 1995 *Talking from 9 to 5*, William Morrow & Co., London, p. 46.

It's not enough to be different. You also have to value the skills of others. Play acting at confidence takes up too much of the mental energy you could be spending on improving your skills.

Confidence is also the courage to recognise when you've changed your mind publicly. That's tough, as vulnerablity is not a comfortable place for leaders of either gender to inhabit. Plus, as McGinness points out:

> *It's particularly hard for senior women to demonstrate any*
> *vulnerability. This is something they've had to suppress*
> *for years to get to the top with the guys. We've been taught*
> *'don't cry, don't show your emotions'. I'd love to see a shift*
> *with the new generation of leaders.*

Similarly, Silka Patel is a senior woman working in the technology sector in Scotland and would be considered confident by anyone who knows her. However, even she prefers to show vulnerability when necessary and responds well to it in others. Patel was tapped on the shoulder to become a Board Member for Technology Scotland years before we spoke. She was cautious about her invitation onto this all-White male Board. Patel, an Asian woman, laughs recalling:

> *In the interview, I was getting on well with the CEO so*
> *asked: 'Are you looking at me because the deeply technical*
> *men you already have are all at least 50 years old and all*
> *White?' He leaned back in his chair, slightly embarrassed*
> *and said 'I'm not going to lie to you. You do tick many of*
> *the boxes I'd like to fill. But I need someone confident and*
> *capable enough to hold their ground in a boardroom. It's a*
> *tough crowd of alpha men.'*

Patel laughs: 'It was a lightbulb moment for me! It made me realise the brand I'd spent years creating around being a confident woman of colour was actually working!' Patel wanted to continue to break down stereotypes of Asian women in technology, so joined their Board. What made her listen to him? She replies:

> *His honesty. I was scared of asking him for fear of the*
> *answer. But he meant well and that he probably was just as*
> *afraid of saying the wrong thing, so I believed him. He had*
> *a vulnerability, and I could see his squeamishness.*

There was a willingness in him to go with an uncomfortable, but true answer. Patel was unequivocal: 'Showing your vulnerability *is* confidence.' She explains:

130

When people admit they don't have all the answers, I find that endearing. They may say: 'Things aren't great financially, but I think the team we have now is the right one.' But if a stereotypically confident person comes into the same situation, pretending all is fine, my alarm bells go off sounding: 'Alpha Male, Alpha Male!' I just don't trust him. The funny thing is I'll work harder for the first person. They've shown a vulnerability over the person who assured me that all was under control when it clearly wasn't.

Patel joined the Board two years ago. For the first several months she watched, listened and only contributed if it was in her 'wheelhouse' of competencies. A few months in, she began to weigh in more regularly explaining:

I'm never going to shout the loudest. I had to do it via my quiet observations and the questions I ask. After they've argued between themselves, they'll turn and ask my opinion. It takes time, but it's where their expectations of my ethnicity, gender and my focus on competence have positively played a role in getting me that respect.

Patel is willing to take the role of referee amongst a group of more traditionally confident people. However, she's only got to that point by being competent in her quiet approach in those settings compared to the argumentative styles of her peers.

Seek feedback, by asking:

- **Your team: Whats working well and what they'd like to see more of.**
- **Your boss: Why they give you certain responsibilities. What do they see in you that you don't see in yourself?**
- **Your previous employer or sponsors: Why they thought of you for certain roles.**

Like many, Lynne Cadenhead is all for rebranding confidence and is interested in how we use 'self' to precede 'confidence'. For example, why do we undervalue confidence when we advocate for others - as opposed to prioritising self-confidence - as we expect people to do? Cadenhead agrees that speaking up on someone else's behalf is a type of confidence, but again one we don't readily recognise. She questions: 'Should the person who routinely asks for promotions for themselves be deemed more confident than the person who asks for promotions for others?'

If the answer revolves around 'self'-confidence versus a confidence in others, that's an issue. Honestly, is the person who thinks primarily about themselves really the best person to reward with a leadership role? Cadenhead raises a very valid question, but one we don't ask often enough. She reflects:

> *Is the person who demands their promotion confident or are they self-centred? Equally, is the person who celebrates their colleagues' achievements before themselves, 'under-confident' or are they more of a '21st century leader'?*

GETTING BACK ON YOUR HORSE

A big part of growing your competence is in recognising the failures you've had. Only when you own them can you adapt accordingly to get back on the proverbial horse. If your confidence means you don't acknowledge poor choices you made, *you'll keep making them.*

I grew up struggling with maths and let that define me for much of my life. Not getting better was my poor choice. So, when deciding on how to collect the data I'd need for my PhD, I specifically chose statistical modelling. I knew it would be painful, but I had to shed my fear or risk always defining myself as 'weak at maths'.

The interviewees all recognised *real benefits* to under-confidence. It means they had to look wider for answers when things go wrong. Alejandra Corona is a Marketing Executive, who has spent over 20 years of her career working across FMCG and Financial Services. She's done this in the UK, Chile, Venezuela, Panama and her home country of Mexico. She recalled a particular situation where she grew her competence only by understanding what had gone wrong with a critical project. Turning the situation around ultimately improved her confidence, via improving her competence. Corona describes:

> *When I began leading my area of the business – 'baby care', our nappies had slowly lost market share over several years. We slipped top in market share to number two, and then from two to three. It was more of a slow 'boiling of the frog', so no one before me was particularly worried. There was always a good excuse, normally about a competitor's fantastic new campaign. Then one day, we lost our biggest market – and the only one in which we'd held onto the top slot – Argentina.*

Corona sighs remembering:

Overnight our confidence went, and with no explanation
as to what we'd done wrong. We'd been following the
standard practices set out by global HQ for marketing,
based on what had worked in other markets. It was a stark
realisation, but from a non-dramatic slide downwards.
It made everyone doubt themselves. They weren't just
wondering how this happened when we were doing
everything right, but how could it happen over such a long
time?

Corona continues, thinking about where the turnaround came from:

Our nappies were working for the rest of the world, but we
eventually discovered our entire Latin American market of
new parents thought our lining felt too much like plastic.
To them, it was like putting their newborn in a rubbish
sack! Immediately, we saw a million things we were getting
wrong and made immediate changes. The self-doubt we felt
that made us look harder for the right answers, even if they
weren't the right answers for other regions. The turnaround
was amazing and within three years, we crossed the 1
billion mark for sales, and we'd regained the top market
share across our main markets.

In Corona's next role for a different organisation in a different sector, her new employer was also experiencing that same type of downward slide in market share. They similarly reassured themselves they were still ahead of increasingly smaller local competitors. She points out:

Their boiling frog was that they were losing market share
because their antiquated online banking systems didn't
work well with mobile technology. But if anyone pointed
this out, they were immediately attacked. The confidence of
the top guys didn't let them see what was going wrong. With
too much ego they just blamed others.

Toby Mildon has worked in fields ranging from media to accounting. Like others, he'd also experienced dips in his own confidence levels due to setbacks at work. For Mildon, having supportive friends and even former colleagues was a godsend.

Toby's advice to anyone considering leaving an employer where your confidence has dwindled? 'Seek an external sounding Board. I've seen too many people have a long, drawn-out internal battle as to whether they should stay or go, so that objective outsider was vital.'

As an executive coach, that's one thing that draws clients. We all have our own version of what is 'best' for a loved one in need, so the objectivity Mildon speaks of can be vital.

Lindsey Porter was a former banker of over 20 years who now runs a successful yoga and well-being business. She agreed there were upsides to under-confidence, and they often came after a setback. Porter's confidence was at a low point after returning to work post-maternity leave. She recalls: 'Hitting rock bottom, when your confidence is at its lowest, can actually be the *perfect trigger to do something different*. It got me thinking about how else life could be. It's the silver lining to under-confidence.'

She retrained as a yoga instructor while still at her role in financial services. However, as Porter's mastery of yoga grew, so did her confidence in how and where to use it. Demonstrating a great deal of confidence, she'd start the senior meetings she hosted between UK and Indian employees with some basic yoga – a highly unexpected but innovative move. She'd explain: 'We have a lot to cover today, but I'd like to start with a 2-minute meditation. It challenged their mindsets as to what a great meeting could be.'

No doubt that surprised her audience, but as she explained it, those two minutes likely also grounded them in thinking what they'd like to get out of the meeting. It also calmed them down from the last harried meeting they'd rushed in from – a norm for many professionals. For Porter, taking this courageous approach helped marry two industries people don't traditionally associate with one another – yoga and banking.

SEVEN

WHO'S AFFECTED BY STATUS QUO DEFINITIONS

'Status quo' is Latin for 'the mess we're in'
– Ronald Reagan

Bias emerges in how we think about confidence, who deserves to display it and how. Our current definitions work well for certain groups of people, like the status quo, but others lose out. In this book, we'll be talking more about gender, race, socioeconomic class, introversion and disability and how they intersect with confidence only as a starting point. This is because your cultural background and the type of both positive and negative experiences you've had *intertwine* to foster both optimism and ultimately confidence.

We're going to look at these groups not to pitch different types of disadvantage against one another. That's counterproductive and belies the intersectional and overlapping nature of demographic differences. Instead, while the ways different people think about and display confidence is as varied as the groups themselves, and the individuals within, there *are* trends we'll explore. While we will look at some group differences, we cannot look at *all* groups as individually as they deserve, for two practical reasons.

The first is how each 'non-status quo' group interacts with confidence could cover many books, each on their own. I can only add to the conversation and encourage others to take this up beyond what I offer. The second and perhaps more dismaying reason is that there is simply not enough research yet that looks at how our different identities affect confidence and competence specifically. We just don't live in a world where this topic has been adequately researched.

I hope this lack of research on different groups changes and I have added research where I can find it. However, our starting point is simply that your confidence level is affected by all the experiences you've had, and the background from which you come. These experiences include every win and loss, *and* the reactions others have had to you. Whether you *see* them or not, they also include every 'benefit of the doubt' you've been given, and your likelihood of feeling understood. Your confidence was not created in a perfect vacuum where the platitudinous encouragement of 'be confident!' is sufficient, practical or even desirable.

THE TRUTH ABOUT GENERALISING AND IDENTITY

At times, it may seem the research findings I draw upon makes generalisations about groups of people, which may seem odd. However, finding *patterns* in a seemingly unrelated world of individual experiences *is the whole point of research*.

To this potential criticism, I draw upon the linguist researcher Deborah Tannen's salient words: 'If findings of the research aren't generalisable, they are useless. If you can't generalise your findings, you can't talk about them at all. Generalising, that great bugbear of conventional wisdom, is the ultimate goal of scientific research.'[93]

People criticise generalisations as limiting and prescriptive. However, I've also seen them be *reassuring*. Without generalisability, any 'weakness' you assume is personal to you, continues to be merely an individual problem. Knowing it's a trend or an experience you share with others has power. Even if a statistical norm *doesn't* apply to you, it can also be illuminating. It can explain why others may react poorly to your style. They do because you are different from what people *expect*.

Deborah Tannen explained this irony of how close stereotyping is to generalising in her seminal book, *Working 9 to 5*. She points out:

> *It is as if the only research that can be accepted is research that proves the opposite of what everyone previously believed ... If we look at why certain behaviour is common, we can then help dispel myths ... Not talking about stereotypes doesn't make them go away.*[94]

To this point, tendencies shouldn't be mistaken for 'norms'. If research finds a majority does something, then what the minority does shouldn't be seen as abnormal, just less common.

---

93. Tannen, D. 1995 *Talking from 9 to 5*, William Morrow & Co., London, p. 311.
94. Tannen, D. 1995 *Talking from 9 to 5*, William Morrow & Co., London, p. 313.

EXCEPTIONALITY IS NOT EVIDENCE

In discussions I've had, status quo members often quickly point to a senior woman or BAME person they know of, who 'bucked the trend'. Their success doesn't dismiss the much larger evidence-based pattern, showing a lack of progress. Equally, we've all heard people talk about 'how fast things are changing'. However, in many ways, progress has been slow, particularly given how rapidly people from historically disadvantaged groups have accessed education.

This progress in higher education rates can be a distraction from how little progress has been made in the workplace. It works on the assumption if higher numbers of people access further and higher education that guarantees their career success. Alternatively, it's presumed all inequalities will be rectified *with a bit more time*. As evidence of this, people love to point out 'exceptions to the rule'.

This is the battle cry of 'but we have a senior Black guy in my organisation!' or 'I've got a disabled lady in our department' that I and perhaps you have heard. I've been challenged by many status quo members with 'You can't open a newspaper without seeing some powerful woman or talk about pay gaps on the cover.' These examples are notable *because* they represent such a change from the expected status quo. However, the existence of exceptions often gets far more attention than the more significant observation of 'Yes, but the other eight members on our leadership team are all White people or men.'

Being an 'exception to the rule' is a risky place. If a non-status quo person struggles or is even just 'controversial' this is problematic, for three key reasons. First, it sends a message to other non-status quo candidates to be wary of raising their head above the parapet for fear of the same spotlight.

To have someone 'like you' fail sends an unconscious signal that undermines confidence, particularly when there are so few models who are both failing and succeeding – as members from any groups do. Second, it puts additional strain on the candidate while in their role because they will be aware to many, they represent a larger identity group. Third, these exceptions reassure people the 'battle for equality' has largely been won when the *evidence* proves otherwise.

The plural of anecdote is *not* data. This statistical reality is vital to recognise as holding fast to 'exceptions to the rule' can have adverse effects. It gives a false reassurance that the mechanisms of discrimination are unravelling quicker than they actually are. Additionally, these stories can create resentment in status quo members who feel *they are the new* threatened species despite the *evidence* showing the cards are still very much stacked in their favour.

OVERCONFIDENCE IN THE PROGRESS WE'VE MADE

Many argued the US was in a 'post-racial' age after the election of Barack Obama as President. Instead, what happened in the subsequent election is what happens at organisations across the world. A status quo member again took the White House, largely in a reaction to the racial status quo who felt 'unheard' during Obama's time in office. This created a type of discomfort for them to which they were unaccustomed given *every previous* president in US history had been a White man.

Worryingly for diversity of thought, status quo ideals are again making some headway across organisations, in particular relating to gender balance. In 2017, 90% of the 279 companies surveyed by McKinsey & LeanIn said they prioritised gender diversity. However, that dropped to 84% just a year later. Similarly, 56% of employees said they were personally doing what it takes to improve gender diversity in 2017, which fell to 45% in 2018.[95]

Over-optimism in our progress prevails in spite of the statistical evidence. For example, nearly half of the men (44%) in an American study *where only 10% of their leaders were women*, actually felt women were 'well represented in leadership'. A quarter of their female colleagues (28%) felt the same way, which still seems overoptimistic given the statistical reality of women in leadership roles in those companies (10%) was so dismally low.[96] This is huge as these American organisations represented 13 million employees – a huge swathe of the national workforce.

Worse yet, this research found no real progress on gender balance in leadership was made in the US since 2015, let alone between 2017–2018 when these two measures were taken. While the data shows no significant progress has been made, people, and particularly the status quo, *feel* that it has. To this point, only 12% of male senior leaders at these organisations said they'd *seen* gender bias against women in the previous year, compared to their senior female peers – nearly half (43%) of whom say they have witnessed it.[97]

Ultimately, the status quo assuming progress has been made when it hasn't, is not helpful for anyone. First, it means leaders won't look harder at the organisations, systems and teams the people in their organisations are inheriting. Second, it also means leaders won't reflect on how the *structure may have contributed* to someone's downfall or indeed the success of others.

95. Krivkovich, A. et al. McKinsey & Co. & LeanIn.Org, 2018 Women in the Workplace study.
96. Huang, J. et al. McKinsey and Co. and LeanIn.Org, 2019 Women in the Workplace study.
97. Huang, J. et al. McKinsey and Co. and LeanIn.Org, 2019 Women in the Workplace study.

The classic 'glass-cliff' greets many non-status quo leaders when they enter senior roles. They are in a very precarious position if not adequately supported at all levels. In the third place, it also means we won't look more closely at what *causes* the proverbial 'lack of confidence' that we think we see.

It is essential to understand that of course 'exceptions' exist, but the standard they have to hit is so much higher than for status quo members. I am optimistic when American research shows Black people with *unambiguously strong qualifications* are evaluated fairly against their White counterparts.

However, the same research shows stereotypes *do* strongly influence judgements[98] when requirements and criteria *are ambiguous*. The hesitancy in my optimism about this finding is that we all know some ambiguity is involved in *most hiring and promotion decisions*.

Similarly, other research also shows Black job candidates with *stellar* records receive high evaluations. However, Black candidates with mixed records will face discrimination when they are compared with White candidates with *equally mixed* records. This again proves the status quo's preference for exceptionality when letting in new people.[99] This understandably feeds into the resentment at having to be 'twice as good' that non-status quo groups feel.

PRAISED FOR 'BEING DIFFERENT FROM OTHER ...'

Our preference for visible *exceptions to the rule* are notable on their own. However, we still must address how people have to often move *closer to the status quo* to receive the same benefits. This often happens if your non-status quo identity is mostly invisible, you can 'pass' for someone closer to the status quo or have other similarities that wouldn't be obvious immediately.

I once met a status quo leader very loyal to his secretary, taking her with him to several different organisations. No doubt she was well-organised and professionally competent, but after his retirement, I discovered she also helped conceal his partial hearing impairment. This was vital in helping him 'pass' for someone with no physical disabilities – as he perceived his peers to be.

For example, disabled people sometimes take jobs that draw the least attention to their differences. A wheelchair user may opt for roles where others may not even be aware of their disability. These choices were highlighted by Jenny Morris, a wheelchair user and author of 'Pride Against Prejudice' detailing the challenges in the perceptions of disability she and others face.[100]

98. Gaertner, S. L. and Dovidio, J. F. 1986 The Aversive Form of Racism, in Dovidio, J. F., Gaertner and S. L. (eds), *Prejudice, Discrimination, and Racism*, Academic Press, Orlando, FL, pp. 61–89.
99. Hodson, G., Dovidio, J. F. and Gaertner, S. L. 2002 Processes in Racial Discrimination: Differential Weighting of Conflicting Information, *Personality and Social Psychological Bulletin*, 28: 460–471.
100. Morris, J. 1991 *Pride Against Prejudice Transforming Attitudes to Disability (PDF)*, Aylesbury, Bucks, UK: The Women's Press.

Certainly, as we'll see, for career progress, it's been adaptive for people from under-represented groups to minimise differences between themselves and the status quo. Alternatively, they'll accept praise for their deviation from the under-represented group from which they come. I am reminded of the devotion I felt towards my primary school gym teacher when he praised me for 'running fast for a girl' or university suitors who told me I 'was funny for a woman'.

Equally, plenty of my female clients in male dominated fields have been praised with: 'you're just like one of the guys'. These statements are intended as compliments. However, to accept them, you're distancing yourself from what people *expect* of your identity groups.

While adaptive, this fundamentally undermines the idea that there can be power in difference. Even worse, it isolates under-represented people from identifying with similar others for the sake of being accepted. For me, the better response to those 'compliments' would have been: 'Well, if I'm so different from what you expect, then you haven't met enough women, because we're pretty funny.'

To this point about feeling distance from an identity group, Silka Patel said she only noticed her status distance *after* she moved out of London for work. She recalls:

> *Race only really occurred to me after I moved to Scotland.*
> *I was now in a visible ethnic minority. I was suddenly not*
> *just an Asian woman in a male-dominated field but very*
> *senior which you don't see much of. In fact, I was the only*
> *senior Asian employee for this big technology multinational*
> *in Scotland at the time. It was only during the end of my*
> *tenure, ten years later, they even hired another Asian man*
> *for a big role.*

STATUS DISTANCE

Identity is vital for us to address as it feeds our ideas of what confidence looks like. Our identities largely revolve around both visible, such as race or gender, and invisible factors, such as disability and sexual orientation or nationality. We all have multiple, overlapping identities as we navigate our career. There may be times when you acutely feel your difference to the status quo and other times when you may seamlessly blend in. This is the pressure of status distance, and it's felt most by people who are furthest from the status quo.

For example, in many ways, I am part of the status quo. I'm a heterosexual, White woman who is able-bodied and a native speaker of the same language in the country in which I work – English. My only real point of difference is that

140

I'm a woman often advising top teams of men. When you suffer from 'status distance', you'll highlight any similarities you have, and downplay differences. However, exclusion at its core forces people to change who they feel they are, affecting both engagement and well-being.

In discussions with professionals, active in their employer's BAME or disability networks, many said these topics came up routinely *amongst themselves*. However, for their employers the 'official party line' was about progress.

However, some remarked people from non-status quo backgrounds weren't expected to go as far up the career ladder. Instead, comments from colleagues implied they should 'Stay in your lane' or 'Who do you think you are?' Instead, there was almost a code of managed expectations so that no one's goals were set *unreasonably* high.

Status distance also suggests how *entitled* people feel to power. Those who are closest feel the most entitled. For example, we see the way women's networks historically have been driven by White, heterosexual women. Conversely, those furthest from the status quo may feel frustration at the speed of progress. Unfortunately, this sense of realism can be misinterpreted as a lack of confidence.

Douglas Morrison, a STEM educator for many years, had an interesting take on how status distance affects expectations. The City of Glasgow College, where he works, runs campaigns encouraging people from under-represented groups to consider STEM fields. When they do, he says the overwhelming response is gratitude, which is somewhat *frustrating* for Morrison.

Morrison says: 'These groups have been overlooked for so long in these fields, they want access and integration. By comparison, overrepresented groups want progression. They've already assumed they'll get the access and integration the others seek.' This is status distance in practice. Morrison, himself a heterosexual White male, says:

> *It's nice to be thanked for our work but expecting them to be grateful doesn't sit well with me. It buys into this belief we've 'given' them this extra opportunity rather than they 'earned' it through their hard work. They have to work hard just to get accepted in the first place. It's not a favour we're doing for them, that's the wrong mindset for us all to have.*

Others highlight Morrison's point. If someone shows merit and dares to expect progression, we can't label them as 'uppity' or 'ungrateful' if they don't get it.

Toby Mildon and I also talked through these issues. Mildon, who is gay and physically disabled, agrees the *closer* you are to the status quo, the *less* likely you are to notice status quo benefits. However, a change in those circumstances can happen in an instant. I see this too with status quo professionals who only notice discrimination when they start dating someone from a different race, or has a child with special needs, or has a sister who comes out as a lesbian.

Mildon says: 'Most of us at some point in our lives will personally experience a disability, though it's always a shock and a struggle when it happens.' Developing this new lens beyond your *own* identities often creates more empathy and a new understanding of colleagues. Mildon continues about the new newly disabled:

> *They can hide it, but they may become angry. They now realise all the privilege they didn't know they had. They have to now identify with a less powerful identity. It's a shock to the system and no doubt to their confidence. Some now see the injustice around them, and so become evangelists for change. I personally love this group! They were already part of the status quo, so have their trust and influence. They can become an ally now that their perspective changed.*

Mildon and I discussed why certain groups react to the injustice they now see and suggests:

> *A man who transitions to becoming a woman hasn't forgotten her earlier life. The same thing happens with disability. If someone has an accident, becoming quadriplegic overnight, they have to change their identity. They are harshly reminded they're now living in a world that wasn't designed for disabled people.*

Mildon explains:

> *It's the cumulation of tiny things like the fact that a favourite restaurant has three steps at its entrance that they never noticed before. You either become angry with the world or you transition into someone better than you were before. They're thinking 'I used to be listened to before this change, so I feel entitled to being heard.' It can create a helpful militancy.*

Two Ears, One Mouth

Writing on different identities was challenging for me, and for good reason. Over one-third of the people I interviewed had been ethnic minorities in the countries in which they worked. Nearly one-quarter were men. Neither were populations I'd specifically addressed in my previous books. Indeed, as I've said, I'm a member of the status quo found in most Western organisations, so didn't see how much I was initially missing.

However, as I progressed through these interviews, informal conversations and my own reading, my understanding around the topic slowly grew. As it did, so did the need to address these issues. I am no expert on all the experiences of people from different status quo or non-status quo backgrounds. However, given the inequity of the modern workplace, we need more people to be part of the discussion so we can find wider solutions.

The sensitivity around, yet lack of understanding of how race affects workplace relations is something Uviebinené highlighted in *Slay in Your Lane: A Black Girl Bible*. Her advice to anyone who wants to be more confident in understanding and discussing race? In our interview, she describes to me:

> *Don't expect others to be an unpaid 'race whisperer'. I get*
> *frustrated when people want to disagree when the topic*
> *of race comes up, but lack empathy. They don't listen to*
> *understand. They're listening to critique and jump in and*
> *tell me where I'm wrong.*

Uviebinené continues:

> *We have two ears and one mouth for a reason. We could all*
> *do with more listening on these topics rather than weighing*
> *in when we see the first online quip we don't agree with.*
> *If you're looking for easy answers to tough issues in 140*
> *characters, you really shouldn't engage.*

There is value in recognising that you don't have equal power in that conversation, something I felt acutely while interviewing people. Those from a non-status quo background will always feel a pressure to not 'rock the boat'. In the workplace, there is an unspoken pressure to diminish how much these issues affect them, simply to not offend the majority group member. This feeling no doubt happened in my interviews.

However, it's not sufficient for status quo members to disengage simply because these are hard topics. Nor is it appropriate to brush off comments with 'Terrence knows we're joking' or 'I'm sure if Anna had a problem with what I said, she'd speak up.' It's even worse when all eyes of the majority group turn to her and say, 'Isn't that right, Anna?' It's merely a method of survival to go along with the majority group assumptions.

Uviebinené's understandable frustration is evident when she writes in *Slay in Your Lane*: 'Repeated attempts to explain phenomena invisible to those not experiencing them can be physically and mentally exhausting.'[101]

This is something I saw when I met Reni Eddo-Lodge, the author of the seminal *Why I'm No Longer Talking to White People about Race* in Edinburgh. Ironically, she largely explained this frustration to a large White Scottish audience. She too seemed relieved if audience members like me had actually previously read the book, rather than expecting her to have quick and easy answers.

As a White, privileged woman, the only way I personally identify with this frustration is in my work. I spend much of my time with teams of mostly White male leaders talking about why they need more women in senior leadership, and how to make progress. I often have to 'sell' evidence-based research about why diversity and inclusion matters to a somewhat incredulous, yet largely senior male audiences who want simple or easy answers.

Sometimes they disavow the evidence or downplay the experiences of others. Alternatively, they'll explain why the mountain of evidence *doesn't apply to their organisations* or to them personally – even if what I've collected is about their organisations or teams specifically.

This is where we start by looking at just some of the identities with which people identify and how they are affected by the issues of confidence versus competence. We'll start with the topic I know because of my work and research. It's also the main dimension on which I differ from the status quo: gender.

---

101. Yomi, A. and Uviebinené, E. 2018 *Slay in Your Lane: The Black Girl Bible*, 4th Estate, London p. 122.

EIGHT

GENDERING OF CONFIDENCE

What counts for most women is having the confidence to make their own money
– Cardi B

As we'll see, women actually enter the workplace just as ambitious and self-confident as men. However, their confidence *in the system*, particularly if they are in the minority at work, is tested as they progress. The unique challenges they'll likely face are similar to other non-status quo groups as they include a toxic mix of micro-inequalities, a lack of identifiable role models and expectations about likeability versus ambition.

Plus, they often have to contend with a gendered division of caring responsibilities inside the home. In the male dominated fields where I work, when a man fails, he was a bad hire. When a woman fails, that burden is watched and experienced by all the women in the organisation. To muddy these waters, we expect confidence to be a panacea in remedying all these systemic issues.

The big question when it comes to breaking the glass ceiling shouldn't be 'how do we help women become more confident?' Instead, the question should be: 'what happened to the confidence she had when she started her career? How exactly do modern workplaces, even unintentionally, erode that confidence over time?' Understandably, we often avoid these questions. As we'll see, keeping women out of male-dominated fields seems profitable to many.

Gender is what started my interest in looking at competence versus confidence. Over the last 20 years, many professional women initially came to me because they felt overlooked. The fact they also displayed high levels of competence, often corroborated by feedback and deliverables, was confusing at best and frustrating at worst. I have had the good fortune to work with impressive women. Both they and I have been described by colleagues at various times as bitchy, shrill, aloof, ruthless, icy, angry, frumpy, hysterical and most negatively; the mother of all c-words – cunt.

Before we go further, it's worth thinking about how and when the c-word gets used. If like me you have been on the receiving end of this label it's likely because you captured attention, were assertive, spoke out and held your ground when challenged. These attributes also describe a person with 'confidence'. The fact is that 'confidence', much like the word 'cunt' is commonplace, but misunderstood. Where the words differ is how they are perceived versus what they really mean.

As we've seen, confidence appears as one of the most desirable qualities to have, yet it often hides a lack of competence. We are too far away from what confidence originally meant; having trust or faith in someone or something. Now, by comparison, overconfident people are sometimes the *least* trustworthy. Competence is the c-word for which we should actually be aiming. It's far more valuable and confidence is just the side effect. Swearing is an emotional and social construct, but *so is confidence*.

You've no doubt heard the phrases 'man up' or demeaning exhortations to not be 'a pussy'. It implies an inferiority, an inadequacy, when in fact this word represents an enduring place of strength from which we all came. I also don't know why people say tackling something challenging 'took balls'. The truth is, as a heterosexual woman with a loving husband, father and brother, some of my favourite people have balls.

But let's be honest, as anyone who has ever handled a pair knows, balls are sensitive, weak and shrink in the cold. You are hugely vulnerable with a pair of balls. In fact, if you are looking for a part of the anatomy that withstands the trials of menstruation, births and even abortions or sexual assault, that's a c-word that should be synonymous with strength!

So what do these common linguistic phrases, and the way we use them, have to do with competence or even confidence? Both our use of the c-word and the way we talk about confidence are highly gendered. Women confident in their demands are 'castrating' or 'ball-breakers'. Showing ambition or having an opinion you stand by is described as being 'ballsy'. Contrast this with the weakness we ascribe to being a 'pussy' or 'hormonal' – a common phrase we use for women who inconveniently object to poor treatment.

Simply put, what are the larger implications when we have transferred so much hatred, anger and ridicule onto the word for the totality of a woman's entire reproductive organs? It becomes a word that *must be talked around*. We also talk *around* confidence, assuming we're all displaying and valuing the same behaviours.

We get distracted by talking about who has it and what it feels like. However, what we too frequently ignore is how different it can look and *why some people seem to have more of it than others*. Answering this question, and how to then build your own confidence, is the focus of this book.

THE TIGHTROPE OF EXPECTATIONS

In the modern workplace, women must balance certainty with modesty. Too much of the latter, and women's achievements get overlooked. Too much of the former, and they can face what experts refer to as the 'backlash effect'. These are the social and professional sanctions for failing to conform to gender norms.

McKinsey & Co. with LeanIn.org conduct one of the most comprehensive surveys of American workers on an annual basis. The surveys are based upon five years of research engaging over 600 companies. They collected data across sectors on 13 million people and also surveyed 64,000 employees from those companies. Dismally, virtually no progress had been made in women's representation, at almost every level between the years 2015 to 2019.

Despite the headlines, in reality women's representation is largely stagnant, other than in the one area most companies have been putting concerted effort – the C-suite. On this rarefied level, there's been a 24% increase between 2015–2019, largely because of the vast amount of data on the positive correlations between financial performance and the number of women in C-suite roles. It hardly sounds like something worth cheering but given how dismal the rankings were – it is indeed progress. Women now make up just three in every 10 of C-suite leaders.[102]

However, women of colour fare the worst in those statistics, holding only 1 in 25 of these top roles.[103] This progress, though primarily at the top levels, is no doubt owed to the governmental focus on equity in Board composition over the last few years. As the screws turn and the media pays closer attention, small inroads are made, though the road ahead remains long.

While the situation needs to improve everywhere, gender issues in the workplace are additionally affected by the national cultures in which you work. Reem Hayati worked successfully for US-based multinationals abroad for most of her career. Yet, she experienced far more sexism once she began working for smaller companies in her home country – Egypt.

Hayati explains:

102. Huang, J. et al. McKinsey and Co. and LeanIn.Org, 2019 Women in the Workplace study.
103. Krivkovich, A. et al. McKinsey & Co. & LeanIn.Org, 2018 Women in the Workplace study.

*Multinationals are clearly no utopia, but suddenly I was
told I was 'tough'. I reminded them my toughness was whey
they hired me to get their product to market – which is what
I can do. I'd say: 'Don't compare me to what you expect
from other women, compare me to any colleagues you'd
pay to do this job'!*

Hayati felt she benefited by working for a multinational who accepted her
version of confidence. Whether she hears these criticisms or not, others do and
see their impact. Nearly three-quarters (72%) of over 700 women at VP level or
above in Fortune 1000 companies felt stereotypes about female leadership were
career blockers.[104] This blockage occurred despite the evidence showing female
directors were likelier to prevent and stop disagreements, paid more attention to
subordinates' needs and gave more feedback than their male peers.[105]

However, as we'll see in this section, over time, I began to notice that it wasn't
just women affected by our historic definitions of confidence. It was anyone
who didn't live up to the expectations the status quo had for them. These were
employees from cultures where self-promotion isn't valued, introverts, people
with disabilities and other non-status quo groups.

Before we go any further, I must point out I know *not all men* fit within the
expectations of the status quo. Many men, particularly those who want to
define success for themselves, also need new definitions. The old definitions no
longer work for them either, as we'll discuss later in this chapter on gender.

Even identifying with those definitions does not make most men, and the
families and communities in which they live, better off. Male suicide is at an
all-time high, and there is a growing distrust of the current patriarchal and
Western systems in which many of us operate.

THE MOTHER OF ALL LIES: WOMEN'S UNDER-CONFIDENCE

We have started looking at how intersectionality affects our current definitions
of confidence. However, let's unpack the biggest myth we have on this topic,
that women have lower confidence. This is a difficult nut to crack. Despite
the way we may feel as individuals at times, hundreds of studies show the
confidence levels of men and women are very similar.

104. Wellington, S., Kropf, M. B. and Gerkovich, P. R. 2003 What's Holding Women Back? *Harvard Business Review* 81(6).
105. Van der Walt, N. and Ingley, C. 2003 Board dynamics and the influence of professional background, gender and ethnic diversity of directors. *Corporate Governance* 11 (3).218-234 .

Whether looking at employees,[106] students[107] or entrepreneurs,[108] the evidence shows men and women are equally confident *in themselves*. These findings are vital for us to recognise. They help us understand that women's lower confidence, a factor even many women blame for their lack of progress, *isn't the real story*. Where there is a gender discrepancy, there is still not much to give cause for concern. Any differences are found mainly in *how men and women are viewed by other people*, not how they see themselves.

Ibarra and Obodaru looked at students from 149 countries over five years. On the Global Executive Leadership Inventory (GELI) women outshone men in eight out of the nine most essential leadership dimensions. This trend came from the 360° assessments of those 3,000 INSEAD business school students. These were the results they received from the 22,000 colleagues with whom they worked most closely.[109]

Women were only rated worse on a single dimension; 'envisioning' and then only were rated worse *if the rater was male*. 'Envisioning' was described as recognising new opportunities and developing a strategic direction to capitalise on it. Interestingly, the researchers also found *no evidence* of a female 'modesty effect', again suggesting that confidence was not an issue for the women.

The researchers looked closer at this weakness on envisioning, wondering what decreased women's scores? They said:

> *It was male peers (who represented the majority in*
> *this sample) who rated women lower on envisioning.*
> *Interestingly, female peers did not downgrade the women,*
> *contrary to the frequently heard claim that women compete*
> *rather than cooperate. Our data suggest it's the men who*
> *might feel most competitive toward their female peers. Male*
> *superiors and subordinates rated male and female leaders*
> *about the same.*[110]

The research also shows the infamous 'Queen Bee' or 'Catfight' excuses don't exist. By contrast, a lower rating was most likely given only by male peers who may have felt threatened for their own progression, by her success. To this point, when men gave their opinion about women with *whom they'd not likely compete*, their judgements were more favourable.

---

106. Ibarra H. and Obodaru, O. 2009 Women and the Vision Thing. *Harvard Business Review* 87(1): 62–70.
107. Shibley-Hyde, J. and Kling, K. 2001 Women, Motivation and Achievement, *Psychology of Women Quarterly* 25(4): 364–378.
108. Zhao, H., Seibert, S. E. and Hills, G. E. 2005 The Mediating Role of Self-efficacy in the Development of Entrepreneurial Intentions, *Journal of Applied Psychology* 90(6): 1265–1272.
109. Ibarra H. and Obodaru, O. 2009 Women and the Vision Thing, Harvard Business Review 87(1): 62–70.
110. Ibarra H. and Obodaru, O. 2009 Women and the Vision Thing, Harvard Business Review 87(1): 62–70.

It's not all good news though. Conversely, women were the most negative about theoretical women with whom they'd never worked! A 2008 study asked over 1,000 executives from nine countries (all alumni of executive education programs) to give their impressions of men and women *in general* as leaders. Both men and women believe the two genders had distinct leadership strengths, with women outscoring men on some behaviours, and men outscoring women on others.

Here's the catch: when people were asked to rate the behaviours' relative importance to *overall leadership effectiveness, the 'male' behaviours had the edge*. Across countries, 'inspiring others' – a component of the 'envisioning' dimension mentioned above – landed at the top of the rankings. It was considered the most important to overall leadership effectiveness. However, as we're seeing, there are many ways to be inspiring. Crediting men with 'envisioning' is no doubt related to more frequent displays of confidence, in both themselves and their plans.

What about the areas of leadership where men thought women were stronger? Women's standout advantage? Conveniently for them, it was women's skill at 'supporting others'! However, that skill ranked *bottom* of the list in terms of importance.[111] As a component of overall leadership effectiveness, it wasn't considered critical, but merely a 'nice to have'. It's worrying how being supportive is considered of such low value for modern leaders. The best leaders most of us have ever worked to take a more 'servant leadership' approach, particularly as all become ever more reliant on their teams.

ASSUMPTIONS AROUND GENDER CONFIDENCE

Even if there is no statistical difference between men and women's confidence rates, that's not how most of us think about gender and confidence. We ascribe under-confidence to women because it is preferable than the alternative for them; overconfidence. As much as we don't like overconfidence or arrogance in men, we *loathe* it in women and will punish those who exhibit it accordingly. Therefore, women may use the aforementioned 'helping out', self-doubt or lack of confidence as a form of self-defence.

Essentially, we put ourselves down before others can. It's also part of why women are more likely to attribute successes to luck and men attribute theirs to 'hard work' or their abilities.[112] This doesn't mean self-doubt and gratitude to others is a cunning act. It's just far more socially acceptable for women to portray humility rather than proudly proclaiming their achievements. That's more acceptable in men – and coincidentally one of the ways we've historically defined confidence.

---

111. Prime, J. et al. 2008 Managers' Perceptions of Women and Men Leaders: A Cross-Cultural Comparison, *International Journal of Cross-cultural Management* 8(2): 171–210.

112. Maccoby. E. and Jacklin, C. 1974 *The Psychology of Sex Differences*, Stanford University Press, Stanford, CA.

We assume women are far less confident, when it may be just that men are overconfident compared to the value they create. Douglas Morrison reflects:

Women then tend to be more poorly treated, compared to how they deliver and the men treated better than perhaps they deserve. That's a shame as the under-confident tend to make the best leaders, as they're the ones willing to admit they don't know everything.

It's also more socially acceptable for women to claim low confidence *than for men to admit they struggle with confidence*. However, that may be changing, according to Jenny Garrett, who also specialises in career development. The findings of her research on over 400 UK professionals surprised even her, given the myths we tell ourselves about low female confidence.

In her study, the gap between male and female confidence was only 12%. Nearly half (44%) of men claimed their confidence 'bothered' them compared to just over half of women (56%).[113] Some men are no doubt becoming more open about their weaknesses. We'll see this isn't just good for competence but also for men's mental health.

Women, on the other hand, are told to be more confident in order to progress. This is hoax given we've seen confidence *isn't the real issue*. Plus, it distracts from the more significant issues of inequality between the status quo and the non- status quo. For example, a push for confidence hides the fact competence alone isn't working out for women as equitably as it should. This is particularly true given the strides women have made in higher education over the last half a century. This has real implications for those who aren't deemed confident and therefore, high-potential. It affects the allocation of resources, which can exponentially help people with 'potential'.

For example, extra resources exponentially aids 'potential'. However, non-status quo people are less likely to be deemed 'high potential' and therefore get less support. For a start, this can mean lower-value accounts, smaller teams, less administrative assistance and even smaller offices.

113. Garrett, J. 2019 Confidence: The Destination Or a Journey? www.jennygarrettglobal.com

THE BUSINESS COST OF UNDERVALUING CONFIDENT WOMEN

I suspect many in the status-quo know exactly the impact they have by claiming visible confidence is vital for progression. For example, they'd likely be wary of redefining the behaviours we'd expect to see in leaders. After all, those behaviours justify how they arrived at their position. Excluding people initially benefits the status quo.

Introducing more non-status quo people in the mix creates more unwanted competition for those who've traditionally held the power. As a former leader who shared his *concerns* about improving diversity once 'joked' to me 'Now it's not enough to be better than 50% of the population, now I have to be better than 99%!'

This is worrying for many in the status quo and for good reason. For example, five decades worth of US census data shows, the more women enter a field, the average pay[114] and prestige[115] given to that sector *decreases*. STEM sectors, and particularly those aligned to technology, where there are very few women, pay very well indeed. In the UK, the legal and medical sectors over the last few decades have also seen this change, with pay rates stagnating as more women entered these fields.

Conversely, industries with many women, such as the caring sector and teaching are some of the lowest-paid fields, and struggle to attract men who feel they are 'worth' more. This short-term gain of better pay for status quo members ultimately limits innovation. This makes it unsustainable for any industry.

As we've started to cover, the skills of the under-represented are directly linked to profitability. For example, McKinsey & Company was among the first to find a link between the presence of women in corporate management teams and companies' organisational and financial performance.[116] They found organisations with at least three senior female leaders had an operating margin and market capitalisation that was more than twice as high as those with no women in senior leadership.

114. Levanon, A., England, P. and Allison, P. 2009 Occupational Feminisation and Pay: Assessing Causal Dynamics Using 1950-2000 US Census Data, *Social Forces*, 88(2): 865–891.
115. Pan, J. 2015 Gender Segregation in Occupations: The Role of Tipping and Social Interactions, *Journal of Labour Economics* 33(2): 365–408.
116. Desvaux, G., Devillard-Hoelllinger, S. and Baumgarten, P. 2007 McKinsey & Co. Women Matter: Gender Diversity, a Corporate Performance Driver report.

McKinsey then identified nine behaviours[117] associated with profitability. When they compared those behaviours by gender, they found men only outperformed women on two of the nine behaviours. Men were significantly more likely to engage in 'individualistic decision-making' and 'control and corrective action'. Let's be clear, both are valuable behaviours and form the backbone of what we 'expect from leaders'. However, they're only profitable when used with *enough of the seven other behaviours*.

By comparison, women and men did equally well at 'Intellectual Stimulation' and 'Efficient Communication'. So clearly, women don't corner the market on communication skills. Women were a bit more likely to outperform men on 'Participative Decision-Making' and 'Inspiration'. However, it was on the three factors of 'People development', 'Offering clear expectations and rewards' and on 'Role- modelling behaviours'where women significantly outscored the men. In short, according to McKinsey, women do as well as, and even outperform men on seven of the nine practices correlated with making money.

A study by Credit Suisse in 2012 of over 1,000 companies in 12 countries found those with executive-level gender diversity were 21% more likely to outperform their industry peers with the lowest female representation on profitability and 27% more likely to create superior long-term value.[118] These results are sustainable, in that another study found large companies with at least one female Board member outperformed those with none by 26% over six years, while small-cap firms performed 17% better.

Identify within your CV for every role you've had:

- **The type, number and ideally the monetary value of the tangible projects you delivered.**
- **How much you saved or earned the organisation as part of your job.**
- **The impact of those projects on your team, your clients or stakeholders and the organisation.**
- **What you learned and how you improved with every role -even unpaid roles like carer.**

---

117. McKinsey & Co. 2008 Women Matter 2: Female Leadership, a Competitive Edge for the Future.
118. Hunt, V. et al. 2018 McKinsey & Co Delivering through Diversity,.

LIKEABILITY ISN'T THE ISSUE

Similarly, an analysis of the 360° leadership-effectiveness scores of more than 7,280 global executives was filled out by a range of their key stakeholders. At every management level, the women were rated more favourably than the men, by their direct reports, peers and managers.

Indeed, the higher the seniority, the wider the gap between how the two genders were rated. Despite these favourable reviews earned by women, the higher the level, the higher the proportion of male leaders. By contrast men were perceived more negatively as they rose to each level.[119]

By comparison, women executives generally maintained their popularity throughout their entire careers. In fact, likeability for women was only marginally lower *before* they reached middle management. Not surprisingly, careless and arrogant leaders can be found everywhere. However, their data showed that among the least likeable, 3% more were men. Contrastingly, among the most likeable, 3% more were women.

This tiny margin should be reassuring to women who fear they will have to trade off likability versus seniority – a common concern. Similarly, this should give pause for thought to those who anecdotally site the 'Queen Bee' syndrome. Women are often raised from childhood to be likeable above all else. Therefore, the 'Queen Bee' lie can unwittingly discourage many women from even applying for management roles, let alone senior positions.

Kainaz Gazder, an Indian VP based in Singapore at a major FMCG, says confidence isn't an issue for many of the women with whom she's worked. However, as I listen to Gazder, I think part of that may come from the interest she takes in preparing her team members. She wants their confidence to be a natural extension *of what they know*. She explains:

> *I've never heard a woman criticised for lack of confidence.*
> *I've only heard her criticised as not having confidence*
> *in her plans or recommendations. Then it's obvious to*
> *everyone that it's our job as senior people to support her.*
> *If that's how she's come across, we haven't done our job in*
> *supporting her well enough.*

Her approach is a notable departure against many employers who invest less time, support and resources in someone deemed 'under-confident' or no longer 'high potential'. Gazder clarifies:

---

119. Zenger, J. and Folkman, J. 2013 New Research Shows Success Doesn't Make Women Less Likable, *Harvard Business Review* ,4 April.

We have to dig deeper to understand why she doesn't have confidence in her plans. Does she not understand the financial projections well enough? Has she not had the right training, is her manager not supporting her? That deep dive is vital! It's all about the 'Why, Why, Why?' If she got to that point in her career but didn't have the confidence she needed, clearly we did something wrong.

Gazder wants everyone in her team to be so competent that confidence is simply a *by-product of their knowledge*. Seeing leaders take responsibility for the confidence of their direct reports is refreshing and it's where the smartest leaders are heading.

The fact that so many women work below their potential actually does hurt them, personally and financially. However, the rest of society feels this loss of competency too. As the OECD explains: 'If for the individual women it means a lifelong income penalty, then for us collectively it means a lifelong efficiency and productivity penalty.'[120] The business impact hits everyone from mainstream employees and employers but also extends to entrepreneurship.

The gender parity gap between male and female entrepreneurs in the UK has widened since 2013. Indeed, in 2013, for every 100 new businesses started by a man, 63 were started by women. Unbelievably, this disparity represented *a high* for female entrepreneurship. However, since then it's diminished to a rate of 46 to every 100.[121]

Of the women I've coached who say they'd like to move up in their careers, some will be reticent to tell peers on the same team if it means friends would now be direct reports. To do so would erode the solidarity' the 'we're all in this together' atmosphere many teams cultivate. I've had plenty of coaching sessions with clients devoted to the tricky challenge of managing people who were formerly peers.

The questions I often get at events where I'm speaking can focus on 'bitch bosses who pull the ladder up'. However, I don't see this as a sign of the 'unlike-ability of senior women'. Instead, it's more an indication of our *higher expectations* of women to be nurturing and collaborative leaders.

These stereotypes are a burden for working women. Women often downplay their authority to keep things on an even keel, but this can backfire if others belittle their seniority and expertise. It can make them more vulnerable to challenge. As linguist Deborah Tannen explains:

---

120. OECD, 2012 Closing the Gender Gap: Act Now, OECD Publishing, Paris.
121. Alison Rose, Review of Female Entrepreneurship, 2018.

Like many conversational rituals common among women, talking 'as if we are all equals' but still expecting to receive support appropriate to the higher-status position depends on the participation of the other person to respect that position.[122]

If women struggle to balance being 'nice' in positions of leadership, this may be a reaction to a legitimate concern of appearing threatening. Another tactic women use to ensure their high status doesn't threaten others is to ensure they don't appear to 'have it all'. I see this with senior women I know who take pains to praise others, downplay their wins and point out their mistakes.

However, as Tannen explains: 'But while it may work well for them by making them more likeable, this conversational ritual of "What, this old thing?" can work against them by interfering with a demeanour that exudes authority.'[123] This 'authority' is the very thing leaders are often looking for when determining new promotions.

TAKING TURNS

No matter how good their points or even how well prepared they are, the communications of men and women are perceived differently. For example, women who use tag questions (e.g., 'don't you agree?') are judged less intelligent and knowledgeable than men who say the exact same things.[124]

Researchers also found that in looking at discussion groups of men and women, women regulated how *much* they spoke, taking up less time, to not appear dominating.[125] I can see this in my work, where women do a subconscious mental calculation in meetings. The assumption is that 'if there are five people in this meeting, I shouldn't speak more than 20% of the time'. They are then often surprised or annoyed when someone else 'takes up' half the time, particularly if it adds nothing of substance – or is another woman who they expect *should know the rules*.

Sasha Mooney, a Barrister at Law, notices women display their competence differently even in the first few minutes of a meeting. She observes:

122. Tannen, D. 1995 *Talking from 9 to 5*, William Morrow & Co., London, p. 178.
123. Tannen, D. 1995 *Talking from 9 to 5*, William Morrow & Co., London, p. 190.
124. Aries, E. 1987 Gender & Communication, in P. Shaver and C. Hendrick (eds) *Sex and Gender*, Sage, Newbury Park, CA, p. 166.
125. Aries, E. 1976 Interaction Patterns and Themes of Male, Female and Mixed Groups, *Small Group Behaviour* 7(1): 7–18.

Women will have heads down taking notes. I've done this too, so know they want to ask well-considered questions with the facts recorded to make their case. Men are more likely to pipe up as and when thoughts occur to them, interrupting when they see fit. You can almost see them thinking things through as they're talking.

I also see this in my experience observing women and men in meetings. By contrast, in those settings women do most of their thinking *before* speaking. Mooney's advice? 'Put your pencil down and start making points or asking questions in the first 10 minutes of a meeting. Waiting until you have it all figured out is too late!'

This challenge resonates for many of the women I coach. In my experience, non-status quo members too often assume crucial decisions will be made at the *end* of the meeting. Not surprisingly, they leave confused or frustrated if it seems the decision *was already taken*, even before the meeting started.

In fact, when observing these meetings, those who are 'in the know' can resent these 'difficult' people for asking detailed questions on the day. To the status quo, the results were already decided either ahead of time or in the first few minutes, because they read the room and could predict the outcome.

Presenting in a meeting:

- **Speak up early to reduce the self-imposed pressure to contribute the 'perfect comment' before a meeting ends.**
- **Building on, or even agreeing with someone else's idea is a legitimate contribution on its own.**
- **Avoid tag questions like 'I'm not alone in this right?' or 'You know what I mean?' as both make you seem unsure, even when you know your point.**

VERBAL DOMINATION

I have scarcely worked with a client who hasn't wanted to make a better impression in meetings. When I ask the rationale, answers revolve around getting respect for their ideas, handling 'idea stealers' or being interrupted. The modern meeting is a setting where too frequently, dominance is rewarded. Asserting dominance via interruptions is deemed 'confidence' and starts even before people enter the workplace.

To this point, male university students are more likely to interrupt female professors.[126] As many women can attest, the same is often true in the workplace. In university faculty meetings, other research shows men's 'turns' in meetings took 11–17 seconds on average compared to women's 3–10 seconds.[127] These statistics show the longest vocal contribution by a woman, on average, is often still shorter than those made by men.

As anyone who has sat in a meeting knows, the status quo seems much more comfortable talking as they are thinking – 'throwing an idea out there' and 'hashing it over'. The observations of my interviewees suggest, women and non-status quo members have to think carefully *before* they speak.

As we saw earlier, interviews are a common place we look for evidence of ostensibly both confidence and competence. However, differences in interview style and the way it affects confidence in different groups is vital to recognise.

In over 50 mock interviews where applicants were always women, but interviewees were mixed, the non-verbal dominance (visual dominance and speaking interruptions) of the male interviewers led to lower self-evaluations by the female interviewees and less positive evaluations made by the interviewer *who themselves did all the interrupting*. Clearly, being spoken over, however, didn't do any favours for the women.

By comparison, how female interviewers conducted themselves didn't predict outcomes for the female interviewees.[128]Even when they are hired, the gender difference in where and how people talk continues. Beyond run of the mill meetings, men talk more often and for longer stretches at seminars, in TV discussions and full-class exchanges in the classroom.[129]

126. Brooks, V. 1982 Sex Differences in Student Dominance Behavior in Female and Male Professors' Classrooms, *Sex Roles* 8: 683–690.
127. Eakins, B. W. and Eakins, R. G. 1976 Verbal Turn-Taking and Exchanges in Faculty Dialogue, in *The Sociology of the Languages of American Women*, Dubois, B. L. and Crouch, I. (eds). Trinity University Press, Linguistics, San Antonio, pp. 53–62.
128. Latu, I. M. and Schmid Mast, M. 2016 Male Interviewers' Nonverbal Dominance Predicts Lower Evaluations of Female Applicants in Simulated Job Interviews, *Journal of Personnel Psychology* 15(3): 116–124.
129. Holmes, J. 1992 Talk in Public Contexts, *Discourse & Society* 2(3): 131–150.

These contexts are ones in which talk is highly valued. Contributions generally have status-enhancing potential and inform how confidence is defined. Moreover, the primary function of these discussions tends to be in *explaining* ideas to other listeners. This means men take an explanatory role and women the 'learner' roles.

By contrast, this same research shows women tend to speak more in less formal settings, often starting *exploratory* conversations instead. Their speech is more likely to be tailored to encourage robust exploration and they are less likely to assume they're explaining things to an uninformed audience. In short, women are more likely to ask for opinions and then skilfully manage the answer, something many of my consultancy clients notice in meetings.

This 'questioning' approach is a huge skill for one simple reason. You'll never know *exactly* how someone will respond in a discussion. Managing another person's answer, with the myriad of potential other perspectives in the room, is tricky to get right. Yet it's *hugely valuable* in getting people on side. By contrast, it is far easier to state your perspective as the 'truth', something people we credit 'confident' people as doing effortlessly.

To equalise turn-taking in meetings, be directive. Research shows *only* when groups are *given explicit directions* to take turns equitably in their feedback do women speak equally to men. By comparison, in groups where students were asked to discuss a topic and told they *could structure the feedback themselves,* women made 17% fewer comments and took 25% fewer turns.[130]

Turn-taking makes sense, not just for women, but for introverts or those who may not immediately share their thoughts in the free-for-all of many meetings. As the researchers noted: 'Whereas the young men in these groups... were more likely to persist until they'd made their point...young women usually backed off and gave up their attempts to speak if they were interrupted.' This reminds me of how many women I know who lament the 'game-playing' and showmanship at meetings – things they don't want to waste time on.

To this point, we all know extroversion technically isn't a leadership skill. However, talking for longer than your perceived 'share' of the time can still be misinterpreted as 'a sign of conviction', 'owning the floor' and a sign of leadership. It's simply not enough to say 'We all have equal opportunities to speak up' as it ignores the realities of how, where, and when different groups have learned to speak up often based on how they are received when they do.

130. Sommers, E. and Lawrence, S. 1992 Women's Ways of Talking in Teacher-directed and Student-directed Peer Response Groups, *Linguistics & Education* (4)1: 1–35.

PERFECTION OR NOTHING – 'FEAR OF B'

I discussed these gender differences in confidence with Dr Elaine Eisenman, the former Dean of Executive and Enterprise Education at Babson College in Boston. In her work promoting entrepreneurship, she notes a difference between the confidence men and women display when considering setting up a business. Eisenman observes:

> *Starting any business is a risk, but men don't doubt they'll be successful. The women spend more time in the 'What happens if I fail?' mindset, looking at the complexity of the situation, imagining all the worst-case scenarios. Women are likely to weigh up what they risk losing if they fail against how long it took them to get the success they have now.*

So for men, it's dichotomous. It's either 'I can achieve that challenge or I can't', with a strong tendency towards 'Of course I can!' For women, it's more often a complex inner debate based on the implications of failure against *what she has now.*

For many groups who are mindful of the precarious balance of what they have now, this mindset is incorrectly interpreted as a lack of confidence. Eisenman finishes: 'Women are more likely to think: "if you can't do it perfectly, don't do it at all". This mindset has real implications for adaptive realism as we've discussed.'

Elaine Eisenman recalled a conversation she'd had with a frustrated father, who identified these issues in his daughter. His daughter had earned scholarships for a bio-engineering degree but shocked her parents just a few months after starting her degree by saying she was dropping the course to opt for education. Eisenman describes:

> *While she was doing 'okay', other students were surpassing her. She recognised she understood enough to teach the concepts to others. However, she didn't think she could excel in being a bio-engineering specialist herself. Her father was horrified at how 'typically female' his brilliant daughter was being since panicking at how she wouldn't meet her own expectations.*

This perspective is something I've also heard from many parents. While sure their children will succeed, they are often more optimistic about the competence their *daughters* show. This is in comparison to the statistical likelihood of future career success, whatever the topic, of their sons.

Women's ultra-high standards *for themselves* is the heavily gendered 'Fear of B' phenomenon. Claudia Goldin, a Harvard professor, noticed that while over half of new university entrants taking her Economics classes were women, less than 30% eventually received degrees in that field. To understand why, she assessed the grades students earned as they began their university years.

Goldin discovered that as a woman's earliest grades fell in the first year *below perfection*, their chances of switching to a degree they perceived as less difficult increased dramatically.[131] In fact, for every B a woman received in an 'Introduction to Economics' course, the chances of her staying with the degree *halved*. Men, on the other hand, who received Bs were as likely to stay the course and earn Economics degrees as their counterparts who received As.

Men genuinely seemed *less concerned* by their lower grades. Catherine Rampell wrote how this ultimately affects earnings. She wrote: 'Male students could be more overconfident ... effectively, college bros shrug off gentleman's C's ... as unrepresentative of their true brilliance.'[132] The tendency for women to leave courses early they fear they can't *perfect* is a concerning trend, particularly as we need far more workers in STEM fields, subjects about which women often have the same reservations.

Women's departure from these degree courses can't merely be explained away as 'changing intellectual interests' – common amongst all undergraduates. If it were, we wouldn't only see women leaving the sciences, and in Goldin's case, Economics. We'd see other women also *entering* those degree subjects, which they don't. Even if they were interested in switching into Economics or other courses such as STEM fields (of which there is no evidence), the need for academic prerequisites rules them out. These decisions mean leaving these fields is all the more precarious for their future opportunities.

ADVANCED QUALIFICATIONS

Lack of competence, as demonstrated by qualifications, isn't what's holding women back. Women are outpacing men hugely when it comes to qualifications. The OECD report 'Closing the Gender Gap' looks at education data on a global scale, highlighting a dramatic disparity in university education. It explains: 'There will be an average of 1.4 female students for every male student by 2025, and almost twice as many women in tertiary education in Austria, Canada, Iceland, Norway and the United Kingdom.'[133]

131. Goldin, C. 2013 Notes on Women and the Undergraduate Economics Major, *Committee on the Status of Women in the Economics Profession Newsletter*, (Summer): 4–6, 15.
132. Rampell, C. 2014 Women Should Embrace the B's in College to Make More Later, *Washington Post*, 10 March.
133. OECD 2012 Closing the Gender Gap: Act Now, p. 100. OECD Publishing, Paris, 17 December.

At university level, 57% of first-time graduates across the OECD are women.[134] Before we delve further, it is essential to understand men's enrollment *isn't actually down* over historical trends. It's just that the rise in female participation has so dramatically improved. With current participation patterns, about 46% of women and 31% of men of any age in OECD countries will complete higher education at some point in their lives – a marked difference. Men are simply more likely to drop-out than women, particularly at higher levels of education.[135]

These gains for women, or lack of qualifications for men, don't always translate into the roles we'd expect. McKinsey's research on 13 million employees at 329 corporates in the US shows women were under-represented at every level, even including entry-level positions (48%).[136] Considering the way women outpace men in attaining degrees, this is nonsensical – given hiring graduates is a priority for most of these organisations.

Notably, women seem the most eager to further their education – even *after* they've entered the workplace. Women of every age are, in the previous three months, more likely than men to have taken part in some form of training.[137] This training again further builds competence, that key component of which most employers need and *say* they value.

However, while this gender difference in demanding further training was seen at every level of prior education, it was most notable in graduates. The difference between male and female participation in 'ongoing learning' in the UK after starting work was a full 10%.

However, the answer isn't in training non-status quo people to be *more competent* than the status quo. That merely creates another hoop for under-represented groups to jump through. We have just a few options. We could stop requiring or waiting for women to have additional and 'optional' training not expected of the men. However, a far better option is for leaders to hire and promote non-status quo people at the same pace enjoyed by the status quo.

When I first started speaking to audiences and coaching, I'd be asked by women if they should get an advanced degree. My response was always 'Only if the status quo people above you already have them. If so, then yes, go for it!' However, this was often met with dismay, as the status quo usually didn't have more or better degrees at all. In fact, that would lead to stories of how comparatively less experienced the status quo often were. They merely surpassed the non-status quo in confidence.

134. OECD, 2014 Education at a Glance, OECD Publishing, Paris Table 2.4.
135. Patrignani, P. and Conlon, G. 2011 The Long-term Effects of Vocational Qualifications on Labour Market Outcomes, Department for Business Innovation and Skills, DBIS Research Paper 47.
136. Huang, J. et al. McKinsey and Co. and LeanIn.Org, 2019 Women in the Workplace study.
137. Office for National Statistics 2016 EMP15: Job-related Training Received by Employees, June–August.

There's an understandable presumption that additional qualifications will magically open previously closed doors. Certainly, this belief is likely a big part of the reason *more* non-status quo students attend university. For example, BAME British youths *are more likely to start university* compared to their White British peers.[138]

By comparison, those from non-status quo backgrounds, but with shiny new certifications often progress no faster than they did before. This stagnation is a waste. It causes frustration and doesn't get them ahead as quickly as they deserve given their superior training and competence.

THE LANGUAGE OF INFLUENTIAL ADVOCATES

It's influence that matters, but it may not always be *your* influence or even something you can drive. Unfortunately, if in a non-status quo position, the best way to gain the trust of the status quo members goes way beyond being well-trained. It's vital to have a senior status quo person *talk about how competent you are – and that's why you were picked for your role.*

This is highlighted by a fascinating, if not disconcerting study, on the efficacy of male advocacy. Researchers asked women to lead a 'Lost on the Moon' decision-making exercise played by teams. A female leader was allocated to primarily all-male teams, to mimic the experiences of women working in male dominated fields.

In each team, her placement as the leader was explained to the teams with three different rationales by the researcher. One-third of participants were told she'd been 'randomly assigned' as leader. For the next third, they gave the female group leader extra training vital to the success of the mission. The last third also had a female leader who had been given additional training. However, amongst this group, her skills *were also vouched for by another man.*

This man told the male group members their female leader 'had special training which may be useful for your group as you make your decisions'.[139] It's hardly the most glowing of recommendations, but it was vital. Interestingly, this external 'advocate' wasn't previously known to anyone in the groups so no one could verify *his* credibility, but that didn't seem to matter. These women who were trained and *validated by a man* enjoyed the most benefits. *These* female leaders were listened to the most frequently by their male colleagues.

---

138. Bulman, M. 2018 Number of White People Accepted at University Drops Despite Overall Rise in UK students, The Independent, 11 January.
139. Yoder, J., Schleicher, T., and McDonald, T. 2006 Empowering Token Women Leaders: The Importance of Organisationally Legitimised Credibility *Psychology of Women Quarterly* 22:. 209–222.

By comparison, leaders who were only trained (but not made credible by a male advocate) had to interrupt more frequently to be heard. They routinely had to re-assert their leadership position, even though everyone *knew* they'd received the most training because she could tell them. They were regarded as contributing less to the group and reconciling differences amongst team members less effectively. The impact on this group was the least favourable. Comparatively, *even the randomly assigned leaders were rated more favourably*, even if they too weren't particularly well listened to.

Overall, the male participants didn't seem to care about her training. Her unique skills only became important if another man 'legitimised' her and pointed out the relevance of her skills. Plus, her knowledge had to be cited by that man *as the main reason she was in the role*. This is reminiscent of the observation many non-status quo people have. They'll mention an idea in a meeting, only to see it ignored until a status quo person 'legitimises' it by picking it up later- and hopefully giving her credit.

While this piece of research focused on gender, its implications are far broader. This need to be 'legitimised' creates understandable frustration for any non-status quo person, but also for the organisational goals if that person is in charge of a project. If an un-legitimised person is both well-trained in tasks we usually associate with the status quo, but hindered in their attempts to use that knowledge – it's a complete waste.

It scuppers both the overall work of the team and is demoralising to the highly competent employee. This trend has enormous implications for the assumptions we make about education *being the key* to equality for non-status quo members. It suggests the special sauce for progression is not necessarily in being better prepared or well-educated. Instead it's in having status quo advocates *publicly* vouch for them.

The fact that more qualifications don't equate to faster progress hasn't stopped a thirst for knowledge. This is highlighted in how women spend their 'free time'. Women are the biggest market not just for books, but for self-help books in particular. However, men *write* far more self-help books than women.[140]

According to GoodReads research, in 2017 men wrote two-thirds of all the top 100 self-help books in the US, female authors penned just a third.[141] This means the majority of women seeking advice, end up getting it from male authors. By comparison male readers seek out *very little* guidance from female authors.

---

140. The U.S. Market for Self-improvement Products & Services – January 2015, Marketdata Enterprises, Tampa, FL.
141. Zhou, Y. 2017 Goodreads Data Show Women Are Reading Self-help Books Are Getting Advice from Men.' Quartz. November 4 www.qz.com

This trend echoes their work-life, certainly in the case of many of my clients; women in male-dominated fields. From university-level onwards, these women are often primarily trained by men, who were themselves mainly trained by the status quo. This trend makes the findings around outcomes of education for non-status quo people all the more vital to understand.

The data we saw earlier around women's higher participation rates in ongoing learning as adults is also interesting. It rather unpicks the argument that women, particularly mothers, are 'too busy' or not committed enough to undertake the type of training employers value. These rates again show confidence, or certainly, ambition is not the problem.

In reality, the overconfident just don't think they need additional training. By contrast, those focused on competence know they can always get better and further training is one of the quickest ways to improve. This belief is particularly true if you, as a non-status quo member, are overlooked for the stretches that make you 'promotion-ready'.

To that point, an American study found Black students *with Black teachers* are more likely to graduate high school. They reported feeling more cared for, interested in schoolwork and more confident in their teachers' abilities to communicate with them. They simply *weren't overlooked* which meant they put forth more effort in school, leading to higher aspirations. These trends were the most noticeable for Black girls.[142]

Ultimately non-status quo groups aren't progressing in their careers at the same rate *as their consumption of additional knowledge*. This disparity shows why context is vital when talking about what confidence looks like versus *what really* gets rewarded. In fact, I predict as status quo members continue to under-achieve in advanced credentials, we'll see a shift in the value people place on these certifications. We'll likely see an increase in the value employers place on hands-on experience, apprenticeships and even the 'school of hard knocks' in place of formal qualifications.

In fact, we now live in an era when doubting expert advice is on the rise. Increasingly, I believe we see this with climate change deniers, parents who fear vaccinations and even now 'flat-earthers' to name just a few. Credible evidence-based knowledge is taking a backseat to how you feel about a topic or what your 'gut tells you'. We have entered an era where competence is less valued than ever.

142. Egalite, A. J. and Bisida, B. 2018 The Effects of Teacher Match on Students' Academic Perceptions and Attitudes, *Education Evaluation and Policy Analysis*, 40 (1): 59 – 81.

SUPPORTIVE, NOT CENTRE STAGE

As we've seen, the problem isn't in *the confidence women lack*; it's the way a wider version of confidence isn't rewarded. For example, confidence in women is only praised when paired with 'prosocial behaviours'. These are the kind of supportive and even modest behaviours we expect in women. However, while we expect volunteering and administrative tasks like note-taking and mentoring more from women, we don't expect these same behaviours from 'confident' men.[143]

For example, while research shows modesty works for all professionals, it works better for some than for others. In one experiment, female characters displayed 'high modesty' saying about a promotion: 'Thanks, but I think it was mostly luck that I got it'. These women were the most positively rated.

By comparison, men only had to demonstrate 'moderate modesty' by saying 'Thanks, I heard about the promotion unofficially this morning' to be well regarded by their managers and colleagues. Dismally, high confidence, as displayed by saying 'Thanks, I just knew I would win' and *even* moderate confidence was far less appealing in women,[144] though *both were more acceptable* in men.

The authors of the study recognised the societal challenge of their findings, saying:

> *In addition to the ethical problems associated with encouraging women to engage in gender-role behaviour that is likely to perpetuate gender stereotypes, it is also unclear that this strategy would be an effective one for women at more advanced occupational levels.*

As you lead meetings:

- **Institute 'turn-taking', ensuring everyone has been heard – not just those who spoke up first.**
- **If someone is routinely slow to speak up, ask what you can do to support them better.**
- **Publicly introduce, legitimise and talk up *why* non-status quo people have the roles they do.**

---

143. Guillen, L, Mayo, M. and Karelaia, N. 2017 Appearing Self-Confident and Getting Credit for It: Why it May Be Easier for Men than Women to Gain Influence at Work, *Human Resource Management* 57(4): 839–854.
144 Wosinska, W., Dabul, A.J., Whetstone-Dion, R. and Cialdini, R.B. 1996 Self-presentational Responses to Success in the Organization: The Costs and Benefits of Modesty, *Basic and Applied Social Psychology* 18(2): 229-242

This expectation of collaboration and conviviality is something most people recognised. Sasha Mooney, a Barrister at Law who is of British-Ghanaian descent, identified with others' experiences of the double standard for women, and women of colour in particular at work. She explains: 'Men are "driven", but if women want to progress, they have "pointy elbows". Mooney is also a NED for several organisations.' She notes: 'When I've asked about budget deficits or refuse to sign something before I understand all the implications, I'm labelled "difficult" or not a "team player".'

Expectations, as well as barriers, are highest for women in male-dominated fields. There is a prevailing respect for male agency often characterised as a 'can-do attitude' with a preference for action over reflection. Women who display similar characteristics are much more likely to be judged as hostile, abrasive, manipulative, untrustworthy and selfish in these settings.[145]

Overall, they're viewed as less compelling colleagues. As we'll see with other non-status quo groups, women working in male-dominated fields are more likely to be criticised by onlookers. Even when they make a single mistake, they are judged less competent.[146]

This type of reaction was also seen in male-dominated fields beyond STEM, such as the armed forces. Peer assessments for over 4000 US Naval Academy students found men were consistently praised for their agency; that is 'exerting power or being in action'. Indeed 'taking charge' is what we might say is the mark of a confident leader.[147] Words used for the men were much more likely to include 'action-oriented', 'instrumental' and 'task-focused'. Women were judged as 'communal'. While peers theoretically agreed these qualities were equally useful, agency was only rewarded in men.

But what if a woman showed more agency? Perhaps not surprisingly, in this research women were described much more negatively than their male colleagues. These military peers, *all leaders in training who would eventually judge others*, respected agency far less in women. In particular, in peer reviews women were deemed inept, frivolous, gossipy, excitable, scattered, temperamental, panicky, and indecisive – a litany of negative female stereotypes. The message inherent in these descriptors is clear: the women evaluated were incompetent and not qualified to be leaders; they're only worthy of being the support act.

145. Heilman, M. E. et al. 2004 Penalties for Success: Reactions to women Who Succeed at Male Gendertyped Tasks, *Journal of Applied Psychology* 89(3): 416–427.
146. Brescoll, V., Dawson, E. and Uhlmann, E. 2010 Hard Won and Easily Lost: The Fragile Status of Leaders in Gender-Stereotype-Incongruent Occupations, *Psychological Science* 21(11): 1640–1642.
147. Smith, D. et al. 2018 The Power of Language: Gender, Status and Agency in Performance Evaluations, *Behavioural Scientist* 80: 159–171.

TRIPLE HURDLES FOR WOMEN IN MALE-DOMINATED FIELDS

Even worse, when women publicly evaluate themselves in front of other people or in stereotypically male domains, they grossly underestimate their skills.[148] Countless studies show that when a woman fails, she chalks it up to a lack of *her ability* while men blame external factors. In studies where a man and a woman each receive the same negative feedback, the woman's self-confidence and self-esteem drop further than his confidence drops. Internalising failure and the insecurity it breeds undermines future performance with longer-term consequences for how she displays confidence.[149]

To progress as a woman in a male-dominated field, while also working within stereotypes, you have to go beyond being confident and competent. You must *also demonstrate how supportive you are to other people*. Women, particularly in fields where there are few of them, also have to demonstrate what people expect from women – prosocial behaviours. For women in male-dominated fields, they have to display a holy trinity of attributes their male colleagues don't: competence, confidence *and* social value.[150]

As the researchers explained: 'The more confident male engineers in our sample appeared to be, the more influence they had ... Women were able to translate their self-confident image into influence only when they also displayed ... the motivation to benefit others.'

This finding reminds me of an assessment I took a few years ago when awarded a Saltire Fellowship. The Fellowship, aimed at business leaders in Scotland, took me to both Boston and China for four months. As part of the application process, we completed an online psychological assessment. Ostensibly this was to see how well we'd get on with the rest of our cohort.

I remember taking my test and berating myself before I got the results back. I was sure I'd come across as selfish and very career-driven, perhaps not even that pleasant to be around. At my debrief with the assessor a few weeks later, he said my scores suggested I'd be 'great glue' for the mostly male group. However, he warned my scores indicated I was potentially *too empathetic* to the plight of others.

---

148. Heatherington, L. et al. 1993 Two Investigations of Female Modesty in Achievement Situations, *Sex Roles* 11–12(29): 739–754.
149. Heatherington, L., Burns, A. and Gustafson, T. 1998 When Another Stumbles: Gender and Self-Preservation to Vulnerable Others, *Sex Roles* 38(11–12): 889–913.
150. Diekman, A. B. et al. 2010 Seeking Congruity between Goals and Roles: A New Look at Why Women Opt Out of Science, Technology, Engineering, and Mathematics Careers. *Psychological Science* 21: 1051–1057.

When I asked for the evidence, he indicated I'd scored in the 96th percentile on the criteria of 'caring'. When I asked him who they had compared me against, he said 'other UK executives'. I'd initially worried that I came across as someone who couldn't care less. However, it turns out, in his eyes, I could care a lot less! To him a lower score would have been more in keeping with what he expected from 95 other UK executives who had scored below me on the 'caring' scale! Being prosocial was still something I clearly felt I needed to be, even perhaps more than many of the new male colleagues I'd eventually meet.

Mother of all confidence blockers - maternity

When I started coaching, many of my earliest clients were new mothers returning from maternity leave. Struggling with confidence came up routinely as a critical issue. Between the individual client and myself, we worked to overcome those feelings. However, very few organisations ever spent quite as long looking at *why* the confidence of mothers had diminished. However, to me, a lack of confidence seems wholly natural and not a weakness at all *when taken in context*.

In the UK, new mothers may have been away from work for up to 13 months or sometimes even longer in parts of Europe. Upon their return they were often met with new team members, clients, and potentially a new boss. They may have forgotten much of the day to day detail upon their return from lack of exposure. Indeed, they are often familiarising themselves with new technology updates, industry changes or relevant new legislation.

Diminished confidence would happen to anyone out of the office for a protracted time. Plus, they often have to contend with how the team managed – or didn't in their absence. Keeping in touch days are undoubtedly helpful, but they do beg the question: How confident can we expect *anyone* to be when returning to workplaces that treat parenting as an inconvenience?

To this point, people were asked to rate job applicants after reading résumés, personal fact sheets, and notes from screening interviews of fictional candidates. After establishing the candidates as *equally qualified*, the researchers told them, in passing, one applicant was a parent. When being considered for the same job, mothers were significantly less likely to be recommended for hire.

Even when they were the favoured candidate, they were offered $11,000 less in starting salary, on average, than childless women. By contrast, fathers were offered significantly *more,* not just compared to the women but also compared to childless men.[151] Raters, whether they are university students or actual employers, assume mothers less competent and less committed.[152] By contrast, we judge breadwinning fathers as *warmer* than their childless counterparts.[153]

As dismal as that is, some of these effects could be overcome, but it's a bitter pill. Some raters were given copies of a performance review showing that this fictional mother demonstrated a *heroic* level of commitment to a previous job. When this happened, mothers weren't judged so harshly. They benefited only by being seen as *equally* competent and committed to other applicants.

However, it took superlative comments such as 'she is one of the most productive employees our division has hired in recent memory' to get around this bias – a very high bar for anyone. Notably, female raters (though, interestingly, not the male ones) still judged the mothers to be less likeable. They were more likely to be judged as 'interpersonally hostile' than fathers and childless women!

In the end, this creates the same result: mothers receive fewer offers and for less money.[154] This result plays out in the workforce as mothers earn less than childless women, but also compared to men regardless of whether they are fathers or not.[155] This research is hard to bear for several reasons. The inherent prejudice against mothers, paired with a preference for fathers, is staggering and a double standard in action.

Furthermore, just to be rated at the *same level* of competence as the men, the mothers still had to jump through exceptionally high hoops. They had to demonstrate their extraordinary skills *beyond what we'd expect to see.* These findings remind me of the expectation of 'exceptionality' we see with other groups of non-status quo members. A mother is fine to hire (though deserving of lower wages) if she can demonstrate 'she's not like *other* mothers'.

As people talk about working mothers, I've heard people say: 'Well, it's her choice to stay at home or not travel for work.' This rationale is positioned as an issue of 'choice' freely made by women. However, we rarely look at what women's choices *actually* are.

151. Correll, S. 2007 Getting a Job: Is There a Motherhood Penalty? *American Journal of Sociology* 112: 1297–1338.
152. Shelley J. Correll 2013 Minimizing the Motherhood Penalty: What Works, What Doesn't and Why? *Gender & Work: Challenging Conventional Wisdom,* Harvard Business School, Boston, MA.
153. Cuddy, A. et al. 2004 When Professionals Become Mothers, Warmth Doesn't Cut the Ice, *Journal of Social Issues* 60: 701–718.
154. Benard, S. and Correll, S 2010. Normative Discrimination and the Motherhood Penalty, *Gender & Society* 24: 616–646.
155. Anderson, D. et al. 2003. The Motherhood Wage Penalty Revisited: Experience, Heterogeneity, Work Effort and Work-schedule Flexibility, *Industrial and Labor Relations Review* 56: 273–294.

If you compare having a job against the 'choice' to have no one caring for your children, food at mealtimes and a welcoming home in which to live, it's hardly a choice at all. The people who see it as an option would rarely expect to leave work simply to make the same 'choices'. This labour is done by someone else who *must* do it, both invisibly and for 'free' – most often women.

BACKLASH AGAINST CONFIDENT WOMEN

A few years ago, I was training a group of 40 early-stage STEM professionals on why their organisation wanted to become more inclusive – particularly around gender balance. Afterwards, a young man asked: 'Did I have any men on my team?' We'd played one of the e-simulations I'd designed on workplace bias so explained: 'Yes. They do more of the technical development, whereas I designed the products, write the scripts and do most of our client-facing work.'

However, I quickly realised *that* wasn't the question he was asking. He responded: 'I agreed with most of your points but would have heard it all better coming from a man.' This was a slap in the face. All I'd talked about had gone right past him.

It also reminded me of a common fallacy. This is the dismissal of these issues with: 'Surely, diversity is something millennials value? We'll see improvements as they move up through the ranks.' The man who asked if any male experts might explain my main points better was no older than 23 or 24. He was part of the new graduate intake for this particular organisation. Confident, but not necessarily competent in *my area of expertise*. However, that wasn't to stop him from pointing out where I'd gone wrong and how a man might better make my points.

I seek feedback where I can, but his queries were not primarily about the accuracy of my message. It was more about *who is entitled* to deliver it. I asked him as evenly as I could why he thought I needed male colleagues to bolster my message. He stepped back, rolled his eyes and said: 'Take it easy, will you?' before giving me a cheeky wink and walking out the door.

We cannot assume that challenging female experts is a problem that will fade away as millennials – a reputedly enlightened generation – age into their roles. Research shows that younger men challenge speakers just as frequently as older men challenge speakers – roughly at a rate of double the number of questions women ask of experts.[156]

---

156. Hinsley, A., Sutherland, W. and Johnston, A. 2017 Men Ask More Questions Than Women At Scientific Conferences, *PLoSOne Journal* 12(10).

Similarly, just as my young attendee was questioning my authority in a seemingly friendly way, others can turn these challenges into virtual compliments. Barbara-Ann King, who has worked for over 25 years in the finance industry, has also seen how nuanced and tone-dependent a 'compliment' can be.

She recalls:

> *Just the other day, I had a colleague who told me: 'You're very forthright!' when we were arguing a point. To his surprise, I pointed out forthright is usually a positive term. However, his tone suggested it wasn't and I was voicing my opinion too strongly. I tried to have a conversation with him about it, but he wasn't going to change his opinion. Ultimately it was my level of conviction that was threatening to him.*

However, the questioning of women, and even girls with knowledge starts much earlier than their working years. These reactions were familiar to Eisenman, who recalls loving school until her teacher called a parent-teacher meeting. Her teacher advised her parents: 'Elaine is disruptive in the classroom because she answers the questions *before the boys get a chance.*' She recounts:

> *She needed my parents to tell me to shut up because I was 'too smart' for who I was – a girl in the 1960s US school system. My parents, who were intimidated by the authority of a teacher, passed on the message loud and clear. So at age 8, I shut up like I'd been told. I was then taken out of the Talented and Gifted classes, and my grades dropped. It took me until university to get my voice back.*

The silver lining for Eisenman? She became a great observer of people. Her listening skills added to her competence, contributing to her success. When she found her voice, she did so wholeheartedly.

Eisenman continues: 'My hunch is that happens a thousand times a day across the world.' Elaine laughs when in our discussion I ask if it would have occurred to her parents to tell the teacher: 'Well, how about you get smarter boys for Elaine to compete against?' This teacher taught for nearly 60 years, affecting no doubt thousands of children's sense of possibility.

Eisenman's parents could have advised their daughter to 'play the system' and wait for others to answer at times. However, instead of taking pride in their child's wins, it's dismaying they may have had to explain to an 8-year-old that there is indeed 'a system to play'. Interestingly, Elaine shared her story with other classmates during a reunion when the teacher retired in her 80s. Other girls, now grown women, confided to her: 'I thought she *only did that to me.*'

172

Similarly, questioning people from under-represented backgrounds as to *how exactly* they got a senior job resonates for Pryde, who earned the role of Head of Commercial Litigation for the global firm DWF. Upon being hired for that top role, she received multiple 'innocent' queries from people asking: 'Did you just get that job because you're a woman?'

Interestingly, while Pryde was the only woman in the pool of applicants for the role, she was unique against her competitors. She didn't initially apply for the job; the firm came looking for her. Pryde's Senior Partner admitted they'd been unsuccessfully recruiting for the position for some months. He said they weren't impressed with the applications from men. When the partners dug deeper into their legal networks, Pryde's name was routinely mentioned both in London and in Scotland – a rarity, but ideal for the Edinburgh offices of this global firm.

This is where the issue of confidence comes to the fore. Pryde says:

> *Oddly enough, if I'd seen the role openly advertised, I wouldn't have applied. I would have thought it was a couple of jumps too high for me. Now that I'm doing it, I see it's completely do-able. That's something I also hear from others who take on that initially terrifying big job.*

Pryde's advice to others who *fear being picked for a role primarily because* of their minority status? She points out:

> *Companies need to make money; no one's going to promote someone they don't think can do it. Don't focus on why you've been offered the role. Just take the opportunity and run with it. People may diminish the reasons why you were selected but use their doubt as motivation. I learned to say: 'I'll take it' and prove why I was the right choice, so they'll send work my way all the time, which they do!*

Pryde's comments remind me of the initial concerns I hear from skilled non-status quo people regarding *why* they've earned a promotion. I remind them: 'How frequently do you ever hear a status quo member wonder the same thing?' They *assume* they've earned it. You rarely hear them lament: 'But what if they just picked me because I play golf well or my referee was a guy I used to drink with at university?' Just as Pryde is advocating; the status quo believes in their ability to deliver, no matter what other factors may have affected the decision to search, hire or promote them.

However, it's crucial to understand *planting the seeds of doubt makes sense for the status quo*. It's one of the most successful power plays ever. If you can get people to question whether they deserve an accolade, there's less competition. Pryde continues: 'There are so many people who want to throw stones or even want me to fail. Remind yourself that hiring someone under qualified isn't something any organisation can afford to do.'

She sighs:

> *A friend of mine made Partner at another firm. When I was talking her up at an industry party, a seemingly jealous colleague remarked: 'Oh, but that's such a small firm. If you looked at their client book, you'd see it's not that impressive.' I was livid! I hate when people tear each other down. What's the point?*

Pryde continues:

> *To add insult to injury, the new Partner is gorgeous, so others tittered that 'she didn't look like a typical lawyer'. I mean, what does a typical lawyer even look like?*

Pryde's flippant point raises a good question. Look at data for how many more women than men earn university law degrees over the last several decades. According to the law of averages, the answer to her question? A typical lawyer looks like an ambitious woman.

Understandably, those stories could leave women angry. Anger, however, isn't an emotion we *like* in women. It's akin to being 'out of control' or based on her personal faults. Male anger, by comparison, is attributed to being based on external causes, such as perceived unfair treatment. Plus, researchers find observers are quicker to think a woman has lost her temper, giving men more leeway to express anger, before eventually judging him harshly.[157]

Schmundt-Thomas recognises this saying:

> *Women who don't conform fail. When they put up a fight,*
> *it's often a fight the company actually needs. However,*
> *she'll get written off for 'stepping on people's toes' or*
> *'being difficult'. Guys who take the same approach, by*
> *comparison are a 'force of nature' or 'admirably committed*
> *to the cause'. That's praised because he's being confident in*
> *standing his ground.*

Interestingly these differences have financial implications. Grenny and Maxfield,[158] found when people saw anger in a speaker, they were more likely to assume the speaker, whether male or female, was incompetent. This penalised the speakers both financially, though women lost out the most.

The perceived competency of 'forceful' or 'assertive' women dropped by 35%, and their perceived worth fell by $15,088. This was compared to a less dramatic competency drop of 22%, worth $6,547 for men. It is vital leaders can manage assertiveness often as a part of their confidence. However, this difference penalises women far more.

Recognising this issue, the researchers experimented with various 'hedges' that might reduce the adverse effect of this judgement. They found *just explaining* the intent of your comment decreased the negative impact by 27%. Before giving a disagreeable opinion, people were encouraged to describe their intention. Participants were merely asked to say: 'I see this as a matter of honesty and integrity, so it's important for me to be clear about where I stand'.[159] This tactic can benefit everyone.

Notably, Cadenhead and other Women's Enterprise Scotland leaders have also faced criticism for being 'too aggressive' from their stakeholders. The irony in giving this type of feedback to an organisation founded to provide women business owners with a voice in government policy is not lost on Cadenhead. She says: 'Some of our male sponsors and policy advisers encourage us and

157. Brescoll, V.L. 2011 Who Takes the Floor and Why: Gender, Power and Volubility in Organizations, *Administrative Science Quarterly* 56: 622–641.
158. Maxfield, D. Grenny, J. and McMillan C. 2015 Emotional Inequality: Solutions for Women in the Workplace, Vital Smarts. www.vitalsmarts.fr.
159. Caprino, K. 2015 Gender Bias is Real: Women's Perceived Competence Drops Significantly When Judged as Being Forceful', *Forbes*.

say we need to be more assertive in challenging when seeking funding. When we do, we're criticised for being feisty and uncooperative.' Cadenhead and the team continue their advocacy work, unperturbed by the criticism. However, in her work as a Board adviser to many growing businesses, those aren't criticisms Cadenhead has ever heard levelled against male leaders.

In our discussion, Cadenhead shared a tip of questioning colleagues on their points to make it more 'palatable' to the listener. To the point above about moderating anger, her approach is more agreeable than using a direct 'I think you're wrong!' Instead, she curiously queries: 'I'm not sure if I fully understand what underpins your recommendation. Help me understand what you're thinking?'

The benefit of this 'curious' approach is twofold. Optimistically, you may increase your understanding of a complex topic. However, it can also highlight if someone hasn't thought through their position from other points of view. It highlights the nuance of the topic to the broader audience. This 'sideways on' approach is a skill used by many people from under-represented backgrounds. By comparison, challenging the status quo *directly* is a risk.

Doing so highlights their minority position very quickly, which is precarious with few advocates from the status quo. It's a risk as it can create a backlash that wouldn't come if the challenge was from a majority group member. In these types of potentially hostile situations, a status quo member 'breaking ranks' to support a non-status quo member is even more uncommon.

This only happens if the status quo person sees an advantage in that alliance superseding their affinity to other members of the status quo. This is the perfect time to act. For example, I've helped some of my female clients create alliances with male peers or superiors, particularly if the status quo person challenging her is regarded as a poor performer or is losing power more widely. However, be cautious about using 'I don't understand …' too frequently, as it can backfire if interpreted as real ignorance.

When expressing disagreement or annoyance:

- **Explain your intent: 'This issue is really important to me, so it's important for me to be clear …'**
- **Ask: 'Can you help me understand where you're coming from?'**
- **Realise you will never be liked by all, but no status quo member ever let that get in the way.**

In the years after I'd started consulting, I was in a session with other business owners discussing PR. There had been increasing media coverage of the profitability of companies with gender-balanced leadership teams. As we brainstormed, one woman encouraged me to apply to a national broadcaster, looking for new experts on a range of workplace topics.

One of the men enthused: 'Yes, that's a great idea, but how will you get on "Woman's Hour"?' When I asked him why he recommended 'Woman's Hour' in particular when business performance issues went beyond a primarily female audience, he exasperatedly replied: 'I thought you wanted my feedback!'

We all know, feedback is not created equally. As my friend's comment highlights, it's based on the giver's expectations. An American study of 28 companies found the majority (88%) of performance reviews for women contained critical feedback, compared to only 59% of performance reviews for men. However, the issue wasn't the sheer volume of criticism women received, as significant as this was on its own – but the quality of the 'advice given'.

The researchers found feedback given to men was more constructive, with *specific ways they could improve*. By comparison, feedback given to women included a sharper edge about *how they came across to others*. It was much more likely to include warnings about her style, advising her to 'Watch your tone! Stop being so judgemental!' These phrases showed up only *twice* in the 83 critical reviews received by men. By comparison, they showed up in the vast majority (71) of the 94 critical reviews received by women.[160]

In her role as Chair of Women's Enterprise Scotland, Cadenhead routinely contributes to panel discussions on the role of women-led SMEs in the UK and European economy. Cadenhead and I discussed a panel she'd attended just the previous week that summarised her experiences perfectly. She says:

> *One of the male panellists rarely spoke, but got applause,*
> *questions or appreciative nods when he did. The women*
> *also spoke up, as we've implored them to for years, but they*
> *received less audience engagement. It's maddening because*
> *if a woman took this quieter approach, she'd likely be told*
> *to speak up and sent for confidence training. You can't win!*

As we've seen, if a woman becomes angry about something work-related, she has 'lost control'. Heaven help her if she cries. 'Out of control', 'hormonal' or 'hysterical' women are penalised for being unnatural, even if only expressing their annoyance at being treated unfairly or having strong views on a topic.

---

160. Snyder, K. 2014 The Abrasiveness Trap: High-achieving Men and Women Are Described Differently in Reviews, *Fortune*. August 26.

For women socialised to 'make nice' and be charming, anger is a shock to witnesses. When they point out injustices or ask for support, women are more likely to be criticised as 'nagging' or 'banging on'.

The belittling question: 'What are you on about?' is something women, in particular, are asked routinely, as if their point is seemingly beyond comprehension. In contrast, asking a White man 'What he's on about?' sounds odd and disrespectful. Non-status quo women are then told to 'relax' or 'not to take it so personally' when they then defend themselves. However, these 'tips' are easier to bear if contributions, ideas or requests haven't been ignored for weeks, months or even years on end.

When I was a teen in Australia, I was bullied by a girl I beat in a debate competition across our town. As part of her tactics, she publicly accused me of 'loving myself'. In Alice Springs, this criticism was an often-used phrase to diminish a girl. In retrospect, I think she thought I was *proud* as I told friends I was excited about the regional competition. It would be a trip to the capital of Darwin 1000 miles away – exciting for any 15-year-old. In her mind, I had to be cut down to size.

The irony is that loving oneself is part of the very expectation we have of confidence. Girls in particular, are taught to be modest early on. This socialisation sticks and goes far beyond adolescent bullies. Research on nearly one thousand mostly female Harvard law school students found women gave themselves lower scores than their male peers in almost every category of skills relevant to practising law, even when they were doing *as well if not better* than their male peers.[161]

Self-promoting women are rated more harshly than self-promoting men, but *much more* negatively than women who do no self-promotion at all.[162] While no one likes a show-off of either gender, this is particularly problematic for women. At its core, self-promotion as modelled by the status quo is vital for promotions or pay rises. As a result, in this research, women who talk about their accomplishments – perhaps too proudly for many – were less likely to be hired as they were deemed immodest.

This is completely counterintuitive to our easy encouragement of women to 'be more confident'. It is particularly dismaying that this study shows women were actually the harshest critics of other self-promoting women. While no one warmed to the self-promoting woman, she was consistently deemed less hireable, less socially attractive and less competent than a self-promoting man.

161. Study on 'Women's Experiences at Harvard Law School' 2004 Working Group on Student Experiences, Cambridge, MA.
162. Rudman L. A. 1998 Self-promotion as a Risk Factor for Women: The Costs and Benefits of Counter Stereotypical Impression Management, *Journal of Personality and Social Psychology* 74: 629–645.

HARASSMENT – REAL WORLD AND ONLINE

This disdain and lack of respect for confident women overlaps, not surprisingly, with harassment. To address 'confidence' and the perceived lack thereof, we also have to understand how easily harassment undermines confidence. A Business in the Community survey looked mainly at mid-career female employees asking 'what their company could do to improve their career development opportunities'. Women were twice as likely to say: 'address bullying, discrimination, harassment and unconscious bias' than 'boost women's confidence' (11% vs. 5%).[163] By addressing harassment issues, you would likely improve women's confidence *by default*.

This ground-breaking survey in the UK found that over half of women (52%) said they had been victims of harassment or bullying *in the previous three years alone*, unrelated to sexual harassment. Of those, rates of harassment were particularly prevalent for women with disabilities (71%), from Black-African, Black Caribbean or Black British backgrounds (79%) and those who were bisexual (61%) or lesbian (54%). A further 12% also experienced *sexual* harassment in the previous three years, again women from under-represented backgrounds being the worst affected.

Unfortunately, harassment in the US echoes these findings. A recent survey of over 1,000 Americans found victims of bullying were nearly twice as likely to be women than men (66% vs 34%). Bullies were more than *twice as likely to be men* than women (70% vs. 30%) but both men and women perpetrators disproportionately chose *non-status quo members as targets for bullying*.[164]

As #MeToo unfolded, another UK poll found 14% of people had experienced *sexual* harassment, with women and the young most affected. Nearly three times as many women said they had experienced sexual harassment compared to men (20% vs 7%), with roughly half of both groups leaving it unreported. [165]

Perhaps this under-reporting isn't because they lacked confidence. Instead they were just more adaptively realistic about outcomes if they did. Much of the time, either employers didn't accept their reports (12%) or didn't act upon them even if they were accepted (31%). The remainder of the time, the offender became involved, but only one-third of the time did the offender even get a warning (31%) or was asked to leave the company (4%). Employers largely looking the other way doesn't inspire confidence in anyone - other than the offenders.

163. Business in the Community, Opportunity Now & PWC, 2014 Project 28-40: The Report.
164. WBI & Zogby Analytics 2017 US Workplace Bullying Survey: Gender & Race.
165. Kirk, A. 2017 One In Five Women Have Been Sexually Harassed In The Workplace, Poll Shows, *The Telegraph*, 2 November.

In the US, sexual harassment has affected two of every five women in corporate America.[166] However, here too, sexual harassment is not distributed evenly amongst working women. Notably, it is women who conform *the least* to gender norms in either their personal lives or their roles, who experience sexual harassment the most with senior women (59%), lesbian women (53%), bisexual women (62%), women with disabilities (51%) and women in technical roles (48%) being the worst affected.

These women have the most status distance as we've discussed, and rates are particularly high compared to the figures for all women overall (41%). Notably that 41% rate refers to women 'overall' meaning women who conform the most to the status quo and female stereotypes are somewhat less affected.

Just like in the UK, how well this is handled is in the eye of the beholder. While virtually all large corporations have anti-harassment policies in place, women are more than twice as likely (9%) to view reporting such incidents as 'pointless' or 'risky' for their careers compared to men (4%).[167] This is essential to understand as we redefine confidence.

Women, and particularly women in under-represented backgrounds do *have confidence in themselves*, but they don't have confidence in the systems in which they have to operate. That type of confidence is far more critical for us to address, as we'll never fix under-confidence in individuals if we don't first address confidence, or trust, *in the system*.

While discrimination against non-status quo people in the workplace has been a common theme for years, it's taken a new twist in the online age. By 2015, Pinterest, Facebook and Instagram had larger female user bases. By contrast, online discussion forums like Reddit, Digg or Slashdot attract a more significant share of male users.[168]

Facebook found women's comments revolve around relationships, such as family and birthday posts. Men, on the other hand, are more likely to comment on topics like politics, work or sports.[169] This difference means when women leave the relative 'safety' of a group of allies to post comments on topics beyond the private sphere, they are entering male-centric discussion circles. This reality is critical to address as posting to different channels is a quick but often anonymous tool. However, the anonymity of online spaces advantages trolls.

---

166. Huang, J. et al. McKinsey and Co. and LeanIn.Org, 2019 Women in the Workplace study.
167. Huang, J. et al. McKinsey and Co. and LeanIn.Org, 2019 Women in the Workplace study.
168. Pew Research Centre, 2015 Men Catch up with Women on Overall Social Media Use.
169. Wang, Y. C., Burke, M. and Kraut, R. 2013 Gender, Topic and Audience Response: An Analysis of User-Generated Content on Facebook, ACM Conference on Human Factors in Computing Systems.

Perhaps, then, it's not surprising research on young (age 18–34) Facebook users found half of the women had experienced harassment on the network.[170] Six out of ten harassed had been sent graphic or abusive content, with 38% repeatedly being sent messages that made them 'fear for their safety'.

This means the world weighs in to 'give feedback' regardless of the intent, quality or relevance. Indeed, on my YouTube channel, years ago one of the first comments from a viewer I ever got was how 'sorry he felt for my husband'. Tame stuff by today's standards – but not exactly confidence building – which perhaps *is the whole point*.

Naomi Pryde routinely makes 'Top 35 Under 35 to Watch' lists and so her relative youth is noticeable within the industry. She's also reminded how much other women also judge her choices with the range of online comments she receives. She says: 'They range from "It's all right for you, you don't have any kids!" to the even more charming: "You've f*^@ed your fertility now!", said as a light-hearted "joke" or a cautionary reminder.' She explains:

> *The day before speaking at a conference, I got a 'helpful'*
> *tweet from a woman I didn't even know 'congratulating'*
> *me on my new senior role. She said she loved following my*
> *career, but that I shouldn't forget about my fertility! I'd love*
> *to say these comments wash over me, but they don't, which*
> *no doubt is their point.*

People feel free to comment on Pryde's personal life, via both social media and in conversation. It's not something she, or others I interviewed, male or female, saw to the same extent amongst male peers. The private and professional lives of men are largely seen as unrelated unless they inappropriately mix the two.

While that is increasingly frowned upon, these relationships have been going on for decades. However, they've only recently earned public attention via #MeToo because of the *risk they create for organisations or public scrutiny they can now earn senior men*. Let's be clear, this increased level of scrutiny was never about the way these relationships historically damaged women's careers.

By comparison, in Pryde's experience, women's professional and personal lives are seen as intertwined and subject to public comment, even before the digital age. For women, the personal and professional have always been inversely related. The assumption is that the more *dedicated* the mother, the less likely she is to work outside of the home. Equally, the more you work for pay, the worse a mother you are. It's a wonder working mothers maintain confidence at all!

170. https://www.survation.com/half-of-young-women-aged-18-34-on-facebook-have-experienced-harassment/

The fact that much of Pryde's online scrutiny comes from other women reminds me of how much potential infighting there can between under-represented groups. There is an almost subconscious assumption belief that the status quo will maintain power, and any 'scraps' are to be fought for between the non-status quo.

There is little appetite for questioning *why* the majority of roles at the top table are still unofficially reserved for the status quo. Instead women are supposed to be grateful for the 30% most organisations are now aiming for at the top levels. This avoidance of the more important questions maintains the status quo. Allowing a few 'diverse' hires at the top table reassures us progress is being made.

One much-lauded online tool to record harassment has been the Everyday Sexism Project. Lauren Bates started this collection of tens of thousands of women's daily experiences of gender inequality explained in their own words. Bates later worked with Amnesty International, who polled 4,000 women from eight countries who described themselves as 'moderate to active internet users' about their experiences of online abuse and harassment. Bates recalled how in the early days of her ground-breaking project she herself received 200 abusive messages a day.

Bates says:

> *The psychological impact of reading through someone's really graphic thoughts about raping and murdering you is not necessarily acknowledged. You could be sitting at home in your living room, outside of working hours, and suddenly someone is able to send you an incredibly graphic rape threat right into the palm of your hand.*[171]

Bates is far from alone in her reactions to trolling. Nearly a quarter (23%) of the female bloggers surveyed had experienced online abuse or harassment at least once, half of which was misogynistic in content. Over half of the female bloggers reported decreased self-esteem or loss of confidence (61%) as well as stress, anxiety or panic attacks (55%) as a result of cyber violence and online hate speech.[172]

---

171. Amnesty International 2018 Toxic Twitter: A Toxic Place for Women.
172. Amnesty International 2017 Amnesty Reveals Alarming Impact of Online Abuse Against Women.

ABUSE AND LACK OF LEGAL RAMIFICATIONS

In its reporting of cyber violence, the British press often implicitly blames the victim[173] mirroring the blame and 'what did you do to cause this?' approach we take with victims of *offline abuse*. 'Helpful' advice encourages the victim to change her behaviour including not responding to abusive language and not taking or sharing private photos.

However, this is nonsensical. Evidence shows us victims aren't always complicit and *may not even be aware* she has been abused online this way. This means it's hardly something against which a woman can 'protect' herself. First, trolls often use images from non-willing participants who never 'overshared' in any way, such as 'up-skirting'. Alternatively, they may be victims of rape and harassment where the incident is recorded, shared and even sold online. Or third, they may be images of the woman but altered to resemble someone else.

This all reminds me how we've blamed assault victims suggesting they 'be careful what you're wearing' and 'to not draw attention to themselves'. The message? Hide any confidence you do feel. You'll be attacked whether or not you have the nerve to show it.

Even if they aren't always so sexually explicit, trolls undermine the confidence of non-status quo groups in the public eye in other ways with comments devolving very quickly into misogyny. Women who blog about politics or identify as 'feminist' in Germany, Switzerland, the United Kingdom and the United States revealed that nearly three out of four (73%) had negative experiences because of their usage of social media. Most of these negative experiences involved not only abusive comments, but also stalking, trolling and rape or death threats, because of their beliefs.[174]

Unfortunately, this dismantling of confidence is effective. Between 63% and 83% of these women made changes to the way they used social media platforms.[175] Democracy is threatened when non-status quo groups are disproportionately silenced into disengagement. Twitter, in particular, remains a hostile space for women. This is because one of its core features is virtual anonymity while allowing direct and immediate contact between users.

173. Lumsden, K. and Morgan, H. 2017 Media Framing of Trolling and Online Abuse: Silencing Strategies, Symbolic Violence and Victim Blaming, *Feminist Media Studies*, 17(6).
174. Eckert, S. 2018 Fighting for Recognition: Online abuse of women bloggers in Germany, Switzerland, the UK and the US, *New Media & Society* 20(4).
175. Amnesty International 2018 Toxic Twitter: A Toxic Place for Women.

Looking more specifically at how harassment affects those tasked with protecting democracy, researchers also sought to understand the abuse women MPs face online. They focused on the six weeks before the 8 June 2017 UK General Elections, routinely a time of greater engagement between constituents and their representatives. Diane Abbott, a Black British long-standing MP, received almost half (45.14%) of all abusive tweets sent to all MPs *on her own*.

This Amnesty International research highlighted how a parliamentarian received 500 rape threats in just four days on Twitter alone. It pays to remember that the MP Jo Cox received online abuse from countless people *before* eventually being murdered by a man who simply disagreed with her views. As we've seen with other types of harassment, intersectionality affects this further. Overall, Black and Asian women MPs in Westminster received 35% more abusive tweets than White women MPs.[176]

Looking beyond the UK, online abuse of government officials is widespread. Nearly two-thirds of the female politicians from the EU were subject to sexist or disparaging attacks online,[177] particularly the representatives most active in equality issues. Certainly, vile social media trolling is broadly perceived as pushing women out of politics.[178] It takes passion and conviction to go into politics; these women don't exactly lack confidence in themselves, but again perhaps in the system in which they must operate.

Further hindering women's participation in public life is the *legal* lack of responsibility for maintaining ethical standards amongst internet intermediaries. While there may be legal change afoot on some aspects, cyber violence and hate speech online is amplified by anonymity. Users interpret the lack of rules and accountability as a 'free pass' to harass at will. Individuals can make threats and jibes with ease. They can be 'whoever they want to be' and easily log-off at the end of a session with few, if any, repercussions.

Online harassers know this, and their perception is entirely accurate from a legal perspective. Social media platforms are legally not publishers, so not responsible for the content distributed via their platform. Online platforms largely enjoy statutory immunity for individuals' postings. Plus, there's little incentive to discourage hostility because inflammatory remarks *drive engagement*, which is the companies end goal in cultivating advertising revenue.

---

176. Amnesty International 2018 Toxic Twitter: A Toxic Place for Women.
177. Interparliamentary Union 2018 Sexism, Harassment and Violence against Women in Parliaments in Europe, *October Issues Brief.*
178. Ryall, G. 2017 BBC: Online Trolling Putting Women Off Politics, Says Union, 20 May.

WHEN THEY DARE TO SHARE AN OPINION

Harassment spans industries from politics to journalism, academia and beyond. Female journalists are targeted by hateful online comments three times more frequently than their male counterparts.[179] Similarly, of the Guardian's ten journalists who received the most abuse online, eight were women (four White, four non-White), and the other two were Black men.[180]

This treatment isn't because of what they write, but more about *who they are* and how they may have covered issues in a way unpalatable to the status quo. This treatment flies in the face of imploring people from historically disadvantaged backgrounds to use their confidence for causes in which they believe. If doing so increases their risk of being trolled, why do we expect more confidence?

This is *not* a new problem. As far back as 2006, researchers sent fake online accounts and their avatars into chat rooms. Accounts with female usernames received an average of just over 100 sexually explicit or threatening messages per day, whereas masculine names received fewer than four (3.7).[181] The researchers explained the nature of the comments received suggested the posts were made by humans, *not bots*. Female academics are also much more likely to experience online harassment when their publications are shared on social media and to attract cyber abusers.[182]

This toxic culture for women in technology seeps beyond social media usage, and technical excellence in coding won't solve it alone. One study looked at contributions from men and women in GitHub, the open source software online community. They discovered women's submissions were accepted *more* often than men's submissions *when raters didn't know the gender of the programmer.* However, when *their gender was identifiable*, men's acceptance rates were higher. The authors concluded: 'although women on GitHub may be more competent overall, bias against them exists nonetheless'.[183]

Online spaces reflect the public sphere of the real world, where contributions by women have historically been less valued if not unwelcome. Visible women who assert their views, challenge the status quo or merely defend their intersecting identities are all targets for cyber violence and hate speech. What's the impact? Women are not taking part in shaping tomorrow, which hurts us all.

---

179. OECD 2016 Countering Online Abuse of Female Journalists. OECD Publishing, Paris.
180. Gardiner, B. et al. 2016 The Dark Side of Guardian Comments, 12 April. https://www.theguardian.com/technology/2016/apr/12/the-dark-side-of-guardian-comments
181. Meyer, R. and Cukier, M. 2006 Assessing the Attack Threat due to IRC Channels, 467-472. 10.1109/DSN.2006.12.
182. Mead, R. 2014 The Troll Slayer, a Cambridge Classicist Takes on Her Sexist Detractors, *The New Yorker*.
183. Terrell, J. et al. 2017 Gender Differences and Bias in Open Source: Pull Request Acceptance of Women vs Men, *Peer J Computer Science* 3(11).

Most (76%) women surveyed by Amnesty, who had experienced abuse or harassment on a social media platform, made changes to *their* behaviour including restricting the topics on which they'll speak or not participating at all. When the non-status quo are pushed from cyberspace, via fear of victimisation or retaliation, it has consequences for democracy as well as those individuals. It also punishes those reliant on the internet and their online reputation for a living – an ever-growing number of people.

The landscape of online *distribution lists* groups is no friendlier for women. On these, people can leave public feedback regarding each other's contributions. The data on the reception women have received in these online forums goes back further than you might think, ushering in our modern online world. Even this initial research is worth considering given how much it has shaped today' online world.

As early as 1992, researcher Susan Herring found that of the e-mail discussions on a 'linguistics distribution list', just five women and 30 men took part on these threads. This may seem small yet what's notable is the lack of women contributing considering *how many were qualified to do so*. At the time, nearly half of the Linguistic Society of America members were women.

Over a third (36%) subscribers to that list were women. Even then they didn't participate, making up less than 15% of all contributions. Additionally, men's messages were twice as long, on average, in comparison with women. Perhaps not surprisingly, modern online discussion groups are more popular with men, 20% of whom say they post comments, compared to just 11% of women.[184]

The tone of comments was also very different. All but one of the five women used a hesitant voice in their posts. Herring explained women were much more likely to say: 'I am intrigued by your comment ... could you say a bit more?' The tone adopted by men was much more assertive, sometimes bordering on combative in the way they 'corrected' other participants. They were more likely to use: 'It's obvious that ...' or 'Note that ...'[185]

However, you needn't be an academic, politician or work in a male-dominated field such as technology to be subject to online abuse. As early as 2005, there was an 11% drop in participation in online chat forums overall from men and women. Pew research found disengagement mainly stemmed from menacing comments.[186] As you'll remember, internet usage at the time was increasing both in frequency, but also in the scope of platforms accessed, for both women and men.

---

184. Pew Research Centre 2015 Men Catch up with Women on Overall Social Media Use.
185. Herring, S. 1992 Gender & Participation in Computer-Mediated Linguistic Discourse, *ERIC Clearinghouse on Languages and Linguistics*, October.
186. Pew Research Centre 2005 How Women and Men Use the Internet, *Pew Internet and American Life Project*.

However, even then, the tenor of discussions affected *who* and *how* people participated. In their report, Pew detailed:

> *In one dramatic exception, participation rates have fallen, entirely due to women. The proportion of internet users who have participated in online chats and discussion groups dropped from 28% in 2000 to as low as 17% in 2005, entirely because of women's fall off in participation. The drop off occurred during the last few years coincided with increased awareness of and sensitivity to worrisome behaviour in chat rooms.*

Interestingly, nearly two decades ago, the researchers didn't disaggregate their data according to gender. This lack of granularity suggests women removing themselves from chat rooms was much higher than 11% (the drop between 28% to 17%) if that was the difference when *combining the chat room usage of men and women*. Women simply tuned out.

Yet we continue to wonder why non-status quo groups aren't more confident? If their day-to-day experience is a toxic mix of being ignored, rebuked or harassed, is it any wonder they are deemed 'less confident' when speaking their mind? I'd suggest the non-status quo are confident in their ideas and goals because they are more certain *people are actually listening*.

Back in the online world, this explains why many turn to closed distribution lists such as WhatsApp. Just as women turn to single-sex schools or African Americans turn to historically Black universities, those from historically disadvantaged groups may gravitate toward groups where they will be heard more equitably.

In the workspace, employee resource groups aimed at particular groups such as carers, BAME, women, disability, LGBTQ groups for networking are popular for a reason. Without safe spaces, they continue to make themselves fair game for anyone with a keyboard and an opinion.

NOT ALL MEN ARE STATUS QUO

Let's be very clear: men are *not one generic enemy* who all determine how we define confidence. I know men are certainly not 'all the same'. For a start, globally, 'status quo men' are actually in a statistical minority. As a start, the world is populated with far more people from a wide range of ethnicities who aren't classified as 'White men'.

187

Similarly, when we look at rates of disability, a sizeable proportion of men, particularly as they age, develop some type of disability. Furthermore, to assume men in powerful positions are all heterosexual also does a real disservice to the LGBTQ community. Similarly, most White men *don't* benefit from inherited economic privilege, nor are they all extroverts – issues we'll be looking at.

Plus, women are not all equally disadvantaged simply because of their gender. I am an able-bodied White woman who is a native English speaker, all of which afford me many advantages I certainly didn't earn. Toby Mildon is well versed in how this type of intersectionality affects confidence.

> *I am disabled and gay, but I'm also a White male. When I started my career, I knew statistically I'd be in the minority, but it didn't affect my confidence. But I do wonder if my White male identity overrides self-doubt to a certain degree.*

Mildon continues:

> *In fact, I probably identify as a White male over being disabled until my disability comes into the foreground, like not being able to get into an office because of steps. My gut tells me people identify with the identity that gives them the most power. It's only when I'm with other disabled people that I take on that identity more readily.*

I would go further and say our current definitions of confidence do a disservice to *most men*, even if they are part of the status quo. Status quo men are in a numeric minority around the world. We focus on them only *because they hold such a disproportionately large amount of power in global organisations*. This is, after all, how they've defined our expectations of confidence for so long. Even then, our expectations of confidence, don't serve most men much better than anyone else!

Jennifer Siebel Newsom, the documentary filmmaker of *The Mask You Live In*, said that, to her, the three most dangerous words in the English language were *be a man*.[187] This saying underpins expectations for men to live up to an ideal, aiming for the expected wins of sex and success. Simultaneously we expect them to reject empathy and hide emotion. As we will see, we all lose when men keep up a confident front according to outdated definitions.

---

187. Wiseman, E. 2016 Depression, Violence, Anxiety: The Problem with the Phrase 'To Be a Man', *The Guardian*, 14 August.

Power behind male c-words

Let's not forget the guys also have their own proverbial c-word with hidden meaning – cock. It too has a power in the way we use it, and mirrors the way we think about confidence and our assumptions about men. Being 'cocksure' refers to the arrogant, particularly when compared to the merit of their ideas. Being 'cocky' is synonymous with vanity, and again confidence. It also has a shade of cheekiness, as if you may be trying to get away with something you don't quite deserve on merit.

Calling someone a cock or it's cousin 'a knob', while pejorative, also has a cheeky tone to it. Going off 'half-cocked' usually refers to someone who is light on facts, but aggressively certain in their beliefs – the competence vs confidence dilemma in a nutshell.

We can go even further with gendered expectations. If someone tediously questions the competence of your idea, they are giving you a real 'ball-ache'. If a mistake is made or something gets bungled or is poorly carried out often because of a lack of foresight, planning or overconfidence, we say it was a real 'cock-up' or that they 'ballsed it up'.

While we sometimes use 'tits-up' in this instance, it's notable the phrase has no definition on dictionary.com or in the *OED*, suggesting 'balls-up' is still the favoured term. Virtually every workplace where I have consulted, there are always those who act like 'the big swinging dick', pushing their views onto others.

When someone feels they are being unfairly questioned, they're likely to fight back with 'stop busting my balls'. To do something boldly aggressive or courageous is to be 'ballsy'. Undeniably, the synonyms for ballsy look like a hit list of the words we associate with confidence: brash, bold, assured, brassy, brave, cheeky, cocky, confident, courageous, daring, dashing, dauntless, gallant, game, gritty, gutsy or heroic.[188]

Helpfully, the word easily translates across languages. When growing up, my Texan father would routinely refer to people taking on a challenge by saying 'that took *cajones*' – Spanish slang for balls. This 'everyday' terminology seeps into our expectations about power, confidence and masculinity.

---

188. https://www.dictionary.com/browse/ballsy

TAKING OFF THE MASK

Men have largely been sold a false bill of goods as to what matters in life. They too are victims of the con job. It's hard to realise that much of what you've been taught to value – money, cars, the house – don't matter much at all. Yet by the time you recognise this, you're on the hamster wheel you can't easily get off. Ultimately, the sense of isolation, of going into work only to feel inauthentic can have fatal consequences for men.

We raise them to keep a 'stiff upper lip' and not ask for help; doing so would render them the worst label of all: a 'pussy'. Without safe spaces to 'take off the mask' of confidence, men at best leave industries in which they are very competent. At worst, they die earlier from poor lifestyle choices and lash out either via violence against each other, their romantic partners or even against themselves.

For Sandy Kennedy, taking off the mask was an evolution at the start of his career. Kennedy observes:

> *When we think about ambition, we assume everyone*
> *wants to be at the top. But if you look up, and don't see*
> *anyone with whom you identify, that goes deeper than*
> *demographics. On the outside, I may have looked like a lot*
> *of the senior guys, but they didn't have lives I wanted.*

When Kennedy became a lawyer in a prestigious practice, he remembers:

> *One day I looked through a list of our partners and noted:*
> *'He's having an affair with his secretary; this one is on*
> *his second family and this one never sees his kids.' They*
> *weren't who I wanted to be, so I had to leave.*

Interestingly, this wasn't a reflection on his confidence, but his *values*. However, when women eschew senior levels, it's often viewed by management as a problem with her confidence and ambition, not a clash of values. To address it as a values clash would require senior leaders to question the *value* of the brass ring they grasped. If it involves a mask of confident bravado and disengagement from your core values, perhaps the ring isn't worth having in the first place? As we'll see, acting on your values should be part of how we rebrand 'confidence'.

190

RISE OF MALE SUICIDE

Recognising this lack of authenticity is profoundly uncomfortable but not doing so has dire consequences. In 2018 there were over 6,500 deaths from suicide in the UK, a 12% increase on even the year before, primarily driven by men. While most who committed suicide were aged between 45–49, the sharpest rise was between young men *up to* 24 years old.[189]

On a global scale, in 2016, there were an estimated 793,000 suicide deaths worldwide, again most of whom were men. Even more worryingly, the World Health Organisation estimates that for every successful suicide, there are likely 20 other attempts. WHO's data show that nearly 40% of countries have more than 15 suicide deaths per 100,000 men. Not even 2% of countries have a rate that high for women.[190]

Not surprisingly, suicide is the single biggest killer of men under 45 in the UK, and many high income countries. There are many reasons for the gender disparity. One is that women may be more likely to be diagnosed with depression, compared to men.

Expected to 'toughen up', men largely don't ask for help or are told to 'get a grip' when they do. This contributes to the shock families face after a man takes his life, stemming from his inability, in a crisis moment, to handle stresses such as financial problems, a relationship break-up or chronic pain and illness.

In these moments, someone may compare themselves to a 'confident ideal'. That's the fictional person we all think has it all together. Compared to this fiction, the sufferer only finds themselves lacking. At its core, suicide is a complete waste of latent potential.

Every person we admire has had their doubts and fears. In fact, they probably have all been told that they weren't 'good enough' at something in the past. There is no such thing as a fearless fighter. It's *the fear* that will make them fighter smarter, by making sure they are competent enough to take on the challenges ahead.

Assuming those we most admire don't feel fear, uncertainty and are always confident does a disservice to us all. However, this is particularly hard on status quo men. It flies in the face of the confidence we, and indeed they, expect.

189. ONS 2019 Suicides in the UK: 2018 registrations.
190. WHO 2016 Suicide Data https://www.who.int/mental_health/prevention/suicide/suicideprevent/en/

What's even more concerning is that mental health disorders are only increasing. Simon Gunning, the CEO of Campaign Against Living Miserably (CALM) explains: 'When there are economic factors we can't control, it becomes very difficult.'[191] However, in an increasingly unstable and volatile world, we are likely to see suicide rise. More factors feel beyond our control, and we have ever-higher expectations of the benefits we wrongly assume confidence can provide.

Between 1990 and 2013, the number of people suffering from depression and/ or anxiety increased by nearly 50%.[192] Mental health issues are something that shouldn't be side-lined. Assuming confidence will be the quick fix is a recipe for despair. Clearly, coming up with better definitions of confidence and what it looks like would serve everyone.

191. Schmacher, H. 2019 BBC: Why More Men than Women Die by Suicide, *BBC Futures*, March.
192. WHO: Investing in Treatment for Depression and Anxiety Leads to Fourfold Return, 13 April 2016 News release, Washington, DC.

NINE

CLASS AND DISABILITY

*There is no greater disability than the ability to see
someone as more*
– Robert Hensel

When I first thought about how expectations of confidence impacted different groups, I initially overlooked both class and disability. However, these often invisible identities very much affect the way someone moves through the world, and how they are received as they do so, much in the same way as gender. Not seeing how these identities affected confidence was a huge oversight, and one we'll be looking at in this chapter.

As invisible as it was to me initially, Britain is known for real societal divides according to class background. Indeed, I first heard the admonishment someone was acting 'above their station' when I came to the UK where even postage stamps have first and second-class demarcations. However, this isn't just a UK issue as every culture has its own systems affected by class and socioeconomic status, and the mythology involved. For example, in the US, we romanticise the idea of 'pulling yourself up by the bootstraps'.

Certainly, economic background often came to the fore in the discussions I had with the people I interviewed. They'd share stories using class-based analogies, talking about how they'd 'worked their way up' or how much easier it was to both enter and then network in professional jobs 'when you're posh'.

We often assume ambition and confidence are synonymous. Indeed, openly expressing ambition in reaching for the highest status jobs is linked to confidence.[193] However, what's more interesting is the intertwining of confidence and family economic status.[194] How these three elements overlap – ambition, money and confidence almost ensures those from wealth will do the best in their careers.

193. Kammeyer-Mueller, J., Judge, T., and Piccolo, R. 2008 Self-Esteem and Extrinsic Career Success: Test of a Dynamic Model, *Applied Psychology – An International Review* 57(2): 204–224.
194. Blanden, J., Gregg, P., and MacMillan, L. et al. 2007 Accounting for Intergenerational Income Persistence: NonCognitive Skills, Ability and Education, *Economic Journal* 117: 519.

It starts with the story the status quo adopts about themselves. They often talk about their personal career trajectory rise as a series of 'good choices' or 'just keeping my nose down and working incredibly hard'. This isn't to say these people haven't made fortuitous decisions or put their effort into the right projects. However, they are *incredibly resistant* to the possibility of any unearned advantages. If they refer to these benefits at all, it's chalked up to 'good luck'.

Sam Friedman and Daniel Laurison, authors of *The Class Ceiling: Why it Pays to be Privileged* used a mix of the UK's largest employment survey with 175 in-depth interviews across elite occupations. It exposed significant differences in how quickly people progressed to the top positions in their careers, according to their social class of origin. The money you were raised with had a far greater impact than 'access'alone. However, 'access' is where most social mobility and diversity programmes focus.

Instead, their research highlighted an uncomfortable truth. Even when employees from working-class backgrounds can access jobs in prestigious industries, they *earned less than their middle-class counterparts*, 16% less on average. Plus, these people progressed up the career ladder more slowly, dubbed 'the class ceiling'.[195]

However, this is wider than the UK. Another set of researchers looked at 150,000 small business owners from both Mexico and the USA to understand these issues more deeply. They assessed how much people rated their performance by first giving them a cognitive test. Additionally, participants indicated their *perceived* social class on an image of a ladder: 'representing where people stand in your country'.

After their cognitive test came a final question: 'How do you think you did, compared with other people?' The findings were stark. The higher someone perceived their social class, the more they *inaccurately inflated their test performance relative to others*.[196] Put simply, those from better off backgrounds *feel* smarter than they actually are, increasing their sense of *entitlement* to any successes that come their way. They are also very slow to acknowledge how much of a helping hand their economic class gave them in *earning* those successes.

195. Friedman, S. and Laurison, D. 2019 *The Class Ceiling: Why it Pays to be Privileged*, Bristol University Press, Bristol, p. 50.
196. Belmi, P. et al. 2019 The Social Advantage of Miscalibrated Individuals: The Relationship Between Social Class and Overconfidence and Its Implications for Class-Based Inequality, *Journal of Personality and Social Psychology* 20: 1–29.

EXTROVERSION AND MONEY

Interviewees often cited extroverted behaviours as evidence of confidence, such as 'she could talk to anyone' or 'he's always willing to give presentations'. However, extroversion does not equate to confidence outright. Nor does introversion predict low confidence. Instead, understanding how money and confidence overlap in career success is important for us to address.

The links between confidence, extroversion and career progress were quantified in the 'Winning Personality' report which drew data from over 150,000 UK residents. Researchers found highly extroverted people, that is those we'd deem most confident, sociable or assertive, had a 25% higher chance of being in a high-earning job. That means they were likeliest to earn a middle-class wage of over £40,000 per year, and these benefits were highest for *extroverted men*.

So, what gives people from at least middle-class backgrounds that added extroversion? As the authors of the study point out: 'The experience of higher family status and prestige may also have a direct positive effect on children's well-being and confidence.'[197] In the case of the Winning Personality survey; 'Better off parents may, therefore, be "handing down" characteristics which helped them become successful themselves.'[198]

If we don't assume a simple 'genetics advantage', the likely answer comes from the relatively stress-free backgrounds in which middle-class children are more likely to live. The middle-class may argue they experienced their share of stress as children. However, confidence just grows in certain settings better than others – and stability is where it flourishes. Being raised in a family with at least one parent earning a good wage, in a warm home with a reliable food source, relatively free of familial conflict, is one of those settings.

In the era of zero-hours contracts, extortionate housing costs, unprecedented food bank reliance and an inadequate universal credit system, this type of certainty is harder to access than ever and is likely to get worse. As detailed in the sobering UN report on UK income inequality by Philip Alston, the Special Rapporteur on extreme poverty and human rights: 'Following drastic changes in government economic policy beginning in 2010, the two preceding decades of progress in tackling child and pensioner poverty have begun to unravel and poverty is again on the rise.'[199] Growing incoming inequality in the West does nothing to foster confidence in disadvantaged families and in the children they are raising.

---

197. Blanden et al. 2007 Accounting for Intergenerational Income Persistence: Non-Cognitive Skills, Ability and Education, *Economic Journal* 117: 519.
198. deVries, R. and Rentfrow, J. 2016 A Winning Personality: The Effect of Background on Personality and Earnings report, Sutton Trust Publications, p. 8.
199. Alston, P. 2019 Visit to the United Kingdom of Great Britain and Northern Ireland: Report of the Special Rapporteur on Extreme Poverty and Human Rights, United Nations General Assembly, Human Rights Council, 41st session. 24 June–19 July.

This happens, in particular, because definitions of confidence incorporate the belief things will go well in the future, *because* they have gone well in the past. These families live in circumstances where there is simply less that can be relied upon – and ultimately about which to be confident. Growing up in economic disadvantage doesn't preclude confidence; it just means there is further to travel to naturally to 'own' that sense of entitlement and belief in the equality of the system.

INTERSECTIONALITY AND ECONOMIC DISADVANTAGE

When it comes to confidence, there isn't one single characteristic of intersectionality overriding all others. Friedman and Laurison carefully emphasise the class pay gap should not be seen as more critical or more legitimate than pay gaps based on ethnicity or gender. Instead, they intersect and don't work in isolation.

As evidence of this they found working-class women are doubly disadvantaged. They earn on average £7,500 less per year than women of privileged origin, who in turn make £11,500 less than men of privileged origin.

This means the pay gap between the average earners amongst most advantaged men and the least advantaged women is 60%! Plus, even beyond this, it's an additional £2,000 *higher than* if we just added the class and gender pay gaps together.[200] Friedman explains in our interview:

> *We looked at how earnings varied by class background. We wanted to see if you could explain the difference by more meritocratic means, such as education or experience. But when controlled for all of that, you couldn't explain it away.*

Friedman continued:

> *Gender and social mobility are something we all need to understand better, as our stereotypes about working-class people are gendered. We have this romantic notion of 'working-class boy done good' but no female equivalent.*

200. Friedman, S. and Laurison, D. 2019 *The Class Ceiling: Why it Pays to be Privileged*, Bristol University Press, Bristol, p. 50.

Upwardly mobile women are seen less as 'working girl made good' and instead judged as vapid socialites; calculating, pretentious and self-interested, some of the worst descriptions you can lay at a woman's feet. This is particularly damning for women when society *relies* on stereotypes of unpaid female selflessness.

To this point, Kate and Pippa Middleton, even after the Royal wedding, were often referred to in the press as 'the Wisteria sisters' for their ability to socially 'climb' like the attractive but destructive plant.[201] Megan Markle, with her African-American heritage, is the most vilified by the British press of all for her 'climbing' – despite the fact she was a high earner before marrying into the Royal family.

When we look further at race, we again see the impact of class background. One BAME interviewee said that the successful BAME people in her field often had their confidence levels more in common with the White peers from privileged backgrounds. She notes:

> *Obviously, people from BAME backgrounds can do quite well here. What sets them apart is their privately educated backgrounds. It gives them a certain polish that's reassuring to the prevailing culture at executive levels, perhaps even more so than competent White people from working-class backgrounds.*

Even though those Oxbridge-educated BAME members are in the minority, they still serve as 'real models'; a term vastly preferred by some of those with whom I spoke. However, they are often able to assimilate to status quo peers via a shared social class.

When I spoke to people from BAME backgrounds, many recalled training White colleagues, only to see them leapfrog over them. One admitted how that impacted her:

> *You feel disheartened, demoralised – it can be soul-destroying. When they go above you, they don't even remember you. But their accent, their background, their articulation ensures they'll get ahead. My face doesn't fit. I, and plenty others like me, have consistently been overlooked, ultimately undermining your confidence.*

Another BAME interviewee sighed: 'There comes a time when you ask, "What more do I have to do to get ahead?" which puts a tremendous mental strain on people.'

---

201. Betts, H. 2016 Kate, Pippa and how to spot 'old money' and 'new money', *The Telegraph*, 22 July: https://www.telegraph.co.uk/women/life/kate-pippa-and-how-to-spot-old-money-and-new-money/

EMOTIONAL COSTS OF MOBILITY

The psychological price of upward mobility is high and determined by who has risen in long-established fields before. Past leaders embed their ideas of what constitutes talent and merit, confidence and competence. To be upwardly mobile, you often go through a change of identities, based on what and who historic leaders chose to promote.

Expected changes, even if subtle, can mean adopting your choices in hobbies and tastes, but also your accent and seemingly simple things like holiday destinations, your clothing and other personal preferences. As one man I interviewed laughed: 'It's a minefield at times. I don't know. Is it beer or champagne? Center Parcs or the south of France? Football or rugby? It's all about keeping up appearances.' I've worked with people who discovered 'new preferences', even subconsciously, that are more aligned to the workplace status quo.

Some status quo clients say they walk a fine balance between being working-class (background of origin) and middle class. After all, middle class is how the rest of the world *now sees them based on their career success*. However, this tightrope can create angst as they straddle the line and try to define themselves anew. Interestingly, it's not always easy for even academics who study socioeconomic difference to classify people as 'advantaged' or 'disadvantaged'.

Many more people self-identify as 'working class' than would be expected if comparing them to the much higher numbers of people in the UK who are in professional jobs. This difficulty in measurement is part of the reason researchers use two ways to measure socioeconomic class. They start with subjective views, such as in 'What class do you feel you are part of?' However, they'll ask about more objective metrics as well, such as the respondent's own earnings or professional category.

Taking 'risks', is a key component of the traditional view of confidence, but one that comes at a high emotional, financial and psychological cost and is highlighted by social class difference.[202] For example, university students from working-class backgrounds are more likely to incur debt to graduate. However, they are less likely to *be accepted into the better-paid industries for which they are preparing*. Plus, after graduation, they are less likely to have the support of their original circle in understanding the social rituals from networking to entertaining colleagues or clients.

---

202. Reay, D. 2018 *Miseducation: Inequality, Education and the Working Classes*, Policy Press. Imprint of Bristol University Press, Bristol

Social mobility is a challenge for most professions, where 'fit', as we've already discussed, is paramount. This reminds me how one of the first online games my company ever created focused on helping law firms *avoid social class bias in recruitment*. This is an issue for the legal sector given how many lawyers were raised by other lawyers.

In contrast, depending on their audience, not everyone *wants* to be considered upwardly mobile. Employees also 'play down the social scale' when it suits them. Many from middle-class backgrounds embraced the narrative of 'working-class done good', while still benefiting from privileges they didn't acknowledge. This meant they were less likely to recognise the help they'd had in the past as particularly unique or advantageous when it no doubt was.

We must be careful not to assume talking about class structure is written off as irrelevant in 'the modern world'. A disproportionately high number of the successful people I interviewed were from middle-class backgrounds, something I didn't initially notice. Many came from families where fee-paying schools were a norm, even if they themselves had earned scholarships.

These experiences helped set their path, expectations and their confidence levels in the right direction. Far from a historical issue, the changing structure of employment in the UK over the past century has superficially pushed many initially from working-class families into the middle classes. However, the differences in incomes between social class groups are more significant than ever before because gaps *are actually growing*, rather than reducing.[203]

Sam Friedman, explains this psychological impact in our interview:

> *The further someone has moved along the social class scale, those we call the 'long-range socially upwardly mobile', the more destabilised they can feel. We all have a psychological source of identity tied up in friends, family and place of origin. The cultural assimilation required to be upwardly mobile shifts them away to those very sources, leaving them in some ways culturally homeless.*

Defining confidence is complex, and, as we've seen, it often depends on who is creating the definition. Friedman continues:

> *When I asked people why there was a pay gap between people of different social backgrounds, most people used the word 'confidence' somewhere in their answer. It's an ambiguous term people reach for when talking about the benefits of privilege. That feeds their version of confidence.*

No doubt 'confidence' is a much more palatable explanation to yourself than recognising the unearned benefits your family background gave you.

---

203. Social Mobility Commission: State of the Nation 2016: Social Mobility in Great Britain.

Games of risk with a winning hand

In their research, Friedman and Laurison found confidence was the catch-all term for a whole host of characteristics and their benefits. For example, it was often equated with a willingness to take a risk. That 'sense of adventure' however, was underpinned by the resources someone had available to them, usually in the shape of a financially supportive family. This critical benefit certainly shows up for adult children of privileged backgrounds. It facilitates moving to a new city or undertaking unpaid work experience or a studying for an advanced degree.

However, some have pointed out to me women should be able to take risks because they are supported by men who are 'responsible' for a family. After all, the logic goes, these women have extra resources via that male partner. This assumes many things – most of which are false for a majority of women. First, there is an assumption that all women are heterosexual. It also assumes they are attached to working men who earn as much, if not more, than they do. It also disregards single women or mothers raising children on their own. These situations preclude a higher male income upon which to rely.

Similarly, most families need to have both partners working, simply to offset the pay gap other aspects of intersectionality create. Everyone has varying degrees of financial responsibility. However, with the endemic pay gaps suffered by non-status quo groups mean they can't always as easily afford to take the risks we credit to confidence.

Instead, it's 'cultural capital', not confidence, that is one of the critical factors in determining who gets on in certain professions. If you live a life with economic security, it allows you the time, space and access to common reference points to cultivate 'a presence'.

Presence and its close cousin, 'gravitas,' can be manifested in all we demonstrate on the job. This ranges from the way you dress to the way you speak. Gravitas, while interviewees found hard to define past 'a presence', is 'cashed-in' in most workplace settings.

Capitalising on your social advantage has even wider effects than only workplace advancement. Your cultural capital also signals to *potential romantic partners* your class background, and currently where you are on the socioeconomic scale. These choices all feed into our ideas of 'merit'. It would perhaps be more accurate to describe 'merit' or 'confidence' as aligned to 'cultural capital'. Understanding this distinction will be a challenge, but one that is worth addressing. Sam Friedman tells me about his research:

The areas where privilege seemed to make the biggest
difference were in roles where the 'competence' or 'merit'
was somewhat ambiguous and open to interpretation – for
example, commissioning in television and advisory services
in accountancy. The value of the end product is hard to
predict. To reduce uncertainty, people used confidence
as a proxy for competence in areas that can't actually be
definitively demonstrated in that moment.

It reassures an audience they are dealing with an authority, even if they
aren't. Friedman, in our interview, elaborates on how difficult it is to unpick
confidence from privilege when they perpetuate random social norms. He
mentions:

There are some very well-meaning charities assuming
working-class kids have something missing from their skill
sets that need to be tweaked. The truth is you can do all
the confidence-building workshops you want. If the social
structure people enter is coded to primarily help certain
types of people succeed, you're always to inhibit those who
don't fit. But it's going to manifest as a lack of confidence.

NARRATIVES OF ORIGIN

As a way to maintain their confidence levels, people from privileged
backgrounds often adhere to a working-class family narrative often starting
with variations of 'I come from a long line of …' even if it that disadvantaged
start goes back generations. In our interview, Friedman explains:

We romanticise meritocracy and the upward trajectory, but
people distance themselves from any inherited advantage.
One way to do that is to subconsciously use a parent or a
single grandparent's social mobility story as if it was their
own story, forgetting their parent's destination was actually
their origin.

His comments remind me of the leaders I've worked with who proudly talk
about their own humble origins. They see themselves as non-status quo
even when they have gained from the benefits. Certainly, there are shades of
disadvantage and advantage into which we all fall. However, for people trying
to maintain a sense of 'hard-earned success', the legitimacy of where they are
now is wrapped up in people's perception *from where they came.*

As someone who has led teams as they talk about their own privilege, I know this is psychologically adaptive. It is deeply uncomfortable to self-reflect on your unearned advantage. Most leaders have their narrative finely honed, even if unintentionally. It feeds their identity and sense of entitlement. Perhaps unsurprisingly, addressing unearned privilege *and who misses out* threatens confidence to the core.

DISABILITY

Disability also affects confidence *because it's about the interaction* between the characteristics of a person's body and features of the society in which he or she lives. Some form of disability is estimated to affect more than one billion people globally, or 15% of the world's population.[204] I should have been addressing disability from the start, particularly as its likelihood only increases as people age into the workforce. It is with humility I say, like most able-bodied people, I initially didn't see how commonplace disability is.

As of 2016, there were just over 13 million disabled people in the UK, which is almost one in five of the population.[205] That might sound higher than you think, and *that's part of the issue*. With those numbers we'd expect to 'see' disabled people everywhere. However, most types of disability whether physical or mental, like other identities people carry, are often largely invisible.

It's similar in the US where one in four people have a disability.[206] That research highlights that mobility disabilities are the most common type of disability in the US, followed in prevalence by a cognitive impairment. However, even then only one out of the four who have a mobility disability use a wheelchair, cane, crutches or a walker. This means even the two most common types of disabilities (mobility or cognitive) *aren't actually visible most of the time*.

Cognitive disabilities include learning difficulties, but also mental health issues. These can be anything that makes it harder to concentrate or make decisions, including depression and anxiety, both of which are also on the rise. Similarly, in the UK there are approximately 2 million people with sight loss[207] and 12 million people with hearing loss, both becoming more pronounced with age.[208]

The visible signs we see for these groups include using sign language or braille

204. World Report on Disabilities. 2011 World Health Organization/World Bank https://www.who.int/disabilities/world_ report/2011/report/
205. Department of Work and Pensions 2017 Family Resources Survey 2015/2016, March 16 www.gov.uk/government/ uploads/system/uploads/attachment_data/file/600465/family-resources-survey-2015-16.pdf
206. Centers for Disease Control and Prevention. Disability and Health Data System (DHDS) [Internet]. [updated 24 May 2018, cited 27 August 2018]. Available from: http://dhds.cdc.gov
207. 'SightAdvice' Royal National Institute for the Blind help.rnib.org.uk/help/newly-diagnosed-registration/registering-sight-loss/statistics
208. 'Facts and Figures', Action for Hearing Loss: https://www.actiononhearingloss.org.uk/about-us/our-research-and-evidence/facts-and-figures/

or speech-enabled technology but can also include corrective glasses or hearing aids. These are all *physical* manifestations of how the disabled must adapt themselves to the environment.

Recognising the prevalence of disability and how it develops over time is vital. This is particularly important considering many work environments aren't well-adapted for the disabled. Toby Mildon, who I mentioned previously, is a wheelchair user and during our interview, he remarked how tired he was from the previous day when he'd travelled across the country for a single meeting. He understands how workplaces, and the systems upon which disabled people rely *just to get work done,* aren't as adaptive as we might expect, and the negative effect this can have on confidence. He explains:

> *If two people go on a train journey, the person who has a physical disability is going to find every aspect much harder. They have to get through turnstiles, get a ramp on Board, make sure the accessible toilets are nearby and indeed working – all before they even got to the station. All of this puts an additional mental load on them. There is just so much more to think about at every stage, not to mention more strangers to rely upon.*

When reflecting on his 16-year career, Mildon felt his confidence was greatest at the start of his career. It only diminished over time, often based on how different employers judged or adapted to him. This sense of *confidence slide* was mentioned by other non-status quo members as well. Mildon remembers:

> *When I started at one job, I felt hugely confident and ambitious and even wanted to become a senior leader. For example, right after I joined, I was looking forward to the first Christmas party. I quickly discovered they'd picked an inaccessible venue, so I couldn't attend. I left them 18 months later feeling terrible about myself. I had endured 18 months of being constantly reminded of my disability, which undermined my initial confidence to the point of depression. Even though I'd been hired to look at inclusion issues, the overt message was disability wasn't a priority.*

Unfortunately, the evidence shows Mildon is correct. In the workplace, addressing disability isn't a priority for the able-bodied, and the lack of regard in many ways *is actually getting worse.*

Troublingly, the able-bodied think prejudice against the disabled is getting better, *an impression the disabled don't share*. In 2000, 37% of disabled people and 34% of non-disabled people saw prejudice around disability as an issue.[209] Then, the disabled and non-disabled were mainly in agreement; roughly a third of *both* populations saw discrimination against the disabled as a real problem.

Since then, however, the gap between the disabled and non-disabled people's perceptions of prejudice has *dramatically widened*. The 'Disability Perception Gap' report, using data collected in 2017, showed that 32% of disabled respondents felt prejudice against them was a problem. However, the number of non-disabled people thinking it was an issue had dropped from 37% in 2000 to 22% by 2017.

It's concerning if non-disabled people *erroneously* think disability prejudice has now been eliminated. As we've seen from other groups, the feeling 'this has been fixed' hinders efforts to tackle discrimination. The status quo thinks the job's already been done *when the data clearly says it hasn't*.

ASSUMPTIONS ABOUT DISABILITY

A frequent assumption is that disability is something with which you are born. The belief is that if you are 'lucky' enough to be unaffected at birth, you'll unlikely ever face disability yourself. This myth couldn't be further from the truth, as it's an identity that compounds with age. In fact, only 17% of disabled people in the UK were born with their disabilities. Indeed, around 7% of children have a disability, compared to 18% of working-age adults and 44% of adults over State Pension age.[210]

Mildon is also a gay man and a D&I professional. When sharing his opinion about which groups of people suffer *most* from a lack of confidence he says:

> *If I were a betting man, I'd say disabled people probably have the least workplace confidence. However, that probably also extends to those with other types of invisible differences like members of LGBTQ groups and those who are gender-fluid. It depends on what you feel you can disclose at work.*

Mildon continues:

---

209. Dixon, S. Smith, C. and Touchet, A. 2018 Disability Perception Gap: Policy Report, Scope.
210. Department of Work and Pensions 2017 Family Resources Survey 2015/2016: March 16   www.gov.uk/government/ uploads/system/uploads/attachment_data/file/600465/family-resources-survey-2015-16.pdf

Gender-fluid people might have different ways they present at work, female or male for example. However, company systems make it difficult, for example for them to get two different security passes, each with a different photo. All of this erodes confidence. It means these people have two jobs; one that is the day job and the second is handling the pressure they face.

Jenny Morris, the disability campaigner and author of *Pride Against Prejudice*, highlights the false assumptions made about the value and the activities of the disabled. She points out how multifaceted assumptions range from naivety and resentment to envy or disgust. In her book she discusses how people assume those with disabilities lead sheltered lives or can't accept their condition, assuming they're putting on a 'brave face'.[211]

She also talks about how the able-bodied believe those with disabilities don't have or can't fulfil sexual needs. If they do, their partners are being 'generous' or are 'taking advantage of them'. These are just a few falsehoods Morris points out. Indeed, any resentment those with disabilities have, won't stem from envying anyone else specifically. Instead, resentment would be for the ease in how easily the able-bodied manoeuvre a world designed solely for them.

BEYOND ACCESS

In the UK, the 'economic inactivity' rate for those with disabilities is nearly three times as high (44%) compared to those without disabilities (16%).[212] This means three times as many disabled people are either not in work or not actively looking for a job, compared to the able-bodied. Of job seekers, disabled people are more than twice as likely to be unemployed as non-disabled people.[213]

The frustration of trying to access roles in work environments that don't value you explain why the disabled sometimes 'give up' looking for work, thereby rendering them 'economically inactive' by government definitions. Advising people in this circumstance to simply 'be more confident' is woefully ignorant at best and condescending at worst.

211. Morris, J. 1991 *Pride Against Prejudice Transforming Attitudes to Disability*, The Women's Press, Aylesbury, Bucks, UK, pp. 21, 22.
212. House of Commons Library Briefing: People with Disabilities in Employment, 7540, 17 May 2019.
213. Office of National Statistics, 13 August 2019: Labour Market Status of Disabled People.

Even when the disabled are in work, they aren't in the top jobs. When we look at intersectionality further, disabled people from working-class backgrounds are around three times less likely to be in 'top' jobs than non-disabled people from privileged backgrounds. However, even individuals with disabilities from more privileged backgrounds still encounter huge barriers. For example, they are 30% less likely to enter professional occupations in comparison to their non-disabled peers.[214]

Toby Mildon, who has worked in many large professional settings, explains about a situation he recently saw:

> *A colleague with a fluctuating health condition was told they'd have to 'hot-desk'. Typical perhaps for many people, but for a person whose health is unpredictable from day to day, it's hugely stressful. If you arrive after 9 am, which is likely with a time-consuming and challenging condition, it's hard to find a place to sit, potentially having to go to different floors. It's a strain that doesn't occur to most able-bodied people. The easy solution is to make 'a reasonable adjustment' – just give this person a fixed desk.*

Mildon continues:

> *This created so much bureaucracy and endless conversations, the stress actually made her condition worse. This is all before they even start managing the 'normal' strains of a working day we all face.*

Mildon and I discussed the cognitive load disabled people carry. Cognitive load is the additional psychological strain of doing the most basic of tasks that people from a minority group (the disabled in this case) have to do, yet are invisible to majority group members. So how does cognitive load look? It goes beyond the everyday stresses everyone carries and affects people in different ways.

It's the plans mothers disproportionately organise for their children's school holidays. It's the decision to disclose to colleagues your LGBTQ status by displaying or hiding family photographs on a desk or screensaver. It's asking for an unoccupied prayer space. It's the reliance a physically disabled person has on accessible parking spots to get into the office on time. It's being challenged by security as a gender-fluid person if your appearance that day doesn't match your security badge.

---

214. Social Mobility Commission: State of the Nation 2016: Social Mobility in Great Britain.

It's a million small things that cumulatively create a cognitive load; the strains of working in systems that weren't designed with you in mind. All of which can diminish a sense of 'belonging' and ultimately confidence.

As Mildon explains:

> *In one company, a lack of easily accessible toilets was so difficult it became part of the reason I left. Equally, I've worked in companies where there were plenty of the right toilets, and I could just get on with my work as any able-bodied person. But in the previous job, just finding the right toilets on the right floor is one more thing to think about, before my day job! If that compounds every day, it's not surprising it inhibits confidence.*

The issue in this instance isn't solely access, it's also about accommodation. Most professional settings that want to hire people as astute as Toby will provide 'accessible toilets' for example. However, good employers also ensure these toilets are maintained just as well as the non-disabled toilets and aren't used for other purposes like storing cleaning supplies, nappy changing or breast-feeding – all of which I've seen. Cognitive load affects most non-status quo members. It's each time you are reminded of your difference thereby cumulatively undermining confidence.

For a reminder of where you already rock, for your 'down-days', surround yourself with:

- **Certifications, qualifications or other awards you've earned.**
- **E-mail folder of thank you notes and compliments about your work.**
- **Images of and books by people you admire.**
- **Photos of loved ones who already think you are fantastic.**

DISABILITY AND ISOLATION

Not surprisingly, the disabled are more likely to live below the poverty line.[215] Although finding a job may be difficult for disabled individuals, stabilising that role can be even trickier.[216] This happens whatever your disability and is largely down to two main factors: production skills and social skills. Disabilities, and the way people interact with the world, affect both. These abilities and limitations can affect the networks they can build and ultimately earnings.

Additionally, those with visible disabilities face stigma. This manifests itself as a range of adverse responses in others ranging from fear, pity, embarrassment, patronisation, intrusive gazes and rejection. This means the disabled don't access social spaces to the same degree, and the benefits these public places can provide.[217]

Disabled writer/researcher Jenny Morris describes how stigma functions to marginalise people with disabilities:

> *Going out in public so often takes courage. How many of us find that we can't dredge up the strength to do it day after day, week after week, year after year, a lifetime of rejection and revulsion? It is not only physical limitations that restrict us to our homes and those whom we know. It is the knowledge that each entry into the public world will be dominated by stares, by condescension, by pity and by hostility.*[218]

The marginalisation Morris explains sheds light on how disability can affect confidence. As one woman with a physical disfigurement told me: 'to do it day after day, year after year and face a lifetime of rejection and curiosity would break even the strongest'.

Interestingly, in her home, this working mother rules the roost and is very confident running the household, and the lives of everyone in it. It is only when leaving the house that she needs the help of her able-bodied teenage children.

215. Lindstrom, K. A., Hirano, C., McCarthy, C. Y. and Alverson, C. 2014 Just Having a Job: Career Advancement for Low-wage Workers with Intellectual and Developmental Disabilities, *Career Development and Transition for Exceptional Individuals* 37(1): 1–10.

216. Banks, P., Jahoda, A., Dagnan, D., Kemp, J. and Williams, V. 2010 Supported Employment for People with Intellectual Disability: The Effects of Job Breakdown on Psychological Well-Being, *Journal of Applied Research in Intellectual Disabilities* 23(4): 344–354.

217. Reeve, D. 2004 Psycho-emotional Dimensions of Disability and the Social Model, in Barnes, C. and Mercer, G. (eds) *Reeve Chapter 2004*. The Disability Press, Leeds, UK, pp. 83–100.

218. Morris, J. 1991 *Pride Against Prejudice Transforming Attitudes to Disability*, The Women's Press, Aylesbury, UK, pp. 21, 22.

As she explains, often being with her children helps her 'pass' as a normal mum who is just sitting at a restaurant table or sitting in the driver's seat waiting for them in the car. For her, this is preferential to wheeling herself down a public street to passers-by who stare or offer 'help' when none is needed but react badly when she rejects their offers. She called this 'condescension under the guise of help'.

The campaigner Jenny Morris had a disfiguring accident as a young mother. Like most people with a disability, she spends her days surrounded by able-bodied people who she loves, but also on whom she is reliant. She explains how the world's reactions affect her confidence. She says: 'all these undermining messages become part of the way we sometimes think about ourselves and even other disabled people'. Put this way, why do we expect the disabled to display confidence in exactly the same way as the status quo? The disabled, like anyone else, deserve better definitions of confidence.

Ten

Race and confidence

> *Do what you have to do, to do what you want to do*
> – Denzel Washington

I used to think it was enough to 'not be a racist' and that I could be relatively passive because racism was about hate. Because I have family members and friends I love from different races and backgrounds, I thought that was sufficient. Passive racism, however, is the *not seeing racism* or looking the other way when you do. My daughter (from my husband's first marriage) is mixed race. For me, passive racism would have been trying to straighten her hair for the school she attended and the offices in which she now works. In doing so, I'd accept that being *White* is the de facto identity in many Western settings.

A more progressive stance would have been asking chemists why they didn't stock more selection of products for Black hair or hairdressers why they couldn't style her hair or looking further for those who could. It would have been actively buying from boutique brands set up by Black women that cater to this market. Regrettably, I got to this second approach, and found products she now loves, but only after 15 years of raising her.

Racism is hard to talk about, which is why we don't. You may feel uncomfortable right now. I know, because as a White woman raising these issues, so do I. But I also know that if we don't talk about it, nothing will change. We aren't merely talking about whether we are promoting women or ethnic minorities fast enough. We aren't merely talking about why certain groups may superficially have less confidence.

We are talking about centuries-old systems and how they favour certain groups of people, White people like me. However, we too often ignore racism and its implications. When recruiting, we reassure ourselves we're doing nothing wrong; our industry simply doesn't get many 'diverse' applicants.

However, we should be asking 'And why is that? What is it about our culture that is so unfriendly to them? How should we change to make it more appealing?' We rarely ask the most important question of all, 'How can I use my power, however limited it feels at times, to help fuel that change?' That is a confident approach because it works *with* the discomfort, rather than pretend it's not there.

To redesign social systems, we must initially acknowledge the impact they have. Avoiding these topics and arguing over who is more privileged than who is both a distraction and a strategic political tool used by the status quo. Each individual has differing amounts of privilege, affected by the intersectionality of our identities. I'm a woman, yes, so have particular challenges with getting ahead in workplaces designed by men – for men.

However, I'm also straight, able-bodied, White and American – I've held jobs in five different countries, but in each English was the main language. All of these have privilege. Much career progression focuses on aiming for a position of dominance while *denying* that systems of dominance exist. It's the old 'Anyone can get ahead if they put their mind to it!' While technically true, the status quo are simply more likely to be able to 'get ahead'. We *maintain* the myth of meritocracy by being oblivious to the unearned advantages of certain groups.

For example, some heterosexual clients of mine only *noticed* 'gay jokes' after their sister came out to them. Fathers were quicker to see gender bias after their daughters were asked *if* they'd return to work after their maternity leave. Similarly, as a White woman, I was slow to see racism until my own daughter was punished at school for being 'troublesome' in a way her White peers weren't.

Perhaps I first noticed the invisibility of race when I wrote my second book, about the rise of female breadwinners. Much of the data spoke of *women* flooding the job market, during both World Wars but also in the 1970s when women were graduating university in previously unseen numbers.

However, the truth is that women of colour have long been the primary earners for their families. They've historically worked for pay because the systems that benefit White heterosexual women, whose husbands often earned enough to keep their wives out of the workplace, don't apply to *all* women equally.

Racism creates disadvantages for people of colour that make success harder to achieve, but as we'll see all the more vital. However, racism goes further than that. It gives advantages to White people that makes success easier to achieve. It's hard to see those advantages, much less own up to them.

White allies shouldn't take on the role of saviour or fixer. Instead, allies should talk with other people who have had unearned advantages and discuss the many benefits *they've both had* as a direct result of someone else *not* having those benefits. This is hard, because admitting status quo systems around race, gender, and disability to name just three, have played a part in our success means acknowledging *meritocracy doesn't work equally well* for everyone.

My specialism of working with women in male-dominated fields means most of my clients have had the experience of being the 'only' in the room. They might be the only Asian woman, the only Black woman – often the only woman of any description. People who have been unique in a meeting room have been called everything from 'tokens' to 'numerical minorities' or, my least favourite, yet initially used by some clients, 'diversity hires'. These women don't feel the comfort status quo members feel when surrounded by people who, at least superficially, look like them.

In corporate settings, the screw is tightened for female 'onlys' on virtually every measure. Being an 'only' in meetings is twice as common for senior-level women (35%) and women in technical roles (34%). Research shows that 'onlys' are more likely to be on the receiving end of microaggressions (80%). Compared to other working women, they are more likely to feel routinely scrutinised, held to higher standards and excluded. They also are the least likely to talk about their personal lives with colleagues.[219]

Certainly, even in corporate settings, occasionally men will also find themselves in meetings as the only man. However, when we compare women and men 'onlys', it's a very different picture. Compared to male onlys, female onlys are more than twice as likely to feel they have to prove their competence beyond peers (51% vs 20%). They are more likely to say they've been addressed in a non-professional way (35% vs 19%). Also familiar to many of the women I've worked with, female onlys are also nearly three times as likely to have been mistaken for a junior hire (35% vs 12%).

When the researchers dug deeper to understand what it *felt* like to be an only, there again was a stark difference. The two most common responses for women (out of the list given to both genders) was 'under pressure to perform' (38%) and 'on guard' (31%). This is a stark difference compared to the most common feeling selected by 'male onlys', which was 'included' (26%). Notably, only 7% of men felt that their actions in those rooms 'reflected on people like you' (7%). Only 8% felt their actions were 'closely watched' compared to nearly three times as many women who felt that they were considered 'a representative of their group' or 'closely watched' (22%).

---

219. Krivkovich, A. et al. McKinsey & Co. & LeanIn.Org, 2018 Women in the Workplace study.

Before we go any further, let's acknowledge the disingenuousness in saying you 'don't see race or ethnicity' or indeed other protected characteristics. Saying you 'don't see race' is mostly said by people who unconsciously enjoy the benefits of being part of a majority.

It also suggests they're willing to *overlook* the 'onlys' difference. This, however, is dependent on if they too can swallow the bitter pill of acting like one happy equal family – when the evidence is to the contrary. Saying you 'don't see' a demographic trait also suggests you're *unwilling to accommodate someone's difference* to understand how they may experience the world differently. Let's be clear, these thought processes are often unconscious, but all underlay the meaning when people say they 'don't see' the difference for a category of people.

For the purposes of this section, I've drawn upon research about various groups of people of colour, and where available, I have labelled where and which groups were part of any research I cite. I know they *do not all experience* the world the same way. There is more difference amongst these groups, and certainly the individuals within, than similarity. However, what they do share is that if working in Western workplaces, it is the White status quo who determine what counts as confidence and competence. That overlaps with the non-status quo person's comfort in how they portray themselves. Business says they want everyone to be authentic, but as we're seeing, that's easier for some than for others.

Understanding how authenticity affects 'engagement', that magic elixir of most organisations, is important to grasp because it directly affects how optimistic and confident you feel about your career prospects. Accepting that, it is then worrying that in the US more than 35% of African Americans and Hispanics, as well as 45% of Asians, say they 'need to compromise their authenticity' to conform to their company's standards of demeanour or style.

Furthermore, roughly a third of people of colour surveyed felt 'a person of colour would *never get a top position* at my company'.[220] These prognoses are dismal yet borne out by how quickly Black or Brown people actually earn top jobs. That means that the survey result is based on reality. When looking at the statistics of who holds those roles, how confident do we expect people to be?

Even when they are confident, how well do others react to that confidence? Demonstrating confidence is too often deemed being *angry, aggressive or uppity* often when pushing for better treatment. They'll be told they need '*to know their place*' or be patient for change and *grateful* for the opportunities they now have.

220. Centre for Talent Innovation 2012 Vaulting the Color Bar: How Sponsorship Levers Multicultural Professional into Leadership report.

As we'll see, this is the workplace in which many people from BAME backgrounds across Western workplaces find themselves. Even the supposed 'positive' of 'sassy' or fierce' labels have rather patronising tone when used by the status quo to describe someone of colour. However, *given the lack of respect* to which we attribute these words, it's easy to see how a logical extension is harassment.

This is where the effects of terminology become all the more stark, but relevant. Harassment diminishes confidence in even the most competent of professionals. However, it's important to recognise workplace harassment isn't spread evenly through the workplace or society at large. Harassment is usually reserved for those who have the *fewest advocates* amongst the status quo.

Perhaps, then, it is not surprising that nearly three out of ten BAME employees in the UK (28%) have directly experienced or witnessed racial harassment or bullying *from their manager* in the last five years. This is compared to less than one in five (17%) White employees.[221] Worse, these numbers are on the rise, particularly since the Brexit referendum.[222]

Certainly, by 2018, the number of recorded hate crimes in England and Wales more than doubled to over 94,000.[223] So why look at racist *crimes* when talking about workplace behaviours? These attitudes spill over into the workplace. Trades Union Congress research which found over a third of BAME *employees* experienced racism in the first six months *after the Brexit vote* in 2016.[224]

Discussing race in the workplace is important to address as it's where people engage with the widest section of people *outside* of their close network. Beliefs held by colleagues don't just affect progression, but also affect confidence in the non-status group in *even believing* progression is possible. People from a Black background reported the highest increase in discrimination,[225] within that same research, with minority ethnic women reporting the most dramatic increases in experiencing discrimination.

Business in the Community found even *before* the Brexit vote, 69% of Black women experienced bullying or harassment at work in the previous three years, compared to 52% of women overall.[226]

221. Business in the Community 2015 Race at Work report.
222. Business in the Community Race at Work Scorecard Report 2018: The MacGregor-Smith Review one year on.
223. Home Office, Statistical Bulletin, Hate Crimes 2017/2018 – England and Wales.
224. TUC Poll: 17 March 2017 Racism at Work since Brexit.
225. Booth, R. 2019 Racism Rising since Brexit Vote, *The Guardian*, 20 May.
226. Business in the Community, 2014 Opportunity Now: Project, pp. 28 – 40, 1 April.

Looking more specifically at the *types* of racial discrimination faced, over half of BAME individuals (55%) had experienced a racist comment said 'in jest'.[227] But we know 'jest' covers a multitude of assumptions about what's funny – and what isn't, depending on both the audience and the object of the 'joke'.

BEING 'BOTHERED'

Jenny Garrett carried out unique research into the overlap between confidence and race. Interestingly, Garrett, who is an executive coach who speaks on these topics, surveyed 400 UK professionals from a range of backgrounds. Garrett found BAME men the most 'bothered' by their confidence levels (59%) compared to *any other demographic group*. This rate was particularly noticeable when compared to the number of White men who said the same (38%).[228]

Garrett, who is a Black British woman, explained BAME men don't always know how to demonstrate confidence in a way that isn't interpreted as *threatening* to White people. She explains:

> *Black men are more likely to be misinterpreted as scary or aggressive. The same behaviours would be seen as 'assertive' in others. Similarly, assertiveness is not a characteristic we particularly associate with Asian men, so again, the challenge is in navigating what acceptable confidence looks like.*

Looking at intersectionality and the role of gender, BAME men may be dissatisfied with how many *more* benefits White men enjoy as part of a patriarchal system. Instead, BAME men may be expected to accept the reality of low rates of career progression and all its knock-on effects – like women of all backgrounds have come to expect. Understandably it doesn't sit well and can affect confidence.

They have every right to be angry. BAME men, irrespective of ambition or levels of education, are more likely to be excluded from higher-wage industries and earn less than their White male counterparts. In the US, 87% of industries are still racially segregated. Indeed, in the US, every $10,000 increase in the average annual wage of an occupation is associated with a 7% *decrease* in the proportion of Black men in that field.[229]

227. Booth, R. 2019 Racism Rising since Brexit Vote, *The Guardian*, 20 May.
228. Garrett, J. 2019 The Destination or a Journey? www.jennygarrettglobal.com
229. Hamilton, D., Austin, A. and Darity, W. 2011 *Whiter Jobs, Higher Wages: Occupational Segregation and the lower wages of Black Men*, Economic Policy Institute. Washington, DC

While that research is American, things are no better in the UK where Black people are more likely to be unemployed, especially during recessions. Even when removing the 'economically inactive' including students, in the last recession the unemployment rate of young Black people ran at 50%. This is compared to the rate of 20% amongst Whites people of the same age.[230]

As the authors of the study note: 'There is greater ethnic inequality in Britain than in the US for both sexes – if you are Black, you are more likely to be without work in the UK.' To that end, it's not perhaps not surprising if satisfaction with career progression and being concerned about your confidence levels are notable amongst Black men in particular.

By contrast, in Garrett's research BAME women weren't as 'bothered' about their confidence levels. It may be that Black women expected, like most women *of any race*, to play supportive roles or are indeed pleased with the gains they have made *as individuals*. These perspectives may mean it's slightly easier for women of colour to navigate organisations. When discussing the relationship between confidence and success, Jenny Garrett reflects:

> *How you define success depends on where you are coming from. If you are the first person in your family to go to university, travel for work, pay your mortgage, have a nice car – things your family dreamt of, that's a huge success.*

Garrett continues:

> *For me, my first visions of success were buying my mother a washing machine and a fur coat. Even by that standard, I've well surpassed it. It depends on your initial expectations. If you are from a majority group, you'd expect a good job, the house, the car to come more easily. But if you are from a minority group, the way I am, your version of success is simply different.*

This outlook explains much about confidence, but also how vital it is to understand *context* before making judgements about who and how people demonstrate it. This only happens, however, if BAME women maintain 'backstage' roles or remain 'grateful for what they have', which shouldn't disproportionately be a goal for any group. It's likely being a support act just isn't a role men from *any* background readily accept, something I certainly saw when writing *Female Breadwinners,* about women who are the main earners in heterosexual families.

---

230. Institute for Public Policy Research 2010 Recession Leaves Almost Half Young Black People Unemployed.

However, status distance, as we discussed earlier has real implications for Black women in particular. American research found when individuals are shown photos, Black women's faces were *the least likely* to be recognised by White people of either gender. Furthermore, in team exercises that mixed people from different races together, the verbal contributions of Black women were the most likely to be *incorrectly attributed to other people*, both by White people, but also by Black men.[231]

This sobering finding reminds me of a work dinner I had in Beijing with Scottish colleagues several years ago. We were hosted by our guide; a young Chinese woman. At the table, one of my young White male colleagues in his twenties asked her to look around the table and guess everyone's age. He thought it would be 'fun' though many groaned and tried to dissuade him from the idea.

Expectantly, he looked at her to 'start the game' but her reply was swift: 'I couldn't do that, all you White people look the same to me.' I burst out laughing at her response and how dumbfounded he looked. It's a stark reminder of how limited interactions with a group of people means you tend to see them as an undifferentiated group. This limits us all and his hubris was called out beautifully.

Reflecting the double bind of gender and race further, American Black women in leadership positions are also the most likely to be criticised or punished when making mistakes on the job.[232] Again, this highlights how difficult it might be for those who look so different from our stereotypical image of leadership to remain optimistic and confident.

However, remain optimistic they do. When 2,000 American women were surveyed, researchers found African American women were *far more confident* than women from other backgrounds. Nearly half (44%) described themselves as 'successful' compared to 30% of White women and 21% of Hispanic women.[233] That's consistent with other studies highlighting how African American high school students are also more confident than any other demographic group at that age.[234]

231. Sesko A. and Biernat, M. 2010 Prototypes of Race and Gender: The Invisibility of Black Women, *Journal of Experimental Social Psychology* 46(2): 356–360.

232. Rosette, A. S. and Livingston, R. 2012 Failure is Not an Option for Black Women: Effects of Organisational Performance on Leaders with Single vs Dual Subordinate Identities, *Journal of Experimental Social Psychology* 48(5): 1162–1167.

233. Dreisbach, S. 2017 Black Women are More Confident than Other Groups: Survey, *Glamour*, 1 August, https://www.glamour.com/story/black-women-more-confident-other-groups-females-survey

234. Bachmand, J. et al. 2011 Adolescent Self-Esteem: Differences by Race/Ethnicity, Gender and Age, *Self Identity* 10(4): 445–473.

CODE-SWITCHING

The writer Maura Cheeks who interviewed senior Black women in the US for an article in *Harvard Business Review* noted her interviewees claimed part of their success was due to *code-switching*. Code-switching involves modifying your language usage and references to reflect the dominant culture then switching back to a more authentic way of speaking when around friends and family.[235] For those she interviewed, while adaptive, it was taxing and a mental strain, something experienced by other non-status quo groups.

This linguistic tightrope, while a professional necessity for many, forces employees to decide on a daily basis how 'authentic' they want to be. To this point, in *Slay in Your Lane*, Elizabeth Uviebinené admits that in order to secure an interview at a financial services firm, she removed the word 'Black' on her cv from an award she'd received earlier in her career; 'Google Top *Black* Talent'.

These issues around juggling for success also came up when interviewing Carol Stewart. Stewart is a British-born executive coach of Afro-Caribbean descent who told me a story about a Black coaching client, Jeanette. Jeanette felt overlooked because of the racism in White men who led her organisation, and by one man in particular who harshly criticised her in a recent meeting. To Stewart's eyes, whether Jeanette's assessment of racism was accurate or not, her assumption would likely become a barrier for Jeanette. To succeed, Jeanette would *have* to create positive relationships with members of the status quo.

Relatedly, while only half of White women are likely to socialise with their managers outside of work (48%), only a third of women of colour do (35%) highlighting the gap in familiarity.[236] However, this too has implications for confidence as support from a manager impacts both promotions and a desire to stay with the company. Stewart explains:

> *I asked Jeanette how she would have interpreted his criticism if it had come from someone of her same race. This was a lightbulb for her as she admitted she'd be much more willing to take what he'd said on Board.*

235. Cheeks, M. 2018 How Black Women Describe Negotiating Race and Gender in the Workplace, *Harvard Business Review*.
236. Krivkovich, A. et al. McKinsey & Co. & LeanIn.Org, 2018 Women in the Workplace study.

We need broader conversations about differences in the workplace and how *power* affects these relationships. However, Stewart was only able to move her client on by asking Jeanette to find the grain of truth in his criticism. A coach can only ever work with who they have in that session. Jeanette's colleague may have been racist. However, Stewart could only make progress if she focused on Jeanette's *responses to that colleague.*

This allowed Stewart to dig deeper on how those self-limiting beliefs were affecting Jeanette, which she does with many of her clients.

Stewart continues:

> *So instead of focusing on the incident with this one guy, we spent our time talking about incidents where she had been supported by other White men. This was profound for her, as she was in danger of writing off a group of people entirely. This shift allowed two things: first, she could now see them as individuals. Second, it gave her evidence that she did have advocates even amongst this group. She focused her time on building better relationships with those advocates and spent less mental energy on lamenting how badly this one guy had treated her.*

Stewart smiles: 'I'm a big fan of picking your battles.' This approach is no doubt helpful to her clients. Working *around* bosses, in an assertive but not threatening way, is a challenge for most non-status quo members.

Unfortunately, this approach still means it's up to the person in the minority position to change *their* behaviour for the realities of a racist system. It's undoubtedly adaptive but could be seen as a much larger piece of *behavioural* code-switching, careful not to make the *offender* uncomfortable.

When your skills are challenged by others, ask:

- **What *specific examples* can they give me as to where I'm going wrong?**
- **Can this person accurately judge my skills *in this area*?**
- **What is their criticism *trying to prove* or even trying to hide?**
- **How would I hear the feedback if it came from *someone else*?**

ABUNDANT ASPIRATION AND AMBITION

We must be clear, ambition and confidence to aspire for more is *not the issue* for people from BAME backgrounds. In fact, university enrolments from White students is declining, while we are seeing double-digit gains in the proportion of successful applications from BAME students.[237] This inconvenient fact creates much hand-wringing amidst those more concerned about White male underperformance. What then is ignored is how after they've started, Black university students are 50% more likely to drop out than their White and Asian counterparts.

Specifically, more than 10% of Black university students drop out in England, due to a range of factors from financial to inclusion. This is compared to 7% of the whole population of university students.[238] This may seem a relatively small difference to some. However, it's significant for the individuals themselves as well as the growth industries they are leaving. To this point, Black girls are the only ethnic group that *outnumber* their male peers in studying for STEM A-levels.[239]

Additionally, female students from mixed ethnicity and Black Caribbean origin are more likely to study STEM A-levels than White female students.[240] Given the workforce we need, these subjects have the *most opportunity* for growth and high earnings. However, this isn't translating into wins for BAME graduates.[241]

Even so, experiencing systemic racism doesn't get in the way of ambition or *how important* progress is to people. In a study of nearly 1,300 employees across the UK, more than twice as many BAME employees (25%) said 'career progression was an important part of their working life' compared to those from White backgrounds (10%).[242] Ambition and wanting 'to get on' certainly categorise the life of Sasha Mooney. As a Black British Barrister at Law, she holds a senior position in the criminal justice system.

237. Bulman, M. 2018 Number of White People Accepted at University Drops Despite Overall Rise in UK Students, *The Independent*, 11 January.
238. Social Market Foundation 2017 SMF and the UPP Foundation to Investigate Continuation Rates in Higher Education in London.
239. Shaw, B. et al. 2016 Social Mobility Commission: Ethnicity, Gender and Social Mobility, 28 December.
240. Codiroli, N. 2015 Inequalities in Students' Choice of STEM Subjects, Working Paper 2015/2016, Centre for Longitudinal Studies, UCL Institute of Education, September.
241. Acas.org.uk. 2013 'Minority Ethnic Women Face Compounded Workplace Discrimination', Acas Workplace Snippet, January.
242. Acas.org.uk 2013 Minority Ethnic Women Face Compounded Workplace Discrimination, Acas Workplace Snippet, January.

Only 3% of leaders in the criminal justice system come from BAME backgrounds, compared to 7% of senior leaders in FTSE100 companies and 7% of leaders in public services.[243] While the law may be a particularly poor representation of BAME leaders, it is not unusual.

Business in the Community found only 6% of top management positions in virtually *any sector* are held by ethnic minorities.[244] The low numbers of BAME leaders is particularly shocking given 14% of the working-age population in the UK described themselves as BAME in a 2016 review.[245] This is estimated to rise to 21% by 2051.[246] Despite the rapidly changing face of the UK workforce, 35% of Pakistani, 33% of Indian and 29% of Black Caribbean employees feel they've been overlooked for promotion *because* of their ethnicity.[247]

This low representation of BAME professionals *in the law* is particularly problematic, partially because BAME people are much more likely to be jailed than their White counterparts.[248] In London, despite 40% of the population being from ethnic minority backgrounds, they make up only 23% of magistrates, the same lay people affecting legal decisions.[249]

Worrying, the legal industry doesn't seem to think racial underrepresentation is an issue. When asked to comment on the lack of ethnic minorities amongst magistrates, the Magistrates' Association told *The Guardian*:

> *We take the view that the bench [does not need to be]*
> *representative of society. Justice is blind, after all. [But] we*
> *do want to see a bench that ... engenders confidence in it.*
> *One under-represented group is age rather than ethnicity...*
> *We want employers to be flexible enough so their staff can*
> *contribute to the administration of justice.[250]*

While a lack of *young* magistrates may be their perceived problem, it is partially explained by the fact these roles are voluntary. They draw people who can give their time without compensation – not a reality for most millennials. It may be an issue of money, but it may also be a reticence for people to give time freely to legal institutions that disproportionately disadvantage them.

---

243. Green Park 2017 Public Service Leadership 5000 Report.
244. Business in the Community 2015 Race at Work.
245. Office for National Statistics 2016 Annual Population Survey.
246. Wohland, P., et al. 2010 Ethnic Population Projections for the UK and Local Areas, 2001–2051, p. 140.
247. Business in the Community 2014 Benchmarking 2014 Analysis and Top Ten Analysis.
248. The Lammy Review 2016 An Independent Review into the Treatment of, and Outcomes for, Black, Asian and Minority Ethnic Individuals in the Criminal Justice System.
249. Office for National Statistics 2011 Ethnicity and National Identity in England and Wales.
250. Bowcott, O. 2017 Why We Need More Black and Minority Ethnic Magistrates, *The Guardian*, 4 July.

Similarly, if justice is as blind as the Magistrates Association purports it to be, why should age matter at all? What is interesting is that even the Magistrates Association in their official statement above mentions 'confidence'. They recognise people need to have confidence or *trust* as seems to be defined here, in the system. Yet their lack of willingness to look at how trust is fostered in different groups seems perplexing.

This lack of confidence or trust in the system extends far beyond the legal sector, and for good reason. Nearly half of UK based BAME employees also felt their career progression so far hasn't met their expectations (40%). This was highest for Black people in particular (44%), compared to less than a third of Whites (30%) who felt the same.[251]

This finding echoes Jenny Garrett's comment that if you assume you're entitled to career progression, then you can prioritise *other* issues such as work-life balance. Work-life balance by contrast was the most important priority of White people (66%) in that survey. Comparatively, people from BAME backgrounds rated pay and benefits as their *top* priority (63%).

Racial inequality can seem like one of the trickiest workplace topics to tackle. As I talked through these sensitive topics, I was reminded of the advice from Neil Stevenson on how he tackled difficult issues. It's worth taking on board when planning ways to handle potentially controversial equality issues. He advises:

> *If you want to take on a more controversial issue, bring in someone from another organisation who has already tackled that same issue as a case study. They aren't there to tell your audience why this is necessary for your organisation, but only to share why they thought it was a topic worth addressing at their organisation, how they handled it, and the results. This can distance you from overtly proclaiming: 'This is an issue we need to address here!' as it's merely a case study. If it's accepted, you'll still likely get the credit. If it isn't, you can say 'we wanted to look at many different ways to solve this. We need to understand the range of options and what's worked for others'.*

Even that approach is useful as it highlights publicly what leaders *aren't* willing to do. As I find with my own clients, understanding that gets you closer to the stretches they *will* take.

251. CIPD: Addressing the Barriers to BAME Employee Progression, December 2019.

GREAT OR GRATEFUL

Shoku Amirani is a British-Iranian radio producer for the BBC and has worked for nearly 20 years in media. She is also the Chair of BBC Embrace, the internal staff network for ethnic minorities. It's a position which also brings her into contact with a broad range of external diversity experts and BAME networks and forums in the public and private sector.

Amirani's remit as the Chair gives her a fuller perspective on the overlap between majority group status and confidence. As we talk, she highlights how confidence is a natural state for majority group members – those who designed much of the modern Western work world. She notices how being part of the ethnic status quo or majority creates a sense of entitlement. Amirani observes:

> *If you are told you can be anything, then it's easy to assume you'll get what you want. It's the feeling of pushing against an open door – probably because fewer doors are closed to you. No one questions your credibility or right to be there.*

The implications for confidence are clear to Amirani who explains:

> *When ethnic minority people are not progressing in their careers, or being overlooked for promotion, no matter how brilliant their contribution, it starts to chip away at their confidence. I find they start to doubt themselves, which unsurprisingly, affects their confidence.*

This is particularly true when we recognise confidence is related to *the number of past successes* from which someone has benefited. These are the 'easy wins' status quo members often take for granted. For many of those in the non-status quo groups I've met, no single 'win' feels particularly easy. However, expecting ethnic minorities to be 'grateful' for their achievements isn't the answer.

Amirani has advised people on interview panels to close the status distance. She says:

> *If you have great people in front of you who are equally qualified, choose the person you'd least likely go on holiday with. This is the person who would not normally be part of your social circle, which, as we know, is usually made up of people who are similar to us! It almost always guarantees more diversity of thought. It also means you have to be okay with any discomfort you may feel. But you'll learn more and won't get the echo chamber that limits leaders' thinking.*

She is feeling more optimistic as she sees changes in working practices being introduced at the BBC. These include a pool of BAME interview champions to ensure diversity on interview panels, and different methods for assessing people's skills and experience for a job.

Comparatively, Silka Patel, the founder of Scotland Women in Technology, said that race wasn't initially something she thought about in her early career. She simply aspired to be a great leader in IT. A native Asian Londoner, Patel says:

> *I was one of those people who'd say that 'I didn't see race' earlier in my career. But I recognise now that I was more junior then and surrounded by people of colour. It was London for goodness sake!*

Her point is apt, given 40% of people living in London are from BAME backgrounds.[252] When asked if the move to Scotland affected her confidence, she reflects and says with a hint of surprise:

> *Well, yes, it must have done. When I first moved up, I suddenly felt much more alone. I'm not sure I would have identified it as a lack of confidence at the time. However, I felt inspired to create the external Scotland Women in Technology group (SWiT) which now has thousands of members.*

Patel reflects:

> *I certainly didn't know many senior Asians working women. But even at our first events, I saw hundreds of women working 'alone' in tech, many of whom happened to be Asian. Before the network, I'd ask the few other women I met where they got their support.*

Patel continued:

> *When I realised, they didn't have much either, that suddenly wasn't acceptable to me. How could there be dozens of networks in London, but nothing here in Scotland? If I think about it, the network was probably born from a need I was trying to fulfil for myself.*

252. Office for National Statistics 2011 Ethnicity and National Identity in England and Wales.

LEANING IN, BUT UNSEEN

This is about who we see and *how* we see them. For example, in the US, there is a tendency to label confident Latinos as 'fiery' and assertive people of Middle Eastern descent as 'radical'. Elizabeth Uviebinené explains how the myth about 'lack of confidence' affects women of colour in particular. She says: 'Black women do lean in and want to be counted. But observers are more likely to view them as "angry".' Uviebinené clarifies in our interview:

> *Not everyone is charismatic, but their work still has great value. People skills are essential, but we overestimate how important confidence is compared to the level of competence we need in today's workplace.*

As explained in her book *Slay in Your Lane*:

> *Half of us are leaning in and being read as aggressive, while the other half are so frightened of that outcome, we don't lean in at all ... Ironically, Black women often have the most to prove but the least means to prove it ... The mental toll of essentially wearing 'White face' to work, suppressing cultural identity and shrinking oneself is inevitable – and things get even more difficult when the subject of race itself is brought up.*[253]

Microaggressions are small acts which, in my experience with clients, often end with someone doubting themselves or if they should take offence at a supposedly 'innocent' slight. Slights, often excused as mistakes or forgetfulness range from being assumed you are the junior person on the team or being left out of crucial correspondence.

However, things can become more hostile. This can range from hearing demeaning remarks about you or people like you, to needing to provide more evidence of your competence and skill than other colleagues. No matter how stark any individual microaggression feels in isolation, the danger is in the *cumulative* effect of facing them every day.

Even when they highlight their competence, people aren't listening and are quicker to question Black women in particular. An American study of senior leaders in corporate settings found that Black women's competence and capabilities are more likely to be challenged and undermined by their White colleagues.[254]

253. Yomi, A. and Uviebinené, E. 2018 *Slay in Your Lane: The Black Girl Lane*, 4th Estate, London, pp. 120–121.
254. Holder, A. M. B. et al. 2015 Racial Microaggression Experiences and Coping Strategies of Black Women in Corporate Leadership, *Qualitative Psychology* 2(2): 164–180.

These experiences aren't unique to corporate settings, as Black female scientists in the UK are also more likely to be asked to 'provide more evidence of competence than others to prove themselves to colleagues'.[255]

To this point, American research found women (38%) are more likely to have had their judgement questioned in their area of expertise than men (29%). Similarly, twice as many women (30%) feel they must continually 'provide more evidence of their competence than others do', when compared to men (14%).[256] Indeed, bisexual women (46%), women with disabilities and (52%) and Black women (40%) feel this pressure most acutely – a rate that is nearly three times as high as White men (14%) who say the same.

The situation is clearly endemic in the US and certainly no better in the UK. A UK survey of over 300 BAME female leaders found that over three-quarters felt the leadership style of White women was more positively perceived in the workplace. A further 80% felt White women's communication styles were better regarded.[257] In the US, Black women were the most likely to 'hear others surprise at their language or other skills' (26%), at a rate nearly three times that of men overall (8%).[258]

Sasha Mooney, a Black British Barrister at Law, also identified with this. From the Midlands, she too felt her minority status most acutely when outside more racially diverse locations. When she travels for work, she's often praised by majority group members for how well she speaks to large groups. She reflects:

> *My shoulders aren't wide enough to have chips on them*
> *for long. They simply haven't seen many people like me,*
> *so have low expectations. I'll normally brush it off with*
> *a pointed joke such as 'Yes, it's amazing what leading*
> *conferences for 2000 people can do for your speaking*
> *skills!' or 'I guess in the 20 years I've spent as an Advocate*
> *has paid off!'*

She admits these slights affect her confidence, but 'if I don't make a sharp comment like that back, they'll ignore the assumptions they made, then they'll just do it again to someone else'.

In addition to her professional accolades, Mooney is also a mother of three. She travels regularly each week for all her responsibilities. While not the most senior of all the people I interviewed, she seemed perhaps one of *the busiest*. As we've already mentioned, I routinely heard from other interviewees how their confidence primarily came from their competence.

---

255. Williams, J. and Phillips, K. W. 2014 *Double Jeopardy? Gender Bias Against Women of Colour in Science*, WorkLife Law UC Hastings College of the Law.
256. Huang, J. et al. McKinsey and Co. and LeanIn.Org, 2019 Women in the Workplace study.
257. Prowess Women in Business: UK Female Entrepreneurship: Key Facts.
258. Huang, J. et al. McKinsey and Co. and LeanIn.Org, 2019 Women in the Workplace study.

This subconsciously overlapped with *needing to prove* competence, not just to themselves but to others who'd otherwise question them. I saw this most particularly with the BAME women I interviewed. As we talk, I raise this potential pressure with Mooney who replies:

> *My parents were pragmatic. I was raised with the*
> *expectation that I'd have to be better than everyone else*
> *just to get an equal chance. I'm not sure I ever thought*
> *about it deeply but needing to prove my competence makes*
> *a lot of sense.*

Her sentiment, as well as what I heard from other BAME women, echoes American research of 13 million employees across 329 organisations. It showed Black women (80%) and Asian women (83%), are *the most ambitious* about getting to the next level. They were more ambitious even compared to those we assume are driven by default – men overall (75%).[259] Certainly, other US-[260] and UK-based[261] research also highlights higher ambition levels from BAME women.

The drive of Black women is notable, particularly for how their *motivation differs* from the status quo. In the US, the motivation to progress for Black women (49%) and lesbian women (48%), in particular, is tied up with being a 'role model for others like me'. This is particularly important when compared to how that specific goal is valued less by men overall (30%).

Despite their ambition, in the US, Latinas and Black women ask for promotions and pay rises *at the same rate* as White women, but with worse results. Dismayingly, they get fewer promotions and less pay for comparable work.[262]

When we talked about motivation with Mooney she confirms: 'It's pointless to wait until I retire to make a dent on the social changes I'd like to see now. Waiting for retirement before I can give my time to great causes, like clearing the path for others like me, would feel like an excuse.' Mooney's husband, a White man, found her frenetic pace somewhat puzzling.

However, as with other women of colour I interviewed, they noted their husbands did not feel the same self-imposed sense of pressure. Mooney laughs: 'Realistically, I probably don't need to do so much, but we're a long way from accepting that "being good is good enough".'

259. Krivkovich, A. et al. McKinsey & Co. & LeanIn.Org 2018 Women in the Workplace study.
260 Centre for Talent Innovation 2015 Black Women: Ready, Willing and More than Able to Lead report.
261 Business in the Community 2015 Race at Work report.
262. Hegewisch, A. and Williams-Baron, E. 2018 The Gender Wage Gap by Occupations 2017 by Race and Ethnicity, Institute for Women's Policy Research.

Her concern is realistic. As a non-status quo member, mistakes are highly visible and difficult to live down. 'Mistakes' also may even hinder the willingness of status quo members to take a risk with *people like you* ever again. Even if you do something well, people see you as the exception.

Paradoxically, it seems while mistakes are seen by all, overall, you're largely invisible, overlooked for promotion and expected to be grateful for what you have.

Relying on resilience

In talking with Uviebinené, I was reminded why the racial stereotypes of 'resilience' could be as essential to resist as those of 'anger', one we more readily see as problematic. The resilience of Black people shouldn't be assumed. Trying 'twice as hard', as many Black people are encouraged to do, would take a toll on anyone. As pointed out in *Slay in Your Lane*, this unfair expectation leaves you 'twice as self-conscious and half as confident in your ability'.[263]

We must challenge myths about the 'resilience' of the non-status quo. It's a convenient excuse we give ourselves for accepting Black people in particular can handle tougher treatment and poorer outcomes. While resilience is a skill for *any* aspiring professional, there is a real danger in assuming BAME people and Black employees in particular can carry this extra burden.

These myths historically served to assuage any White discomfort with the harsh conditions during slavery, Jim Crowe laws in the US, medical experimentation and now mass incarceration. All are stains that have relied far too heavily on the *resilience* of Black people. While we'd like to think these issues are separate from 'confidence', they are interlinked.

As Uviebinené writes in *Slay in Your Lane*:

> *As Black women, we really do know how to get on with things in the face of adversity ... these slights can and do cut deep. Inappropriate and offensive comments matter because they are symptoms of a larger underlying problem in society, and to play it down is to underestimate how these tiny cuts can, over time, develop into larger wounds that make you feel a shadow of your actual self.*[264]

263. Yomi, A. and Uviebinené, E. 2018 *Slay in Your Lane: The Black Girl Bible*, 4th Estate, London, p. 87.
264. Yomi, A. and Uviebinené, E. 2018 *Slay in Your Lane: The Black Girl Bible*, 4th Estate, London, p. 108.

I am reminded of Sasha Mooney's confidence and resilience levels when she shares a personal experience highlighting how much progress still needs to be made. It is important in the context of the story she tells to note that Sasha is British, and of Nigerian descent.

In one criminal case she worked, the defendants were all from a specific region within Uganda. As proceedings got underway, it became clear there was no translator for these men. The judge, uncertain how to proceed, turned to the courtroom and asked: 'Perhaps Mrs Mooney can do the translating for us?' Mooney recalls:

> *I was the only person in the courtroom other than the defendants who were Black, so perhaps it made some sense to him? I ignored him several times, hoping he would realise his mistake because of my silence in the chaos. Eventually, he continued until I had to answer: 'I'm sorry, but in Bristol where I was raised, there was no need for that Ugandan dialect. I've had experience with other parts in the UK though, so if you'd like me to try a Scottish accent, I could give it a go!' Everyone burst out laughing, but I was the only woman or person of colour in the room other than the defendants, so my response was a risk.*

Mooney reflects:

> *Just because I'm Black doesn't mean I can speak every Black language in the world! The judge apologised, but I would have expected better from him. He was a gay man who'd talked about his diversity training and the injustices he'd suffered. His particular Inn frowned upon him being openly gay when he was considered for the very role he now held.*

Mooney continues:

> *The irony was that before this reached a head, there had been an interpreter who left the room. But no one had thought to seek her out because she was an Albino woman! Everyone assumed she was White so wouldn't speak that particular African language. Clearly, there are still issues about race and gender. It's far less overt, though I notice Brexit has emboldened many to voice racist views.*

DIVERSITY WHEN IT SUITS

In some cases, BAME members are brought into settings partially *because* of their non-status background. This too is a tightrope for them to walk, as if they can add *diversity of thought* single-handedly, or are representative of everyone from their specific background. That's an impossible task for anyone.

Mooney is also a non-executive director for an arts foundation. She reflects:

> *I've always been the odd one out on our Board of mostly*
> *upper-class White men. But I was willing to join because*
> *the Chair told me: 'For us to survive, this theatre needs*
> *to attract audiences who look more like you, than me.' His*
> *recognition of the challenge and humility convinced me to*
> *give my time.*

However, the issue of race became even more apparent for Mooney when they then hired a new creative director. He was a Black man, which was a first for them. Mooney explains:

> *He was from London, largely unknown to our Board, but*
> *with a fantastic reputation. But the question I'd hear from*
> *others was: 'Will he be confident enough?' I don't think they*
> *were doubting his confidence in doing the job. I interpreted*
> *it more as a concern as to whether he could stand up to our*
> *main donors – other White men, just like them.*

Mooney's point is an interesting one. People often hide their questionable assumptions under the guise of '*I* think he's great, I'm just worried what *other, less enlightened* people will think.' This excuse provides an acceptable way of expressing their own biased views but veiled in the interest of the public good.

The Creative Director wasn't the first person her arts organisation had hired from an under-represented background. A few years previous, they hired a lesbian woman for a senior role. Different from their usual previous hires; the Board also appointed several other White men in *advisory* roles for that woman. Notably, advisory roles for that role weren't deemed necessary before she started.

Mooney, exasperated, says: 'She spent years trying to get out from under their shadow, while the organisation also got the public kudos of a "diversity hire"'. Before the woman's departure to a larger theatre, she admitted to Mooney her struggles with the Board was in how the men criticised her leadership style. For her, that was particularly difficult as it impacted her confidence. Ironically, during the woman's tenure, the theatre moved towards gender and racially blind casting. The theatre became financially very successful, something that was overlooked when criticising her *style*.

ELEVEN

AGE AND INTROVERSION

An expert in anything was once a beginner
– Helen Hayes

A big part of confidence is knowing that you can get through the travails that life inevitably sends your way. This may rely on how much experience you've had, as well as how comfortable you are in publicising your wins and all that you know. Both factors are affected by age and where you fall on the introversion versus extroversion scale. These are the identity groups we'll delve into within this chapter.

Let's start with age and how it overlaps with confidence. Consider this: compared to yesterday, do you know more, are you more comfortable in your skin, are you more certain in your value? There's an interesting paradox in saying we value experience while simultaneously spending so much time and money on looking younger. In my experience, most older people wouldn't go back in time to 'do it all over again'. They've grown into their skin; learned a lot, experienced some highs and no doubt, some lows.

But there can be a real confidence in ageing. Comparing yourself to others and worrying about what they are saying about you is exhausting. As Shirley MacLaine joked: 'In your 20s you worry about all that people are saying about you, in your forties you stop worrying about what people are saying and in your 60s you realise no one was talking about you in the first place.'

Age can give you a sense of perspective, wisdom and resilience. Speaking to the benefits of a more measured viewpoint, Chamorro-Premuzic, who has written extensively on confidence observes:

> *What would a less confident world look like? People would start each day better prepared' there would be fewer arguments and fewer mistakes. Indeed, many of the major global disasters of the past few decades, which have been attributed to confidence excess, might never have happened. In time, the world would be a more competent place if we could lower people's confidence.*[265]

---
265. Chamorro-Premuzic, T. 2013 *Confidence: The Surprising Truth About How Much You Need and How to Get It*, Profile Books, London, p. 221.

Heightened anxiety and lower confidence may partially explain why women tend to outlive men in every culture. Anxiety and relatedly caution, could be a saving grace. It might be part of the reason women are more likely to arrange visits to the doctor; less likely to drink, smoke, or consume illegal drugs, and less likely to have weight problems.

Clearly, we must address age if we look at how confidence is spread through different populations, and the workplace. In terms of numbers, millennials are now the dominant group in the workforce, and now represent 50% of workers, and 75% by 2025.[266]

TEMPERING YOUTHFUL HUBRIS

Superficially, modern millennials seem to have it made when it comes to confidence. As we dig deeper, however, we see the wider picture, and *how it affects confidence,* isn't any better for them. Starting at the basics; millennials are now are the most confident generation since records began.[267] For example, in 1980, just 12% of 20-year-olds agreed with the statement 'I am really special'. Incredibly, by 2010 80% of 20-year-olds claimed the same thing.[268]

The research of Jean Twenge, who writes extensively on this topic, highlighted an even steeper increase in narcissism between the 1980s and mid-2000s. Importantly, we find these effects even when studies control for the influence of age on generational or cohort effects. In other words, it is not only true that young people are more narcissistic than adults. Modern millennials are more narcissistic *than all previous generations were at the same age.*

In fact, representative studies of US universities estimate that up to 15% of students in their 20s now meet the criteria for narcissistic personality disorder or display pronounced narcissistic traits.[269] This will have a considerable impact on the workplace, as millennials become the dominant workers. This trend will make self-awareness, especially of one's limitations and impact on others, all the more critical, but more challenging than ever.[270]

My question is not *why* they are more narcissistic, but what are the implications for the workplace, and relationships in general? What does it mean that the dominant generation of our time sees itself as individually extraordinary and destined for unique greatness? What does our collective future look like?

266. PWC report 2012 Millennials at Work: Reshaping the Future.
267. Twenge, J. 2014 *Generation Me: Why Today's Young Americans are More Confident, Assertive and Entitled – and More Miserable than Ever Before*, Atria Books, New York.
268. Twenge, J. M. and Foster, J. D. 2010 Birth Cohort Increases in Narcissistic Personality Traits Among American College Students, 1982–2009, *Social Psychological and Personality Science* 1(1): 99–106.
269. Waugaman, R. M. 2011 The Narcissism Epidemic, by J. W. Twenge and W. K. Campbell (review) *Psychiatry Interpersonality Biological Processes*, 74(2): 166–169.
270. Chamorro-Premuzic, T. 2017 *The Talent Delusion*, Piatkus, London, p. 173.

It's a future that needs international co-operation on huge issues ranging from global warming, managing global pandemics to the usage of artificial intelligence. Positively younger millennials arguably have the most to gain from common solutions. However, the challenge is that narcissists are not known for compromise.

Given its prevalence, some leading psychiatrists are making a case for *reconceptualising* narcissism. It could soon be labelled a standard *trait* rather than a psychiatric disorder. Narcissism is *no longer rare enough* to be classified as a mental disorder – something affecting just a fraction of people.[271]

Several interviewees also predict newer definitions of confidence, informed by their work with millennials. As the founder of WeAreTheCity, Vanessa Vallely, OBE, runs dozens of training and networking events for working women across London. She observes:

> *I don't think younger women lack confidence. It's the most*
> *confident generation I've seen. Twenty years ago, you*
> *didn't see conversations about people's earnings – that last*
> *taboo. Now, our attendees are talking about their earnings*
> *to share information. In my experience, lacking confidence*
> *is far more of a problem for those returning from maternity*
> *leave or for whom English is not their first language. They*
> *still have to compete with native speakers as they progress,*
> *but overall confidence isn't the same issue for younger*
> *people it once was.*

Vallely's comments remind me how the rise in narcissism, and the confidence that comes with it, is something to which most of my clients have to adapt as they work with younger people. For example, because of my work with senior teams, most clients are usually just a bit older than millennials. They are having to adapt to ongoing requests for feedback from their younger colleagues.

They also complain about when the next promotion cycle is, even after just a few months on the job or indeed right after a recent promotion. A senior friend in Human Resources once exasperatedly told me: 'They want constant praise and are keen for new challenges – but it's maddening if they aren't yet doing the job they were hired for very well!'

All of this might suggest that millennials are the real winners when it comes to status quo definitions of confidence. However, I've put them with our non-status quo group for two main reasons. The first is despite their confidence, comparatively, they aren't that happy or healthy. The Health Foundation's research on 22–26-year-olds highlighted the impact of the stressful conditions young people are living through compared to earlier generations.

---

271. Reynolds, E. K. and Lajuez, C. W. Narcissism in the DSM, in *Handbook of Narcissism and Narcissistic Personality Disorder: Theoretical Approaches, Empirical Findings and Treatments*. John Wiley & Sons Press, Hoboken, N.J.

This includes an increasingly globalised and competitive labour market, rising housing and higher education costs paired with climate change and self-identity issues, often driven by widespread usage of social media. These are issues, we as the older generation, created for them. The report's authors say: 'The gains made as a society in improving the health of previous generations may well be eroded by the precariousness and instability of the lives that some young people are facing.'[272]

Millennials are also the most likely to experience chronic loneliness,[273] and 70% of American millennials say depression has impacted their productivity at work.[274] All of which, not surprisingly, is part of why the Health Foundation puts millennials on track to be *less healthy* than their parents were by middle age.

The second reason I don't believe millennials are the clearest cut winners in our redefinition, is because of their relative lack of the experience and competencies necessary to create a *robust* sense of confidence. Millennials often seem confident simply because they've *not yet had* the professional knocks we all eventually face. Not having failures *yet* is very different from *never* having them. Indeed, when they face inevitable knocks, they potentially will be the least prepared compared to previous generations. Therefore, expanding our version of confidence could also benefit millennials.

To this point, Jenny Garrett's research looked at confidence as disaggregated by age, ethnic background and gender. She also found the stereotype of the uber-confident millennial was more nuanced than we'd like to believe. In fact, when comparing age groups those under 24 were the most 'bothered' by their confidence levels (73%) and most likely to think *those around them were more confident* (85%) than any other age group.[275]

This suggests young millennials may assume they *should* be confident, rendering them the most likely to notice any 'confidence deficiencies' *when it's missing*. This happens particularly when they compare themselves with their peers; easier than ever in the hyperlinked world.

272. The Health Foundation, June 2018 Listening to our Future: Early Findings from the Young People's Future Health Enquiry.
273. Office of National Statistics 2016/17 Loneliness – What Characteristics and Circumstances Are Associated with Feeling Lonely? Analysis of Characteristics and Circumstances Associated with Loneliness in England Using the Community Life Survey.
274. McCreary, M. 2017 *Depression and Work: The Impact of Depression on Different Generation of Employees*. Morneau Sheppell Press
275. Garrett, J. 2019 Confidence: the Destination or a Journey? www.jennygarrettglobal.com.

School of hard knocks

Promoting people more on their confidence than their proven competence is a real risk for most teams. As we've seen this risk could grow as millennials take over the workforce. We could create leaders *compelling* enough to lead, but who are not skilled, humble or experienced enough to be worthy of following.

This is a real danger as research shows it is managers, millennials and men who are most likely to be narcissistic. They are prone to not just overestimating their intelligence, but also their creativity and leadership potential.[276] Luckily, many will likely lose this overconfident edge as they mature and experience a few setbacks. Career hurdles sound harsh, but they're often incredibly useful. They add to competence. People working through hurdles become better at their job.

Undoubtedly, age and experience often combine to create a real competence that is hugely valuable. PWC surveyed 6000 European professionals, looking for what they called 'strategist leaders'. These were the people who could best oversee transformational change.[277] Strategist leaders were unique in that they individually had a broader range of experience of different settings, used positive language and showed humility. These skills they often earned from earlier disappointments or failure.

That all gave them greater resilience when things went pear-shaped, as they inevitably can do. The demographic group with the most strategist leaders? Women over 55. However, this winning demographic is problematic for businesses. Women over 55 are rare as hens' teeth in most corporate organisations – particularly in the fields that need them the most. We face a massive drain if we don't address how confidence intersects with age.

As an entrepreneur and Chair of Women's Enterprise Scotland, Lynne Cadenhead identified with this point. Her most notable confidence dip came after one of her businesses failed – a new experience for her at the time. She remembers: 'After that happened, I was so demoralised I just withdrew and didn't work for six months.' During this low point, Cadenhead spent time with family and friends and invested in all the other parts of her identity aside from 'successful businesswoman'.

This reconnection with other aspects of identity is particularly important for entrepreneurs. Entrepreneurs often over-identify with their work, sometimes to the cost of other parts of their lives. It leads to a crisis of confidence if the business is the only thing in which they believe they are competent.

---

276. Grijalva, E. and Zhang, L. 2016 Narcissism and Self-insight: A Review and Meta-analysis of Narcissists' Self-enhancement Tendencies, *Personal Sociological Psychology Bulletin* 42(1): 3–24.
277. Leitch, J., Rooke, D., and Wilson, R. 2015 Hidden Talent: 10 Ways to Identify and Retain Transformational Leaders, PWC & Harthill Consulting report.

It becomes part of how they define themselves, which is a considerable risk given how frequently new businesses fail. So how did Cadenhead get out of the slump in her confidence? She remembers:

> *I had over-identified myself with my business. I eventually*
> *gave myself a good kicking and wrote out what I wanted to*
> *achieve in the next ten years, and that was a turning point.*
> *I could again visualise my future. I wanted to give back. I*
> *wrote that I'd like to join four Boards: a government body,*
> *a university, a women's organisation and a major charity. I*
> *thought these were a great way to get back out there.*

Cadenhead's competence was quickly recognised by those with whom she reconnected. She was quickly invited to join Boards of all four types of organisations within just six weeks, a feat she'd expected to take years. Her expertise was highly valued, despite the 'failure' she'd been focusing on for too long.

For Cadenhead, the time to reflect and even 'wallow' for a few months was vital. As she reassures me: 'You are allowed to reflect and think about what you should have done, just don't let it define you. You need to get back out there.' It's why giving yourself the ability to fail, learn, talk about it and get up again contributes to the way she defines confidence.

Conversely, not all millennials identify with the confidence research tells us they supposidly have. Naomi Pryde rejects identifying with the millennial label event though she is right in the middle of that generation. While relatively young for her success, confidence is not a label with which she identifies.

She remarks: 'In a crowded meeting, because of my age and perhaps my gender, I'm often ignored by younger people, many of whom have lawyers in the family.' She tells a story of a young trainee who alternatively interrupted conversations Pryde was having with others or physically pushed past her to rub shoulders with 'important people'. Pryde remembers:

> *Her whole body changed when my colleague said 'Have*
> *you met Naomi? She's our new Head of Litigation'. At that*
> *moment she looked horrified, but then quickly composed*
> *herself as I was the person heading up a department she*
> *wanted to try. That turns me cold as I can't stand bad*
> *manners, it feels mercenary.*

While initially annoying, these instances can be validating for Pryde. They're a reminder her accomplishments are the result of her labour, rather than well-connected parents.

Interestingly, for Pryde, she feels her self-doubt is getting worse with age, not better. She says: 'It used to be easy to tell myself "I'll do that better next time". Now I'm at a level where I should have figured this all out. People are watching me closely, so self-doubt cuts that much deeper.'

Cadenhead and Pryde's honesty may be dismaying to many readers, who hope to seamlessly flow into greater confidence with age. In reality, I think there's a beautiful truth to what they say. Confidence is not a steady slope that increases evenly as we age. It can dip, and you can also have great runs when you are younger, only to find a life change overwhelms your sense of confidence.

This is something I recall many of the women I interviewed for my second book, *Female Breadwinners* talked about. They were the primary earners for their families. Most had not explicitly planned it that way, but managing that responsibility gave them a more certain sense of self-reliance and confidence. Pryde also noticed a difference in the ways millennials negatively respond to the label of competence. She observes:

> *In my experience, millennials have a lot of confidence and even great competence. Even then they certainly don't want to be described as competent. Instead, they want to be recognised as 'outstanding'. Ironically, while I don't identify as a millennial, I probably fall into that bracket.*

Pryde was the youngest person ever to be made a Partner of a law firm in Scotland when she earned that role at 33, becoming the Head of Commercial Litigation just a few months later. Pryde says:

> *Today's trainees speak up, even before they've had a lot of experience or any real competence in a given area. I don't know if they all go to the same training class to learn to do this, but I'm somewhat in awe. It feels pretty far from how I felt in my 20s.*

Pryde continues:

> *There's often a strange mix of confidence and entitlement. I was willing to work until 11 pm to prove myself. By contrast, many millennials both feel able to leave at 5:30 when the work's not done and tell me how hard they work!*

While similar in age to other millennials, why is Pryde's work ethic so different? I'd suggest it was partially her upbringing in a working-class background, which we've seen is part of jigsaw of what we expect from 'confidence'. She agrees: 'As the first in my family to go to university, I couldn't take anything for granted. I just knew I'd have to work a bit harder.'

BIAS FOR EXTROVERSION

We can't discuss which types of people win and lose out with our current definitions of confidence without also looking at introversion and its showier cousin, extroversion. When I asked people about the behaviours they'd expect to see in a confident person, most describe variations on *extroversion*. People would give examples like 'chatty, likes people, charming, happy to speak in front of a group'. However, it's not quite that clear-cut, nor is it accurate to say introverts *aren't* confident. Neil Stevenson points out:

> *Promotions from middle to senior management shouldn't be reliant on memories of 'Who was always quick to contribute?' or 'Who always seemed ready to volunteer?'. If it is, you risk a rather lop-sided senior team where one style dominates. I've found it useful to additionally ask: 'Who did a lot of the work behind the scenes?' or 'Who brought the most technical detail?' or 'Who, even though they rarely spoke, did everyone listen to?'*

Those questions are great at unpicking our assumptions of the inherent value of confidence. Stevenson is describing the classic introversion versus extroversion dilemma.

Let's start with some reasonably basic descriptions. Extroverts crave social stimuli. They prioritise being around other people and often get their energy from social situations. They *aren't* being fake; they simply like being with others and derive their energy from these interactions.[278] Extroverts seek others because it gives *them* a buzz.

However, that's very different from going out simply because you assume *others want your company*, which is something the overconfident would do. The archetypal extrovert prefers action to contemplation, risk-taking to tempered caution, certainty to ambiguousness. They tend to be assertive, dominant, think out loud, are rarely at a loss for words and occasionally blurt out things they may later regret. That's okay though, as they are more comfortable with conflict, just not solitude.

In short, extroverts are gregarious and comfortable in the spotlight. This benefits them in the eyes of any audience. Research shows we even erroneously credit extroverts as being smarter – even through grades and various intelligence test scores (such as SAT) show this isn't the case.[279] Extroversion is prized in much of Western society.

278. Fishman, I. et al. 2011 Do Extroverts Process Social Stimuli Differently from Introverts? *Journal of Cognitive Neuroscience* 2(2): 67–73.
279. Paulhus, D. and Morgan, K. 1997 Perceptions of Intelligence in Leaderless Groups: The Dynamic Effects of Shyness and Acquaintance, *Journal of Personality and Social Psychology* 72(3): 581–591.

One of the biggest compliments you could give a Western parent? To describe their child as 'outgoing'. As they age, that label transforms into 'people skills' which is often shorthand for extroversion. As they enter the workplace, most modern offices are set up perfectly for extroverts. People are expected to work in teams, increasingly in open offices without walls. They are also often 'hot-desking' which may mean interacting, even if only on some basic level, with new people every day.

Kiera Tsenti sees this preference for extroverts in her UK wide recruitment work. Tsenti has seen this work *against* introverts when seemingly 'less confident' voices get drowned out. They may be ostracised as 'boring', 'negative' or 'uncooperative'. She observes:

> *Because of the way their brains process dopamine,*
> *extroverts need more external stimulation. A promotion, but*
> *even an interview itself, is actually 'external stimulation!'*
> *They're often better practised as they're more likely to*
> *put themselves forward even for stretch roles. Plus, I'd*
> *say there are probably more extroverts or at least people*
> *who can manage a confident front, doing the actual*
> *interviewing. Since we all like to hire people like ourselves,*
> *this gives the confident person a double advantage.*

At worst, sometimes extroverts may get an undeserved bad rap for speaking without thinking. While this no doubt happens, it's likely down to the way they process information. Extroverts can actually be good listeners. Perhaps their tendency to dominate a conversation originates in their own nervousness. Or maybe it's a generosity in which they feel compelled to fill uneasy silences to provide flow in a conversation.

However, even *if* extroverts didn't get the benefit of doubt, *they are still winning*. People assume all this additional talking, whatever its motive, actually makes them smarter and more competent – which it doesn't. Sarah Douglas sees the real limitation if confidence veers into overcompensating for lack of competence.

Douglas says:

> *The dark side of talent management is that while we need*
> *confident people, they aren't the ones doing the majority of*
> *the work. I run a business powered by introverts but sold by*
> *extroverts. Extroverts dominate the client-facing roles, but*
> *most of our creatives are introverts. Their skill is in going*
> *into themselves to pull out ideas no one sees coming. We*
> *get the blended skills by hiring both types of people, but this*
> *has longer-term implications for team structures.*

Douglas sees the irony of this. She observes: 'A good proportion of our promotions ultimately go to the extroverts, but this makes sense to me since as a society we are seduced by their noise.' The 'noise' is what Douglas can most easily sell to clients as it most closely matches their expectations.

Building on this, Douglas Morrison, based at the City of Glasgow College, points out how frequently people link ambition with confidence, even when they are entirely *unrelated*. He's seen confident and extroverted people over-rewarded with promotions – *even when they didn't seem to aspire* to progression in the first place.

To this point, not all extroverts are ambitious or driven by career success – some are happy where they are. However, they are more likely to be encouraged into management roles and judged as 'high potential' by others who misinterpret their extroversion as confidence and, *by default*, ambition.

Interestingly, extraversion is more prevalent in cultures where there has been a great deal of immigration. Extroversion as a personality trait is less frequent in Asia and Africa than it is in South America or certainly the US, whose populations mainly descend from transcontinental immigrants. To researchers, there is an undeniable link; world travellers are more extroverted than those who stay in their country of origin – and they pass those traits on to their children.[280]

This link is something with which I can identify. One of the most common responses I got when deciding to emigrate from the US to the UK without contacts or a job and just a few months after turning 22 was: 'Are you crazy?' More benevolently people might say: 'That's confident!' which no doubt often meant something similar to the first question in their eyes!

---

280. Olson, K. 2007 Why do Geographic differences exist in the Worldwide distribution of Extraversion and Openness to Experience? The History of Human Emigration as an Explanation, *Individual Differences Research* 5(4): 275–288.

AMBIVERT ADAPTERS

It's reassuring then to discover how false these 'opposites' actually are in terms of numbers of people. We all fall somewhere on a scale, but there are far more of us in the middle than we like to think. Research on professionals suggests two-thirds of people could be 'ambiverts' – people who fall midway on the scale between extrovert and introvert, and make the best salespeople.[281] I'm one of these people and based on those numbers, you may be too. Notably, your preference can also change over time, which means, like confidence, it's not necessarily a set-point.

On assessments, I fall halfway between the two, with a very slight preference for extroversion. I make a good part of my living speaking to audiences so my ambiversion surprises some. However, I also love the quiet, and some would even say the seemingly mundane work of writing this, my third book. I love research and making linkages between disparate ideas. However, I can only do that quiet work because I'm happy at my desk on my own for days and even weeks on end.

Additionally, it's dangerous to assume that only extroverts can have the confidence to do public-facing work. That risks writing off the 'unconfident' for client-facing work, when they may actually be some of your best people. Ambiverts are flexible in their preference for talking *and* listening. This made them the likeliest to show just enough assertiveness and enthusiasm to close a sale but are also more likely to take on board a client's needs.

Someone who has learned to grow his extroverted side is Douglas Morrison who says:

> *As I climbed into senior leadership, there was an unspoken expectation. I'd have to project a version of myself I'm quite uncomfortable with. I'm actually fairly introverted. I like working in small teams, if not just on my own. I'll never be defined as an extrovert, but I've had to take on that guise as part of 'raising my game'. Introverted leaders just aren't accepted as easily.*

281. Grant, A. M. et al. 2013 Rethinking the Extraverted Sales Ideal: The Ambivert Advantage, *Psychological Science* 24(6): 1024–1030.

Introverts, by comparison, get their energy by recharging on their own. This isn't to say they aren't skilled or even great with people. It's just to indicate introverts prefer small groups to large. They will opt out of large social gatherings in favour of time on their own. This time is dedicated to an activity or a few people they love, but where they won't be the centre of attention.

The most significant difference, however, between the two has to be with the way we *assume* extroverts are confident and introverts simply aren't. When thinking about how we describe children, to label a child 'shy' is sometimes received like a character fault. It can be a concern to parents who often then *work* on 'confidence' with their child, again conflating 'lack of confidence' with introversion.

It's hard to get accurate global data on where people fall on the scale of extroversion to introversion. In the US, some research suggests introverts are between one-third and one-half of the population.[282] However, this is likely to be an underrepresentation largely due to how much the American culture *prizes* extroversion. Introverts may have strong social skills, but after a certain amount of interaction most would prefer to be home or in their own space at work, getting the energy they need. They are very close to fewer people, listen more than they talk, think before they speak and dislike conflict.

Like others, Lynne Cadenhead notes her frustration with the way extroverts are listened to, perhaps more than they deserve. She mentioned a common challenge for many of my clients – how to respond when an enthusiastic colleague raises a point she herself has been mulling over. You may recognise how the person who 'jumps in' with a garbled observation gets the credit for being 'confident' – even if their point isn't well-thought through.

For Cadenhead and others like her, who may have been quieter while thinking through the complexities, they've been beaten to the point by someone quicker. She laughs: 'Nothing annoys me more! So what I've learned to do is to build on it. I say things like: "I was thinking something similar, but I couldn't see how we'd get around X. What are everyone else's thoughts?"'

Derek Watson points out that introverts, while confident, will still need an extra dose of self-belief to stand up to extroverts. Extroverts will challenge them on answers that may have taken the introvert a great deal of time and detail-oriented reflection to create. He maintains:

---

282. Allik, J. and McCrae, R. 2004 Towards a Geography of Personality Traits: Patterns and Profiles Across 36 Cultures, *Journal of Cross-cultural Psychology* 35: 13–28.

I have to remind quieter people they can't just say 'this is the right answer' and expect people to accept it. They need to explain why it's the right answer and what are the implications. They'll also have to stand up to doubters who know nothing about their topic, but whose confidence makes them feel entitled to challenge the expert!

Watson and others agree our workplace bias for extroversion *doesn't lead us to any better ideas*. However, our preference for extroversion is certainly not diminishing. Nor is the assumption that confidence and extroversion are the same thing. Susan Cain, who wrote extensively on this topic in her book *Quiet*, talked about how difficult it is to find self-proclaimed introverts when she visited Harvard Business School, given the way they reward both group interaction and compelling presentations.

Before Cain's visit, she found a Harvard Business School webpage advising students on how to be a 'good team participator'. Advice deemed *helpful* includes: 'Speak with conviction. Even if you believe something 50%, say it as if you believe it 100%' or 'Don't think about the perfect answer. It's better to get out there and say something than never to get your voice in.'[283]

We *all* rely on business leaders to make sound decisions, which makes this advice very concerning. Believing half-truths and taking up time in a meeting just to show you are there, are some of the key reasons we must rebrand confidence for the 21st century.

To identify undersung 'competence-heroes' ask:

- **Who does a lot of the work behind the scenes?**
- **Who brought the detail we actually needed?**
- **Who makes things work, but rarely gets credit?**
- **Who may be quiet, but is someone we all listen to?**

---

283. Cain, S. 2012 *Quiet: The Power of Introverts in a World that Can't Stop Talking*, Viking, London.

TWELVE

CULTURE CLUB

Before enlightenment, chop wood, carry water. After enlightenment, chop wood, carry water
– Chinese proverb

Getting ahead in a Western workplace, as we've seen, can require self-promotion, an individualistic mindset and bullishly standing your ground, all of which favour cultural natives. However, it will also take a tenacity in realising how much more there is *to do*, much like the above proverb. This however needn't favour any one culture. Your culture of origin, that is how you were raised, will also affect your willingness to do the former. However it doesn't affect the latter.

As we experience unprecedented growth in multinationals, we are in danger of homogenising definitions of confidence according to a single, largely Western cultural ideal. This is affected by many things, including which type of status quo we chose to lead, but also the media we consume and even the business education providers we select. All have an ultimate effect on how we value competence versus confidence and was something with which most interviewees identified.

Georg Schmundt-Thomas worked in FMCG for nearly 30 years and spent some of his career leading teams in Japan. While raised in Germany, he worked for non-German Western companies for three decades. He believes confidence is largely a cultural concept – not a global set of behaviours. He observes:

> *To the Japanese, confidence is wrapped up in self-control.*
> *It's part of why we in the West think of Asians as being*
> *unreadable or having a poker-face. For example, for the*
> *Japanese, Donald Trump is considered completely childish.*
> *He does impulsive things they'd expect people to grow out*
> *of by the time they enter their teenage years.*

Schmundt-Thomas' peers and managers were diverse in their style. However, he recalls those who showed the most American type of 'confidence behaviours' – speaking the most at meetings and self-promotion – often progressed quickly. He witnessed the employees most committed to compromise in order to achieve consensus were also the most likely employees to give way, for the good of the team, even if not for themselves.

However, when we look at this demographically, we see it's mostly people from collaborative cultures who are socialised to take this more cooperative position. While compromise is ultimately very useful, this bias has repercussions for who we promote. As we've seen, too frequently we equate 'talkers' with 'leaders' as we do 'pushy' with 'ambitious'.

To this point, the more someone speaks, the more other group members direct their attention *to that person*. This means 'talkers' eventually become more powerful as the meeting goes on, something researchers have also seen regardless of the quality of their content.[284] However, not surprisingly, that expressiveness doesn't get interpreted as confidence *equally well for all groups*.

When defining confidence, Carol Stewart leaned in and used her body language to gesture when describing confidence, a move favoured by a few other interviewees. It denotes the physicality of that feeling. However, as Stewart points out: 'If you're from an Afro-Caribbean background like I am, simply asserting your opinions can be misinterpreted as being "excitable" or "passionate". But this is just how we show feeling.'

In non-status quo groups, enthusiasm is more likely to be interpreted as being 'fiery' or 'fierce'; a somewhat less positive description than it deserves to be. However, Stewart is displaying a belief in what she's saying and a desire to share it with others. If that isn't worthy of being described as confidence, it begs the question, what is?

Cultured ideas of confidence were something Stewart noticed for other groups too. She mentions the viral video of the White man on a televised Skype news interview, interrupted by his marauding toddlers. Stewart points out:

> *Most people assumed the Asian woman who came to grab*
> *the kids was a nanny. But she was his wife. This mistake*
> *says much more about the prevalence of seeing mixed-*
> *race couples. It's about who we expect to be servants and*
> *expecting subservience in Asian women. However, because*
> *we don't expect confidence in Asian women or expect to see*
> *mixed-race couples, viewers didn't initially see it that way.*

---

284. Surowiecki, J. 2005 *The Wisdom of Crowds*, Doubleday Anchor, New York, p. 187.

Shoku Amirani is a British-Iranian BBC radio producer. She explains much of Iranian poetry and literature extols humility and modesty. She points out: 'In Iran, humility behind the greatest of achievements is respected and admired.' She continues:

> I was raised with a famous Persian expression: 'A tree
> that has no fruit to offer remains erect. But when the tree
> is laden with fruit, its branches bend down.' When you
> have genuine humility, it is a sign that you have something
> valuable to offer the world.

She points out this attitude is widespread in many Eastern cultures. Amirani says:

> There is also an Indian proverb which says: 'Empty
> barrels make the most noise', meaning those with the least
> knowledge often shout the loudest to make their presence
> felt. Within these cultural contexts, it's easy to understand
> why 'speak up more to be confident' feels like a personal
> challenge.

For Amirani, the high value humility plays in many cultures creates a real clash for those working in status quo organisations. She explains:

> At job interviews, you are expected to blow your own
> trumpet, but for many cultures such as mine, that's a
> struggle and completely cringe-worthy. It's not that
> candidates aren't competent or even confident. It's that
> the interview panel doesn't identify with the social norms
> around how we display confidence. These are norms which
> we have had ingrained in us – often from birth!

She says it's important for interviewers to see and understand their candidates through a wider lens. Amirani remembers:

> I once talked with a senior leader from an Oxbridge
> background about these cultural norms. He was genuinely
> surprised and thanked me for this insight. He said it would
> never have occurred to him otherwise, as it was not part
> of his conditioning. Throughout his career, promoting his
> achievements and abilities had come naturally to him.

Amirani's colleague, like all of us, is the fish who doesn't see the water he's swimming in. Strength comes from *understanding* the water in which you swim. Seeking different perspectives is a mark of confidence, though not one we currently value.

Working abroad is one way to highlight the perspective your country of origin gave you, for both good and bad. I spent the first 14 years of my life in the US. However, I never understood how American I was in my outlook until I moved to Australia, where I'd been born, as a teen. Similarly, for many I'd interviewed, leaving their country of origin highlighted cultural norms they'd previously assumed were universal.

Ben Capell, the owner of BeCap, a Hong Kong-based management consultancy, remembers his first role as a young professional in the US. It gave him a sense of the expectations he had after being raised in Israel: 'In that first job, I was surprised how ambiguous people could be.' Capell is the only interviewee to call Americans 'ambiguous' in their meaning. In fact, most cite Americans for how literal and upfront they are in their communications. This is something I can also see, after living outside the US for over half of my life. Capell explains:

> On the spectrum, I'd come from a very upfront, even confrontational and much less hierarchical culture. In Israel, you'd never call a professor a 'Professor', that's humiliating for the student. Instead, Israelis approach issues with the understanding: we're all in a room together, why would we need to use titles? Israelis can be misinterpreted as impolite at best and adversarial at worst. Plus, we don't ascribe our behaviour as confidence. Israelis just think of ourselves as 'straightforward'.

Capell smiles as he continues:

> In multinational teams, we're overconfident or even confrontational in our approach. We can be viewed as the 'bulls in the china shop' who can't pick up social nuances. Years ago, an Israeli colleague of mine had lunch in the US. During the meal, she remarked that the soup was 'interesting'. The Americans thought she hated it! However, to an Israeli, 'interesting' means just that – it's complex, unexpected, flavourful in a way she'd never tasted before. She was actually complimenting the soup, and probably even trying to praise the host who decided where they'd go for the meal!

Rise of the multinational

Most organisations now recognise the benefits of a cross-cultural team, and because of the rise of mergers and acquisitions that lead to multinationals, they are only going to increase. If the value of 'diversity of thought' is genuinely recognised, why do high-potential employees tend to demonstrate confidence in the style most recognised by 'head office'?

As many multinationals have headquarters in the US, this means the American version of confidence is being promoted globally, just like the services and goods it provides. However, the danger is that this can ironically *undermine* their entire push for diversity in leadership styles by only creating more of what went before.

Alejandra Corona, a Marketing Executive, sees differences in how confidence is interpreted globally, with significant variations between neighbouring countries. Corona, who worked in Latin America for a US-based company, observes:

> *Those who got on best, no matter where they were from, adapted to an individualistic and competitive style of confidence. It must have suited me because when I left that employer, people from my home country would tease me about how American I'd become! I was originally offended, but then realised I had just adapted my style over time. I had more in common with Americans than I did with other Mexicans. From the Mexicans who said it though, it wasn't praise! I'd just delivered my ideas 'as if I knew better' which is how most Mexicans regard the US, particularly now. They'd call me 'conquistador' – the conqueror!*

By contrast, in Mexico, having formal authority is key to having 'earned' confidence. Corona came to banking after a long, successful career in FMCG. However, the confidence she brought as a very experienced hire was *not* well-received in her home country. The problem? Her experience had been earned in a *different* industry and by a woman.

When Corona began working back in her home country, it was a stark reminder to adjust her ideas. She often had to make them seem like they'd *come from someone else* – just to get things done. This was a stark change for her. Healthy disagreement in her previous employer was interpreted as confidence, but now based in Mexico, she was 'disrespectful' to the senior men surrounding her.

However, as Corona admits, not showing confidence left her very vulnerable and liable to criticism for being weak. She explains: 'Here in Mexico, to influence anyone, you have to go through the most senior authorities. This is particularly true if you don't have the experience they'd expect or formal qualifications specifically for that industry.'

This is ironic given her external perspective was what *the employers originally* wanted. Now Corona had to qualify every idea or opinion she had *before* it would get any traction. She recalls:

> *Before I'd say anything, I'd have to start with 'Well, while*
> *on my Masters' degree I found that …' or 'Based on my*
> *discussions with the Head of our Department, I think …' It*
> *was never enough that I had an observation based on the*
> *20 years I'd had before arriving at the bank.*

Like Corona, Dr Capell, also thinks we should be giving more due to the way a national culture affects 'confident behaviours'. Now in Hong Kong, he agrees with some of the other interviewees, pointing out that in Asia, confidence is less confrontational for the sake of harmony. Capell, raised in Israel, points out:

> *This is particularly important if the hierarchy isn't clear.*
> *In Asia, overall, hierarchy tends to be more important than*
> *in Western culture. While communication between peers*
> *may be less direct for the sake of harmony, there is always*
> *a hierarchy. That lack of directness can be mistakenly*
> *interpreted as being less confident. But that's only based on*
> *a Western ideal of what we expect from confidence.*

However, as Asian companies, particularly Chinese, continue to buy Western companies, this Western view of confidence will look dated and decidedly 20th century. Capell explains:

> *To many Asians, Western confidence is far too*
> *individualistic and non-collaborative. If you have this*
> *approach, in an Asian-owned company you won't be*
> *rewarded for it. You'll need to tone down self-promotion as*
> *it only counts if others do it for you.*

Capell reflects on how being employed by a multinational affects how we view confidence, as it means more 'adaptation' if not from the culture where the headquarters sit. He says:

I see a particular challenge for Israeli companies, who are world leaders in technology when Chinese companies acquire them. Israelis may have to rein in their challenging tone, and the Chinese will likely have to accept it more. If you can't adapt, you're out. But the upside is that previously overlooked people will now have more opportunities.

So is this the way 21st-century businesses will evolve? With a more Eastern approach to confidence? Capell responds:

Not necessarily, as it's also affected by the number of Asians educated in Western business schools and working for multinationals not based in Asia. As they become educated in Western schools and exposed to more Western colleagues, they adapt or leave.

Capell continues:

On the other hand, we will have more Westerners exposed to Asian values. This will happen as China, in particular, becomes the largest economy in the world, and drives more global business decisions than ever.

Capell has a unique insight into these issues having been raised in Israel – arguably a country with a bigger appetite for challenging authority. This may stem from the Israeli requirement that all citizens undertake military service. This expectation means people can take on serious leadership positions by age 22 or potentially even younger. Given the implications of many military decisions, young people are actively encouraged to challenge their superiors' thinking if they don't understand or agree with a decision. Being 'challenging' and assuming relative equality they then take into the workplace.

As more multinationals emerge, employees of the future may be better advised to find *companies that suit their style* of confidence. Capell points out this can be a win for people:

If you could play in both cultures, you'll get ahead faster. If there's a bridge between the two cultures, don't aim for the middle. It will always feel like a compromise. It takes much more skill but is more rewarding if you can jump fully from one side to the other.

To me, this also sounds like a call for more flexible definitions of confidence.

CROSSING CULTURES, CROSSING CONFIDENCE

Maria Camila Vargas, based in Chile, has been in the field for over 25 years. She was raised in Colombia but worked across South American in her FMCG career. For her, confidence is also very influenced by culture – and not as uniformly as people may assume. She clarifies:

> Latin Americans get bundled together as if we were one big group. In Colombia, where I'm from, confidence is about being outspoken and centre stage, focusing on the 'self-made man'. However, in Chile, those same behaviours are deemed phoney, pushy and even corny. Politics enables this. Social unrest, as we've had in Colombia, gives people the chance to redefine themselves quickly. You don't always get that in more politically stable economies.

Vargas recalls a recent conference in Chile of HR professionals she'd attended featuring two successful male entrepreneurs – one from the US and the other from Canada. She recalls:

> The American was self-congratulatory and made sure we knew he was a self-made millionaire by 30. The audience looked on in disbelief, wondering: 'Who does this guy think he is? What a show-off! What's he trying to prove?' No doubt he's used to audiences seeing him as confident. His achievements are no doubt impressive, but the audience didn't warm to him at all.

Vargas continues:

> By contrast, the Canadian spoke of building this multinational company via his people. He was centred, quiet, and engaged the audience so he wasn't always centre stage and people just loved it! He was grounded, which we interpreted as very confident.

Perhaps not surprisingly, Vargas identified with the idea of widening confidence to allow a greater range of people to succeed. When listening to her story, I was reminded of the work of Susan Cain we've already started to discuss, on why we should be valuing introverts more.

In Caine's own book she wrote about the American culture from which she originates: 'If genius is 1% inspiration and 99% perspiration, then *as a culture* we tend to lionise the 1%. We love the flash and dazzle. But greater power lies in the other 99%.'[285]

---

285. Cain, S. 2012 *Quiet: The Power of Introverts in a World that Can't Stop Talking*, Viking, London, p. 169.

By contrast, in Chile, confidence relies more on your network, your place in a recognised hierarchy and your education. She laughed: 'Colombians do more of a "communications dance" that can be maddening to Chileans who are asking: "Show me the numbers, give me the data, so I know *why* you are telling me this big story!"'

In Chile, she explained those without a degree are often more successful in multinationals where *lacking the right education* may not be such an issue. Vargas describes: 'If you don't have the "badges" of confidence expected in your own country, you're probably better off working for an employer who respects the badges you already have.'

When Vargas advises people aiming for a job in a company headquartered in a different culture, her advice is unequivocal. She wholeheartedly recommends:

> *It's not enough to think you understand the local culture.*
> *Go further to see how they judge both competence and*
> *confidence – and the difference between the two. Don't*
> *assume confidence looks the same across cultures.*
> *Alternatively, be prepared to be misunderstood if your*
> *confidence isn't what they expect to see.*

Kiruba Sankar, a native of India, also noted differences in the way different cultures expressed confidence. Sankar has lived and worked across Asia, the Middle East, Australia and now in Canada. He's noticed how different Canadians are in the way they display confidence, particularly in comparison to their near-neighbours – Americans.

> *Canadians will show you the fantastic quality of the*
> *products they're presenting for us to buy, their competence,*
> *but they don't oversell. Overselling just doesn't work for*
> *the local market. That's a surprise for people from other*
> *countries, who expect more of a hard sell.*

Sankar, an introvert, thinks the single most significant factor determining how much confidence groups of people display is not demographics like their gender or heritage. Instead, for him what sets the standard for confidence are the *behaviours that get rewarded* in their industry and, more specifically, national and company culture. Sankar has lived and worked most of his adult life outside of his native India. He explains: 'I've now been in Canada for 15 years. We've hired some great people but I've also seen many leave if they were too full of themselves. That type of confidence just isn't welcome here.'

NATIONAL ECONOMIC PROSPECTS

In discussing what might affect confidence, Kainaz Gazder raised a new factor. For her, the state of your national economy also deeply affected an individual's confidence. Based in Singapore, Gazder is a VP at P&G, an FMCG multinational she's been with for over 23 years. When asking how she defined confidence, Gazder responds: 'Like you've got the world at your feet.'

Gazder was raised in India and began work during the late 1990s when India was beginning to embrace the world economically. This outlook brought foreign investment into the country which increased both the aspiration and confidence levels of its citizens.

When her career then took Gazder to China in the early 2010s, the country had recently gone through the same fundamental shift. This meant that much like India beforehand, younger workers could enjoy high employment rates unseen by previous generations. The Chinese team she inherited was made up of very confident women.

For Gazder, seeing this trend in a *rapidly emerging economy* highlighted how linked national economic security is to feelings of personal confidence. This came via improved job opportunities and an individual's economic spending power and had the potential to change society radically. For Gazder, a nations' financial future outweighed other factors for shaping individual confidence.

As Gazder is the VP in her category across Asian markets, her teams are diverse. This allows her to notice differences in the way people embrace confidence while striving for competence. Gazder noted that Asians from *low income* nations often appear to have less confidence.

She explains: 'Compared to my experiences during the economic booms in India and China, the colleagues I have who are Thai, Filipinos, Vietnamese and Indonesians assume hard work alone is how they'll provide for their extended families.' So for Gazder, confidence is informed by what is going on economically *in your own country of origin*.

As the global economy shifts further East and away from North America and Europe, we could see rising confidence levels amongst people from these nations, or a rebranding of what confidence should be at the very least. Conversely, we could see decreases in Western confidence levels. This shift is a concern.

The US, in particular, is a heavily armed nation that feels entitled to make confident geopolitical moves while their relative standing on the world stage shrinks compared to emerging economies. This creates a real stress for countries like the UK and the US. Both are accustomed to exhibiting more power than they can realistically expect going forward in comparison to many rapidly expanding economies. As we know, competence takes effort and time. Appeals of 'Make America Great Again' only make sense if you feel a *deserved* greatness is slipping away.

THE LINGUA FRANCA OF CONFIDENCE

Related to culture, the role of native speakers in a business also influences perceptions of confidence and competence. Employees will always benefit if they work *in their mother tongue*. This is not just in their ability to master the language, but also to understand the subtle nuances within. This means they are formidable colleagues to compete against, for those who don't natively speak the language of headquarters. Celine Jahn, a French national who works in Germany, explains:

> *When talking with British colleagues, I thought they always sounded so smart. They could play with expressions or cut straight to the point. While they were great colleagues, I eventually realised it wasn't that they were naturally smarter. Their ability to play in their native tongue gave them a huge advantage. I, and other European colleagues, for whom English was often a second, third or even fourth language, felt so much more limited and insecure. We can't always find the perfect words, and certainly not as quickly. So native speakers come across as more competent – even when what we're buying into is their confidence.*

The ways different cultures relate to confidence becomes even more apparent when you look at how the word is defined in different languages. For example, in French, 'confiance' it's more about relationships and building trust between people. In German, the word for confidence, 'vertrauen', revolves more around reliability. Both of these translations get us closer to the original Latin definitions from which English 'confidence' derived.

The difference between the meanings behind this same word, helps us understand why each culture historically *expects and rewards* different behaviours. It also illuminates how far away the English translation, which now seems to focus on an almost showy sense of self-regard, has moved from other definitions.

It's imperative therefore not to assume Western cultures all interpret confident behaviours the same way. For example, the Swedish corporate clients I've worked with derive much of their interpretation of confidence from 'janteloven'. Their historical focus is on democracy, social good and *not* drawing attention to yourself. Setting yourself apart as a confident individual is not wholly positive in a culture that values being approachable, working as a team and being humble.

Reem Hayati is a Cairo-based marketing consultant who, after over 20 years working mostly for P&G, now helps Egyptian food manufacturers take their goods to a broader market. She agreed with others in saying a colleagues' command of English (or whatever language is spoken in headquarters) gave them a double benefit.

First, native English speakers had greater confidence in their own presentation skills. However, it also gave them the benefit of the doubt *from the audience*. They could be understood better than other foreign nationals. This meant sometimes non-native speakers *who had better ideas* but struggled to explain them, particularly to a monolingual audience, weren't as widely credited as native speakers.

To highlight how nonsensical this benefit enjoyed by native speakers actually is, non-native English speakers recommended similar employees focus *not* on more technical training, but on *improving their English instead*. Hayati explained:

> *If you're not confident in your fluency, it's easier on those big international conference calls to keep quiet and not embarrass yourself. It's a shame, because they may have the best point. But if the idea is mentioned 10 minutes later by someone who is more confident in their English, it will never be viewed as that first person's idea. Speaking English gives you leverage and therefore, more confidence.*

When multinationals hire talent from across their markets, they'll recruit most heavily from communities that speak the language of the multinational. English has been a long-standing favourite, but that will eventually change as China and other economies grow further.

In Hayati's case, parents like her send their children to international English-speaking schools. They ensure their children are well-travelled and become at least bi-lingual if not trilingual. This goes on globally and is illustrated by the higher confidence levels we see as these talented multilingual employees move up the socioeconomic scale, something we earlier discussed.

Running remote teleconference meetings:

- Ask non-status quo members, or those dialling in, to speak early – or at least draw them out further.
- Stop an 'interrupting' culture by saying 'I think X was just about to finish …' if they are interrupted.
- Ask participants to send new ideas ahead of the meeting to avoid bias towards extroverts or native English speakers.

GENDER, AGE AND NATIONALITY IN RELATION TO CONFIDENCE

We have already looked at gender on its own, however, it is worth noting there are further differences when looking at the way race, gender and age *intersect* with nationality. Fascinatingly, the confidence gap between men and women appears *largest in high income countries* according to a survey of nearly 1 million people between the ages of 16–45.[286]

In high income nations individuals compare themselves with their *workplace peers* who most often, are *both* men and women. However, in low income nations the gender confidence gap actually *appears* smaller as women tend to compare themselves to other women and men compare themselves with other men.

However, it's not a sign those groups are *equall*y confident. As the researchers explained: 'Individualistic, prosperous, egalitarian, high income nations with higher gender equality had larger gender gaps in self-esteem than collectivist, poorer, low income nations with greater gender *inequality*.'

Because of these levels of inequality, it simply didn't occur to women to compare themselves to the men or vice versa. This is largely because within high income nations women socialise and work with men, whereas in poorer nations, work is more likely to be sex-segregated. By contrast, women in the high income countries seem to compare their confidence levels, even subconsciously, to *their male peers* – thereby noticing difference. It is only in direct comparison to men that women find themselves comparatively lacking in confidence. It's also likely that if you are in a low income nation, you have far more pressing concerns than your confidence levels.

---

286. Guimond, S. et al. 2007 Culture, Gender and the Self: Variations and Impact of Social Comparison Processes, *Journal of Personality and Social Psychology* 92: 1118–1134.

This happens across the world. Other research by Bleidorm shows women consistently report lower self-esteem than men across the 42 countries tested, most of which were in high income countries.[287] However, confidence tended to *increase as people age*. This improvement happened for women in all countries, but confidence actually fell for men in Egypt and Japan. It only decreased with age for both genders in China. Only in Thailand, Turkey and Hong Kong did women's confidence ever overtake men's confidence.

However, even amongst those I interviewed for this book from North Africa and South America most *women agreed gender is a bigger factor* than cultural background in determining how confidence is interpreted and judged. One executive from Latin America describes:

> *I've seen senior women from the US come into our offices give virtually the same presentation as their American male colleagues. My own colleagues will criticise his ideas and content, but criticism against her is more gendered in the way they complain about her leadership style.*

This particularly affected women who *returned* to their home countries if their previous multinational was more progressive than was common 'at home'. Those I spoke with were explicit. In their experience, multinationals were far from perfect. However, when they were back in their own country, local attitudes towards confidence, particularly when displayed by women, were much more punitive.

For them, this only highlighted the temporary reprieve and time of personal growth they'd enjoyed while working for a multinational. It meant re-entry back into the workforce of their home country even several years later was sometimes harder than they'd anticipated. For these women, their personal career expectations progressed, while the way their home nation saw them had *not*.

Alejandra Corona returned to a Mexico City employer after a career spent in multinationals. She explains:

> *Working again amongst all Mexicans reminded me the expectations for women were even tougher. My US-based employer would listen, but then disregard my idea if they didn't like it, which is fair enough. But back in Mexico, if a senior person felt challenged, they'd react with anger.*

---

287. Bleidorn, W. et al. 2016 Age and Gender Differences in Self-Esteem: A Cross Cultural Window, *Journal of Personality and Social Psychology* 111(3): 396–410.

For Corona this reaction is multifaceted. In Mexico, there is a clearer respect for hierarchy. However, she adds men aren't used to being challenged by women, particularly in male-dominated sectors. This was noticeable for her when she moved from FMCG to financial services. Despite Corona's seniority, this led to a combative atmosphere if she didn't toe the line as a woman. So, for Corona, confidence was about 'being able to take the heat by knowing you can withstand the burns'.

Similarly, for women from some cultures, even working *outside the home* was itself a confident move. It challenged convention. Hayati, likewise, returned to her home country after an international career. She explains: 'In Egypt, we only expect women, not men, to do the lion's share of work in the home. But if a woman enters the workplace, those expectations are still there. She gets no slack.' This was repeated by women in virtually every part of the world. It helps explain why improved higher education levels for women hasn't led to rapidly improved workforce participation rates as quickly as we might expect.

INTERSECTIONALITY IN YOUR OWN BACKYARD

Intersectionality also affects people who are working within their own country of origin. So, to people who are both the non-status quo racially and by gender, what affects their confidence more – race or gender? For Patel, the founder of Scotland Women in Technology, her answer is quick: It's her race, but also *ethnicity*. She says: 'I know people expect Asians to be quieter. It's why I'm such a surprise to many.'

Patel wonders that if she had lived in London her whole life, 'ethnicity' might not be her answer, choosing gender instead. It may be that Patel feels this difference all the more acutely as an Asian woman in Scotland, where only 4% of the population claim ethnic minority heritage.[288] Ethnicity also comes into it given she often works with women of the same race, but who live in and were raised in India, whereas she was not.

Interestingly, the real number of BAME people in Scotland *could* be higher, as 10% of the population in the census for Scotland *didn't disclose* their ancestry. Comparatively, in London where Patel was raised, 40% of the population are BAME. Noticing her gender first may have felt more natural in London. In Scotland, the greater sense of difference is in her racial make-up and how she was raised.

---

288. Scotland Census 2019 Ethnicity, Identity, Language & Religion update report.

When we sit outside of the status quo, we often feel our differences *before* any similarities. Interestingly, most of the BAME interviewees I talked with lived in racially diverse cities. They may be less likely to feel the isolation of being part of a visible minority at all. Often the only place they felt their non-status quo status was at work, particularly as they ascended the ladder.

After arriving in Scotland, Patel joined an employer where people often stayed decades. She laughs: 'I quickly earned the seemingly playful greeting of "Here comes trouble". Instead of recognising me as bringing the new ideas they'd said they wanted, I decided to own that troublemaker label.'

This label was relatively straightforward for Patel. She wasn't just a new outside hire; she was also an Asian woman – unlike anyone they'd ever hired previously. Patel explains:

> *Their experience of Asian women originated from the female developers we hired from India. While we may look the same to the leadership, we are poles apart. I was raised and studied here in the UK. Those women had only been brought via our Indian office specifically for much more junior developer roles. Those new women appeared more subservient than I certainly was.*

Patel continues:

> *However, you can't write these women off as 'not confident'. Their technical competence meant if they had a question in a meeting, they wouldn't raise it there, but later based on detailed notes. By comparison, I'll just challenge the idea outright in a meeting, which probably wasn't what any of the White men around me expected either!*

As we discussed confidence at work more, Patel admitted she was often mistaken for the tea lady in meetings. Male mentors reassured her this wasn't related to confidence but was a tactical error in how she arrived at meetings. When asking her female colleagues who had hosted guests in the office more regularly, their advice was clear: 'Arrive at the meeting earlier than the others so you can get your own coffee. Then sit away from the drinks and as close to the Chair as possible.'

Patel feels the pressure of being an Asian woman at work. For her, however, it means she goes above and beyond in giving back to the community, something we've seen expressed by other BAME interviewees. She observes:

*In the Indian culture, we are taught to never be confidently
satisfied, always to go above and beyond. That's not about
earning a certain amount, but about getting recognition for
what you do beyond your day job. That way, you can give
back to others.*

This outlook creates an interesting dynamic for Patel with her husband. He is
also a British Indian yet doesn't feel this self-imposed pressure. The reason
behind their difference she thinks may lie in the nuances of social class and
where they were from in India. While Patel's husband was also raised in the
UK, his family was from the Indian state of Goa; an area colonised initially by
the Portuguese.

Patel explains: 'In Goa, they have a more Western attitude towards many
things. Plus, he came from more money than me and was privately educated in
the UK.' Patel, by comparison, comes from a working-class background. She
notes that while she and her husband may *look* similar to much of the status
quo in the UK, they have entirely different perspectives of the world, and also
their responsibility within it.

Patel's husband identifies well with his primarily White colleagues in Scotland.
However, she notes his closest friend is still a Ghanaian man he met over 20
years ago while they were both dental students. That friend also assimilated
amongst a mostly White population in the dental profession they both share.
She laughs: 'Whereas I will tick "British Asian" boxes on a form, my husband
only ticks the box saying "British". He argues with me why we measure these
things at all!'

Thirteen

New confidence

> *When someone shows you who they are, believe them*
> – Maya Angelou

For me, the most important word in Maya Angelou's quote is 'shows'. It's completely different from the 'tells' of the confident. Confident people can happily tell you who they are and even what they feel they've achieved, but what someone can 'show' you *must be based* on evidence. Showing relies on proof.

If competence is what mattered, more people could own confidence. However, this may initially feel like a hard sell. After all, it's the status quo who has set the rules and have the most skin in the game in maintaining 'business as usual'. However, workplace confidence is modelled on a very narrow set of behaviours that we've been taught to expect, yet ridiculously are most readily displayed by a fraction of the population.

In order to move on, we've got to change the definition and rebrand confidence. It must incorporate both a wider range of behaviours and expect *proof of competence as a prerequisite*. Rebranding is such an overused term that may sound like a big ask. However, as we've seen language is highly adaptive, based on what people need, feel or think. We've seen definitions develop before, so this isn't beyond us. If anything, we need to start by taking confidence back to where it started: *a trust in others based on their reliability*.

As we've seen confidence used to be something you earned or gave to others as a result of your choices and actions, your trustworthiness. Currently it's most commonly thought of as a set of showy poses to hold. Indeed, as one of the most popular sayings about confidence is now; 'fake it until you make it'. However, as we all know, you can't easily fake being trustworthy – that takes evidence and competence.

So how should we progress as we dig deeper into what confidence should mean? According to Uviebinené, the answer is clear:

265

Have no expectations of what confidence should look like. Some people are quiet but certain – they're quietly confident. On the other hand, some are loud and are extroverts, but could have little internal confidence. Images can be a smokescreen.

This is a feeling that Uviebinené identifies with, in our interview: 'The problem with confidence is that it's all about external factors, what people can *see*. If that prototype that doesn't fit you, you're written off.' The irony is that those who often *appear* the most showy and confident have little self-worth. They primarily exist for the gaze of others.

A starting point is in accepting there are not 'confident people' any more than there are 'people with no confidence'. Confidence dips and has many layers, but it's now used as a catch-all description. In reality, how confident we feel about our next challenge is determined by how we've dealt with other challenges in the past.

Atkin, whose doctorate focuses on these issues, also sees the fallacy in thinking you either have confidence or you don't. She points out:

I feel comfortable in talking about myself and across all situations is how we erroneously think of confidence. But if we look back at the history of the term, it originated as a perceived belief you'd succeed at a specific task – not most or even all tasks. Thinking about it as a magical quality you either have or don't have is unhelpful – that was never meant to be the point.

When looking at gender and confidence, career development specialist Jenny Garrett also noted how *contextual* confidence was for people. She explains:

Women tend to amplify their feelings about confidence, men compartmentalise them. So, if she's not a great speaker, she'll lament she's not confident. However, for men, they are more likely to cite just a few weak areas. The fact he's struggling to manage a colleague doesn't affect his confidence overall, just in handling certain people. Even then he'd only share that perceived 'weakness' if we have a trusting relationship.

Vanessa Vallely also sees confidence as contextual – not a static state of being. She clarifies: 'It's unrealistic to think you can be confident in every situation, nor should you be. Even though I do a lot of speaking, for example, I certainly won't talk about things I don't understand.'

266

As we've already seen, that mindful editing is something we need to see as a core part of confidence. It's the difference between 'shooting from the hip' to weigh in on a topic (old confidence) and weighing in *because* you can add more competency-based insight (new confidence).

Carol Stewart is an executive coach with over 30 years of experience, who focuses on self-limiting beliefs. She explains:

> *My version of confidence is simply 'being comfortable with who I am and having the courage to do what I need to do'. It's something almost everyone can relate to, as it speaks to authenticity. You don't have to put up a front. It can take people time to come around to, but not because they don't identify with it. Instead, it's because we're inundated with images of great speech givers and the person who leads the meeting. If you're confident in certain areas, it's usually because of repeated exposure to that type of challenge.*

Ironically, saying you're not confident as a blanket statement warns people *not* to give you that exposure. Worryingly, it also makes 'not confident' part of your self-definition. Neither are helpful. Stewart's guiding point is to treat a lack of confidence as a *simple skill shortage*. You can always get better at a skill, so under-confidence isn't a life sentence. If a client starts with a blanket statement about 'not being confident', Stewart sagely gets them to break it down. She says:

> *What exactly are they not confident about? Is it about interviewing? Is it about challenging people who've taken credit for your ideas? Do they feel confident speaking to a group of ten people, but not 50? Or if 50 is okay, how about 250? What is their weak spot exactly, because that's where we'll focus our attention?*

Stewart's method drills down. Where's the sticking point? Getting a sense of what makes the difference helps you identify what you need to improve. For example, most people have spoken up in a team meeting of just a few people, so focus their effort not on 'gaining confidence' per se but on getting exposure to bigger crowds, or where you are the main presenter.

Stewart continues: 'I'd be more worried about the confident person who's never handled that challenge before. That's a recipe for disaster, their confidence means they won't focus on being competent!' For Stewart, taking this perspective can have a profound impact as she says: 'You can almost see them grow in front of you.' Stewart mentions:

I ask them to write out skills on which they've had compliments. Then I ask them to write out a separate list of what they need to work on or even what they've had negative feedback. After creating this list,, they'll often see the first category is the longest though they spend most of their mental energy on the shorter list of 'negatives'.

She continues:

Plus, I'll ask them how those skills moved from one category to another. Some skills you developed only because you knew you needed to improve. Similarly, there will be skills that are now strong but will humbly have to go into a lower 'rating' after a promotion realising you have to work to a higher set of standards.

In short, being a confident speaker in front of ten people is fundamentally different than being expected to command an audience of 100 or even 1,000 eventually. All audiences, however, start with just one or two people.

Stewart's point reminds me of the work I've done helping CEOs of university spin-outs to pitch their ideas to investors. Let's be clear, this type of pitch practice is not what any biologist assumed they'd have to do when they entered the life sciences. Instead, these pitches require them to sell the commercial value of a lifetime of their work, *often in a few minutes or less*.

Incredibly smart people have to simplify complex research into a bite-sized yet compelling narrative. Their audiences are rarely as skilled as the founder, but the result is incredibly important as it determines if they'll part with their money to invest. It's the ultimate challenge for many technical experts who have made their careers often on a specific competence, rather than projecting old style confidence.

As someone who has coached these start-up Founders, it's often simpler to *not* think of this challenge as building confidence – which always seems like a lofty goal. Instead, for many highly competent people, it's simpler to position pitching as a *new skill* they have to master. A truly competent person will recognise that they can get better at anything *with practice*. It's only via repeated exposure to the challenge that they'll come across as 'naturally confident', no matter how they felt originally.

Clearly, we've got to update our assumptions for the 21st century. After all, the images we have of a risk-taking 'big talker' feel antiquated at best and dangerous for us all at worst. Based on the stories of those I interviewed, it's time for a rebrand of confidence. Competence deserves to be thought of as 'sexy' and outdated versions of confidence, 'ridiculous'. But let's start with the key components that will go into this new definition.

ONE: ABSOLUTE SELF-AWARENESS

Having absolute self-awareness doesn't mean being comfortable with all that you discover about yourself. That would be a 'take it or leave it' approach. Instead it means having the courage to ask how you are perceived. More importantly it means doing better if you don't like the answer.

You can't read other people's minds. You'll go further, however, if you *interpret* their words and actions to understand what they need to build *their* confidence and trust in you. Ironically, if you take this 'other-focus' first, you'll start to feel more confident in yourself because you'll be able to give them what they need. This is the value of emotional intelligence and self-awareness.

Indeed, self-awareness is *the skill* that underpins the competencies, like empathy and listening skills that will move you ahead. To that point, one study found high self-awareness to be the *strongest* predictor of overall success. The study's authors found self-awareness increased a leader's willingness to bring *complementary* talents to the table, rounding out their decisions.[289] Ultimately, this type of confidence is about knowing how to read others and *then act* accordingly.

This type of self-awareness, however, is not about navel-gazing, but in *seeking feedback*. Asking for feedback this way shouldn't be seen as needy or as a lack of confidence.

Nikki Slowey explains:

> *Asking for feedback is about ensuring competence, particularly on a relatively new task. Even if they ask for feedback on something they've done many times before, I'd only assume a desire to improve, not that they're lacking confidence.*

However, reading people well isn't primarily about relying on a tidy 360° feedback assessment collected at quarterly intervals. Instead, it means continually getting and giving informal feedback on your interactions.

Derek Watson manages large teams of people at the University of St. Andrews. He elaborates:

> *I need team members to consider: 'What does this mean for this particular audience? What will happen if they don't make changes or ignore the issue?'*

Watson smiles and says:

---

289 Hausknecht, J. and Faum, J. 2017 *Nice Guys Finish First*, American Management Association & Cornell University.

Of course, I need them to understand their area of work,
but ultimately as they progress, it's a different skill set that's
needed. The further up the ranks you go, the more complex
the issues and implications you'll need to think through.
But at its core, you'll have to take people with you. It's not
about doing more work. It's about different work. You have
to have the confidence to leave the detail behind.

Watson's point about 'taking people with you' relies on self-awareness. Getting a sense of how people see you is key to improving your confidence. It's what a more fashionable author might call 'impression management'. If the feedback you receive is already positive, own those characteristics. Let them sink in. If their input suggests 'room for improvement', however, work primarily on those behaviours which are *visible to other people*.

Lucky for you, your self-confidence, low as it may feel at times, can't easily *be seen* by others. Oddly enough, impression management was initially thought to contaminate on-the-job assessment tools, *as it took into account other people's opinions*. However, in jobs where you have to influence people (all jobs), managing their impressions of you is vital to get right. This is where self-awareness overlaps with emotional intelligence.

This bleed between the two is good news for employers too as emotional intelligence correlates with higher employee engagement,[290] resilience, tolerance to stress, positive organisational behaviours[291] and overall personal effectiveness. Interestingly, there have been objections to citing EQ (emotional intelligence) as a leadership characteristic for its perceived bias *towards women*. By contrast, there's little concern for the ways our historic definitions for confidence favour *the status quo*.

In reality, scores of emotional intelligence *don't overwhelmingly favour women*,[292] as people often assume. While women do tend to outscore men slightly, the difference rarely exceeds 15% on most standard tests of EQ. It's far from a clear 'win for women', and certainly isn't one that's meant they've progressed any faster. Plus, there is no magic to EQ – it's a skill at which *everyone can become more competent*.

290. Akhtar, R. et al. 2015 The Engageable Personality: Personality and Trait EI as Predictors of Work Engagement, *Personality and Individual Differences* 73: 44–49.

291. Baron-Cohen, S. et al. 2001 The Autism-Spectrum Quotient (AQ): Evidence from Asperger Syndrome/High Functioning Autism, Males and Females Scientists and Mathematicians, *Journal of Autism and Developmental Disorders* 31(1): 5–17.

292. Joseph, D. and Newman, D. 2010 Emotional Intelligence: An Integrative Meta-Analysis and Cascading Model, *Journal of Applied Psychology* 95(1): 54–78.

In fact, a study of over 1,300 global managers found feedback-based coaching, aimed at building the self-awareness necessary for EQ, increased managers' willingness to *seek* advice. It also improved their subsequent performance ratings one year later.[293]

This approach and valuing self-awareness is familiar for Naomi Pryde who says: 'I routinely ask for feedback. Believe me, it's not comfortable. Even if they are 99% positive, it's the 1% they critique that I'll still be focusing on days later. But that's worth the angst, because it's the 1% I'll improve upon.'

Pryde's desire to improve is all about growing her competence, even if she knows her confidence may take a momentary knock to get there. The ability to read people using emotional intelligence and make valuable connections, as a result, is something Pryde, identified with, even in the earliest years of her career. She laughs as she says:

> As one of the few women invited to events, you can either be
> affronted, wondering if you've been invited solely for your
> 'minority' status, or you can say 'I'm going to go and use
> that opportunity', which is what I did.

Pryde continues:

> I was easy for people to remember at networking events
> because I was often the only woman. But I'd mostly go
> along because I was skint, and these were free dinners! But
> I'd walk away with a full belly and a pocket full of business
> cards of all these senior people. They make up my network
> to this day.

Approachability and a lack of grandiose confidence worked for Naomi. It made her non-threatening to others who were happy to chat with her and share their insights. Her approachable demeanour has served her well as she's risen through the ranks. However, there is no doubt senior people gave her time because, within a few minutes, she demonstrated her competence and interest in the topic at hand.

Pryde's self-awareness and the resulting emotional intelligence has paid a big part in her success, but it's a skill the rest of us can also improve. A meta-analysis showed that 70% of people coached on their emotional intelligence scores went on to *outperform those who weren't.*[294]

293. Smither, J. et al. 2003 Can Working with an Executive Coach Improve Multisource Feedback Ratings over Time? A Quasi-Experimental Field Study, *Personnel Psychology* 56: 23–44.
294. Theeboom, T. 2013 Does Coaching Work? A Meta-analysis on the Effects of Coaching on Individual Level Outcomes in an Organizational Context, *The Journal of Positive Psychology, 14*. September.

> **To strengthen your network:**
>
> - **For people on whom you rely, *at all levels,* write unsolicited testimonials on LinkedIn, talk them up to others and offer to meet for a coffee.**
> - **Try a 3-D Greeting: Smile, Eye Contact and a genuinely given positive comment. People remember how you made them feel, and can sniff out 'fakery'.**
> - **Distil your goals and current projects to just a few words or phrases, so it's easier for others to remember and think of you when they hear connected ideas.**

Emotional intelligence sounds too 'airy-fairy' for some of my clients. However, when they look at what it boils down to – coping skills, stress management and self-regulation – they see the need. People with the type of confidence worth emulating have this type of both self-awareness and other-awareness – the key components of emotional intelligence. As we move further into the 21st century, these skills will become all the more critical for humans. Emotional intelligence is one of the few things that computers can't easily replicate.

Other people are also concerned about outdated versions of confidence, and how self-awareness and emotional intelligence should be a part of a new definition. For example, Douglas Morrison showed frustration with the much lauded 'competency-based framework' in many organisations.

According to Morrison, most employers only reward people who are visibly doing well on a certain set of *narrow* metrics. These 'competent' employees get bigger projects and larger teams to manage. Plus, they get more budget to oversee. It's all because they're working well to highly visible and *easily measurable* metrics.

However, as he points out, they couldn't do any of it without their more socially skilled, but supposedly less 'competent' colleagues. They're the ones who fix communication problems when tensions between teams emerge, or things don't go to plan – which invariably they often don't. Identifying with this challenge, Morrison sighs:

> *That's when I need those high EQ people at the front. Let's get clearer definitions of competence, even those skills often ignored or hard to measure. If we don't recognise the value of those soft skills as a key part of competence, we're missing a trick.*

So why does Morrison think we don't value those aspects self-awareness and emotional intelligence enough? As a long-time supporter of diversity in the workplace, he smiles and replies: 'Quite often, it's part of the male-dominated sectors in which I operate. Since these are the skills we see women being particularly good at, they are undervalued.'

Amanda Jones also agrees a new definition of confidence could reduce the way non-status quo members are doubly disadvantaged. She explains:

> *We tell women to know their place, but then demand they speak aggressively in litigation. We have to change what we value more. For me it's about courage. Who tells the hard truths, who asks the insightful questions and has difficult conversations? Who not only speaks with passion but knows how to listen?*

Jones is comfortable in her self-awareness and welcomes a rebranding of confidence saying it's overdue. She notes:

> *If the definition includes being comfortable talking on topics you know little about, I don't want to be 'confident'. I have my own internal standards, and need to be able to live with myself. If that first version is success, I don't want it.*

To an outsider not unpicking what confidence means, Jones' answer could be misinterpreted as 'under-confident'. After all, she's rejecting the *status quo ideal* of confidence – the willingness to weigh in on any topic of which you feel strongly yet may not understand. However, she is redefining *confidence on her terms* – which I would suggest in itself is a type of confidence. Jones' advice to those consistently overlooked? 'Go somewhere else. Go for an organisation that values your version of confidence.' She explains:

> *We get far more questions from millennials about our Corporate Social Responsibility policies, our Pro-Bono work, working abroad and equality and diversity. People are redefining success differently to previous generations. The legal sector originally couldn't advertise, now selling is fundamental. Everyone is a potential customer, so teams have to be better at sales. That's why confidence is more prized than ever, whether rightly or wrongly.*

So, does this mean the industry could shift towards a push for confidence or breakdown further between the 'confident finders' and the 'competent minders and grinders' as she calls them? Jones thinks so and says, 'We could get to a place where we have a discrete sales team, perhaps even without legal degrees.'

However, for Jones a re-branded confidence will still have to evolve to include listening skills – a strong skill amongst the self-aware and emotionally intelligent. She explains: 'EQ will be so much more important. Confidence will also be about your ability to read what another person needs and concisely tell them how you can help satisfy that need.' Her unsolicited mention of emotional intelligence confirms what others have said about the value in redefining confidence.

Similarly, Barbara-Ann King, an MD who led the Female Client Group at Barclays, eschews traditional 'confidence' in her recruiting. Instead, she hires for two things: empathy and the ability to clearly explain detailed investments in a non-patronising way. These are again hallmarks of those comfortable in their competence, but with an addition of self-awareness as opposed to the historic version of confidence. In her interview, King was clear – the guys she already had on her team before creating the Female Client Group were great:

> But they were also more likely to err on the side of brash salesmanship. By comparison, our new hires were as likely to come from legal or accountancy backgrounds. When handling clients, they erred on the side of: 'Here's an article or an event I think you'd like, you know where I am when you're ready to talk about your investments.'

As an MD, King, at the helm of building a Female Client Group, was delighted with the team of men and women she'd brought together. In fact, she was routinely thanked by men who appreciated being rewarded based on *their skills*, not just by their hours at a desk or how visible they were in a team meeting. However, when she chose to leave, she realised the culture she'd created for her team was more of a bubble in a broader, less collegiate organisational culture. Dispiritingly, after she left, some of the men and all of the women she'd recruited also left within just a few months.

She'd occasionally meet those who remained longer than she had, in subsequent years. They'd cite the amount of bravado they felt expected to display as a reason they ultimately chose to leave. After her departure, people didn't feel valued for their competence as solely evidenced by their results. King remembers:

> One woman, in particular, was quiet and easy to overlook unless you looked at her stellar results. It was frustrating for me to hear the only fault leaders now found with her was: 'You need to make internal people more aware of you!' This was galling. Let's be honest, her clients – the people bringing in their money to invest were very aware of her!

King's frustration stems from the fact that client satisfaction, and in this case, the amount they invest, should be all that counts. What shouldn't matter was how visible this stellar performer was to her senior colleagues internally.

King reports this former colleague left the industry as a whole. The woman eventually went into education, potentially a field that better recognised this type of emotionally intelligent confidence. To add to King's point, the woman's new employer is now benefiting from her *skill at getting people to part with their money*. Ironically this is a skill most businesses would love to grow yet may be too focused on traditional confidence to actually notice, let alone reward.

For some interviewees, a key criterion of self-aware confidence should be putting a task *above* your own ego. That means leading a course of action you may not get credit for but *will have a bigger impact* – even if it's years down the line. Many of my coaching clients have often been in this 'task first, ego second' position, usually by turning around poor performers no manager before them could or even wanted to handle. King identified with this and explains:

> We need to move beyond simply rewarding the 'loudest
> duck'. It takes real confidence and grit to manage a difficult
> team member successfully, help get an atypical candidate
> through a tough promotion process or turn around a failing
> team. These wins all require confidence but don't get
> rewarded as often as the person who gives a single good
> speech and we then praise for being 'confident'.

King's point is apt as these versions of confidence also require a willingness to highlight *other* people. Instead, as it gets closer to promotion time, employees often visibly try to gather credit for projects, *even for things they didn't do*, to prove their leadership skills. As King explains, 'They'll confidently talk about their "invaluable contribution" when they've played a minimal role. Instead, we should reward those who played a significant role, but did it with less of a song and dance.' This is maddening to King, who saw this over her years in financial services. As she says:

> We'll throw someone a difficult colleague and ask them
> to clean up the mess. But we don't define the person who
> turns them around, as confident. Indeed, they're doing the
> quiet work, requiring a steely determination, but they're
> mainly doing it behind the scenes where it's less likely to be
> rewarded. If the manager succeeds in turning them around,
> it's the difficult colleague who gets noticed. It's not the
> person who facilitated the transformation on the quiet.

> **In discussion with your boss, find out:**
>
> - **Who they've promoted in the past and who likes to work with them.**
> - **How long previous direct reports stayed and where they went next.**
> - **If they've promoted people known for their competence or confidence.**

King's observation reminds me of a middle manager, Sirita, whom I coached for several years in a drug discovery company. In a team shake-up, she was given responsibility for line-managing a difficult underperformer, Jack. Interestingly, 'problems with Jack' had also come up in sessions with *other* clients who also had to interact with him. Jack's tenure however meant he couldn't easily be forced out despite his lack of willingness to do the work assigned to him.

In another organisation, I suspect Jack would have been shown the door much earlier. Instead Jack was passed from one manager to another until he was assigned to Sirita. 'Handling Jack' found its way into many of our coaching sessions. Sirita didn't give up, whereas other managers we'd deem as more confident had, pushing Jack from pillar to post. Eventually we did find ways Sirita could manage him better – something everyone noticed.

Oddly enough, I know Sirita would still not be someone senior management would describe as obviously confident. However, as a mother of two young boys who knew how to misbehave, Sirita knew she could try to turn around Jack's behaviour. Doing so led her to a long-overdue promotion. Putting aside ego, to know you can support and potentially transform a floundering colleague is a type of confidence we need more of in the workplace – and one we'd be smart to reward.

Getting to that right outcome is vital for us all, no matter the industry. For example, some in the legal sector spoke of how frustrating it is to see clients reject technically gifted lawyers who they know do a great job for their clients. Too often, clients opt for a perhaps more egocentric and aggressive, yet less competent lawyer.

As Neil Stevenson explained: 'You can have a poor lawyer sometimes quite bullishly get a client or the bench on side. It means we can default to a public, confrontational and adversarial system, even when the situation doesn't always need it to be.' His comment relates particularly well to litigation, where the only result that matters is what happens in a court; a forum where pantomime, performance and even hyper-aggression *are often expected*.

Litigation is the glamourous, Hollywood version of the legal sector. As Stevenson explains: 'Unfortunately, it's not just the court system that operates to these assumptions; it's all those who are buying these services as well: employers and clients.' His comment reminds me when people say they'll 'have their day in court', it suggests an upcoming battle, not an impending compromise.

This tendency is dismaying. Many disagreements would be better off being resolved *before* they get to a court, something with which Stevenson agrees. He elaborates:

> *Legal mediation plays to a much wider skill set. You still*
> *have to be confident with people, but it's confidence based*
> *on emotional intelligence, not assertiveness. If there was a*
> *shift to mediation, there would be more jobs that would suit*
> *a wider range of people.*

This is an interesting observation. It also suggests the status quo know exactly what they are doing by limiting confidence to behaviours only they readily display, and therefore should be rewarded for. When mediation isn't useful, Stevenson explains:

> *Even then, you still don't have to fight it out in front of an*
> *audience for it to count. For example, expert adjudication*
> *within the legal sector often focuses on a finely-honed*
> *written argument in which the judge makes their decisions*
> *alone. This piece is largely written and doesn't require a*
> *screaming match between two parties.*

When compared to court showmanship, expert adjudication again is something that doesn't play to confidence *as we expect to see it*. However, it does rely on an internal certainty the lawyer is correct in their knowledge, interpretation and communication skills and can be persuasive based on *those skills*. Could this be part of the new confidence? Stevenson explains:

> *In law we expect confidence to be demonstrated*
> *adversarially. But it takes as much confidence to approach*
> *someone who's offended you and explain the impact it*
> *had to create a long-term solution. Perhaps even more*
> *confidence than average, because that's a tricky subject! It's*
> *probably easier to start a 'fist-fight', which, he laughs: 'is*
> *where many men started out'.*

Stevenson explains the downside of focusing on that version of confidence when talking about the law. This ultimately affects how many more people might succeed in the field if the definition of confidence was updated. He says:

> *If you tell everyone that to succeed in this industry, you're going to be judged by how you play in a boxing ring, you'll skew who enters the field. It fundamentally affects what behaviours get rewarded. If success in this field was instead down to who gets a good result for everyone, we'd have a completely different set of behaviours and leaders.*

TWO: COURAGE OF YOUR CONVICTIONS

When people talked about confident behaviours, many mentioned the integrity required to show the courage of your convictions. For example, while it may not be easy, leaving an exploitative job for better opportunities elsewhere takes confidence. Others will go a step further to start something *on their own*. Leaving an employer to *start your own business* or experiment with tricky roles is another way people, and particularly, the non-status quo, demonstrate confidence. In both cases, standing by their ethical code can take courage. However, the inclusion of this type of *integrity* into our definition takes us back to the meaning behind the original Latin term, as it's synonymous with *honesty.*

While embracing risks, such as job changes, has long been equated with confidence, *context* is invaluable. It helps us understand how much more comprehensive our definition could be if we go beyond the platitude of 'believe in oneself'. Indeed, believing in oneself is something with which even the *least* competent people can identify, so should only be where we start – not where we end. Acting on the courage of your convictions is fundamentally much harder than 'self-belief', so should be much more highly valued. Going further, context also helps us understand *why* certain people can more easily demonstrate old-school confidence simply by taking a highly-praised risk.

I'm reminded of Greg, a client credited at his office with being 'hugely confident' because he'd taken an extended sabbatical to climb Mt. Kilimanjaro. By his own admission, mountain climbing is most often only open to those with the financial resources and sufficient 'free time' to train to undertake such challenges. Indeed, as they keep pulling bodies off Mt. Kilimanjaro (or leaving them as the case may be), it's a good reminder that confidence and preparation aren't synonyms, and that just because you have the funds to attempt it doesn't mean it's a good idea.

By comparison, Greg had colleagues who had set up kitchen-table businesses in their free time, risking their own money. However, no one ever credited *these* people with confidence. Notably, I routinely hear the term 'lifestyle business' used pejoratively when describing female business owners.

When I wrote my second book, *Female Breadwinners*, I encountered many self-employed men. None would have identified themselves as running 'lifestyle businesses' even if their wife was financially keeping the family afloat. It's a demeaning term, particularly as *we all work to fund a lifestyle* for ourselves, our families and the people we employ in those businesses.

We need to look wider as to what 'willingness to take a risk' actually means. I've coached many women through the process of being the first person on their team to ask to work two days a week at home. Alternatively, I've worked with others on negotiating promotions *before* they go on maternity leave. In those cases, they were acting on the courage of their convictions and showing real confidence.

Just initiating these conversations creates real risks in how that request will be received by their boss and colleagues. Yet we'd *rarely* credit these women for being 'confident' for these challenging moves. In fact, fathers taking their legal allocation of paternity leave are showing real courage, as it goes against the workplace norms. In both cases, just starting these conversations requires the 'courage of their convictions'; part of our new definition of confidence.

Another way people show confidence is by experimenting in 'intrapreneurship' – that is, starting something new within their *current* organisations. Based on the work I've done with clients; I know these kinds of changes are available to far more people than we realise. In many of the people I met, this type of confidence was fed by the courage of their convictions.

As a former MD within private banking at Barclays, listening to her clients to follow the courage of her convictions was how King knew to set up the dedicated Female Client Group team. She noticed an increasing number of clients asking 'Why do I never get to speak with a woman about my investments?' King knew that by the time clients are complaining, you've missed a trick. Following the courage of her convictions, she eventually got CEO buy-in to create the team. They went on to perform 300% better on new client acquisition than other divisions with the same business.

However, listening to how clients talk about these qualities is not something King thinks many industries do particularly well. She focuses on one of the most useful, but least exciting ways to describe a competent team member.

She smiles and says: 'When you talk to clients, they will tell you they want the "safe pair of hands" managing their money. That makes sense as it's *their money* we're talking about! They'll quickly see through a presentation that "wows" if it can't deliver.'

However, King thinks the 'client-focused approach' most businesses say they live by doesn't affect their hiring or promoting patterns. King observes:

> *We'll spend millions on client entertaining, improving our technology to be user-friendly and branding for websites – all for our clients. But we never ask them about what they want in our people. We just put team members in front of them and expect it to all work out somehow.*

King showed confidence in understanding she didn't know it all, so needed to listen more to what clients wanted. This is a mark of a competence-first outlook. Indeed, there's a hubris in *assuming* 'we know what our clients need'.

Listening, however, makes hiring beyond our personal biases much trickier and time-consuming – something most time-pressed senior leaders want to avoid. For King, the only type of confidence that matters is the confidence *clients place in her*; believing in the service they'll get.

King's view on this issue was no doubt affected by the customer-centred research she did before setting up the Female Client Group. However, it's probably also influenced by how dismaying it must have been to see that initiative mostly fizzle away after she left. She observes: 'We acted on client's advice when we set up. So allowing all of those hard-won female private bankers to leave so easily after my own departure and not addressing what that said about the culture meant the company went *against* client wishes.'

For some people, leaving paid employment to set up *on their own* as a business owner is the only way to follow the courage of their convictions. As Chair of Women's Enterprise Scotland, this is an area Lynne Cadenhead knows well. For her members, choosing self-employment should be directly attributed to confidence, as it's *tough*. She comments:

> *For most of my life, my confidence was based on external validation – winning medals, earning prizes, getting high grades. But when you enter entrepreneurship, there's little external validation – particularly anything positive in the early days. You'll need inner confidence to take things forward. You either sell the product, or you don't. Sales are a type of validation, but not like you're used to. No one pats you on the head, and there is no boss to encourage you further, only a Board who focus on what's not going well.*

To get through this, you need to know the value of what you are selling (competence). Only that will translate into a personal sense of confidence, but that is spread unevenly across the developed world. Indeed, amongst the working population, women run their own businesses at an unprecedented rate in Canada (15%), the US (11%), Australia (9%) and in the Netherlands (9%).[295] This is compared to not even 6% in the UK.

In my experience setting up an e-learning gaming company in a technology incubator space in Edinburgh, it was widely known how gruelling Board meetings were for leaders. They were a real test of confidence. The prize of getting through a Board meeting as a competent leader? No big pat on the back, just another round of cash to continue and work even harder the very next day. Cadenhead observes:

> *When you realise how little of venture capital funding goes to female or BAME-led businesses, it grinds you down. It affects your confidence to take things forward. But it isn't you or even what you are selling that's wrong – it's the system that is wrong.*

Following the courage of your convictions past systems that unevenly reward people is what initially draws many into entrepreneurship. According to the Department for Business, Energy and Industrial Strategy, just 5% of small to medium-sized businesses in the UK are led by BAME people.[296] Of self-employed women in the UK however, 9% are from BAME backgrounds, a rate that is increasing.[297]

Uviebinené explains how both push and pull factors are vital to understanding expanding rates of entrepreneurship amongst African Americans in the US.[298] In our discussion, Uviebinené says:

> *Push factors for Black people in work is about not feeling you can bring your authentic self to work. Any work you do will not likely be as well recognised as if it had come from someone from a different background. It's the daily push of microaggressions that just pile up.*

In her insightful book, Uviebinené discusses the daily microaggressions that Black people suffer in the workplace. There are hundreds of variations but include patronising comments from 'curious' colleagues touching their hair to 'compliments' about the articulacy of their speech.

---

295. Alison Rose Review of Female Entrepreneurship, 2018.
296. YouGov Sept 2019 Leadership of Small and medium Enterprises.
297. Business in the Community & Race for Opportunity 2015 Race for Opportunity Factsheet: BAME Women and Enterprise.
298. Fairlie, R. et al. 2015 Kaufman Index: Start Up Activity & National Trends, Kaufman Foundation.

However, pull factors are also at play, particularly for millennials. In our interview, Uviebinené notes:

> *Black millennials are more confident about their place in the world. They are spotting gaps in the market for services and products in which they've been overlooked for decades. Plus, we're seeing so many high-profile role models of people like us who are doing well. Role models highlight more options. Black women have greater confidence in their ability and might not want to wait around to see if they'll get ahead in a big corporate.*

Sasha Mooney completely identifies with the previously mentioned data on how Black people, particularly millennials, are establishing businesses at a faster pace than any other group. Like most Barristers at Law, Mooney is self-employed and observes:

> *I very rarely work with any Black professionals like myself, but I do see them set up on their own. Millennials are confident, but they're not willing to play the game they've seen their older relatives have to play in corporates. They're impatient with the pace of change, so they may as well establish businesses of their own. Yes, it's riskier, but they are more confident and optimistic.*

Kate Atkin, whose graduate work focuses on the imposter syndrome, saw a clear trend towards making the most of the learning inherent in entrepreneurship, and the requisite courage of their convictions, within her research. She says:

> *Entrepreneurs were the only ones I worked with who used the phrase 'Things that Didn't Work'. They didn't talk about 'failure' per se. I like that. We all need to be able to talk about what we've learned from our failures. How much more validating would it be for people to talk about experiments and experiences as 'Things that Didn't Work' and what I learned from that.*

Avoiding a steady employer may be risky to some. However, it is a risk worth taking for many given 'safer' workplaces have not historically rewarded non-status quo employees or remaining in them challenges your sense of integrity. If you have statistically had less chance of getting to the top, and that you feel *you have to compromise too much* to get there, you'll likely feel you have less to lose by leaving. Therefore, working for yourself is attractive, particularly if it means one less setting in which you have to justify your skill.

Having the courage of your convictions encompasses a willingness to talk about your near misses and mistakes. Realistically, you can only take that type of risk *if you know you'll be supported*. Because they've often been socialised to be humble in order to survive, for the non-status quo widening the definition of confidence to include this type of integrity and self-reflection makes confidence more recogniseable. It's authentic, as it requires owning both our wins but also our losses. Ultimately, this means a wider range of people can empathise with the experience, as *we've all had both*.

Reem Hayati was driven by this integrity in her *values*. It gave her a sense she could get through any challenge. She showed her values by hiring two of the best-qualified candidates she could in the early days of her own tenure, both of whom happened to be Christian, for her Egyptian employer. Being a Muslim helps drives Hayati's actions, but it also *reassures* her she'll overcome any problems – beliefs many would term 'confidence'. She didn't expect her hiring choices to be as controversial as they turned out to be for her fellow Muslim colleagues. This highlighted the cultural mismatch she felt while there. She reflected:

> *For me, there's an overlap between faith and confidence.*
> *My faith drives me to live by my moral values. It also*
> *reminds me that even bad situations will improve and that I*
> *can get through anything.*

Getting to understand organisational culture is vital, and to do so you'll need to observe and ask questions, ideally *before* you start. Organisations have unique cultures; the 'way we do things here'. However, you'll also know each team often has its own sub-culture. Interviewing for a role in a completely new organisation, or indeed a new unit to where you are currently, can start to give you a sense of both cultures.

All interviews are a two-way street. For your sense of integrity, aim to get a sense of the culture you'd be entering, *before* you jump ship from where you are currently. It's better to ask questions, even if they give the interviewer pause for thought, than be in the role a few months, realising it's a terrible fit.

So back at the interview stage, ask the difficult questions. It will be tough to get straight answers but asking does two things: first, it shows you aren't afraid of having tough conversations and getting honest answers. Secondly, it shows that culture and progression matter to you. If they take that approach badly, you probably wouldn't have enjoyed it or progressed in any case. As Uviebinené aptly observes in our interview:

Bean bags and free drinks are meant to suggest fun, but 'fun' isn't a culture. For me, it's about fairness and being heard. At a basic level, if the interviewer talks over you, that will give you an indication of where things are headed.

As a hiring manager, if you are on the receiving end of these questions from an interviewee, don't judge the candidate as being 'difficult' or acting 'above their station'. Instead, recognise the candidate is doing their homework and being authentic as to what matters to them. They have integrity, are asking tough questions and know their value. Ironically, these are the same qualities you'd *want* them to display on your organisation's behalf.

When interviewing a boss or colleague before you accept a job on a new team, ask:

- **Can you tell me about some of your star performers?**
- **What made them stand out?**
- **Can you tell me about your own career trajectory?**
- **Where did the person who did this job before end up?**
- **Can you describe the boss or organisational culture in three words?**
- **What's valued here above all else?**

Kainaz Gazder also exemplifies the confidence in having tough conversations about challenges. Her experience also highlights a truism for us all. If someone is undermining your confidence at work, it could be *unintentional*. Gazder remembers when she told a senior manager the negative impact he was having on her. He routinely walked the floor, asking detailed questions and giving people a hard time if you couldn't give instantaneous answers. Gazder recalls:

After a few months of working for him, he asked me into his office asking how I was finding it all and I blurted out: 'You're the reason I hate coming to work every day!' We were both stunned as I couldn't believe I'd said it, and it probably wasn't what he expected to hear either! As soon as he recovered, he asked why. I shared all the examples I'd been storing up and how it made me feel. He responded that he'd no idea, so this was a lightbulb moment for us both.

Gazder, who stood by her integrity in that difficult moment, elaborates:

> *If you build self-awareness for someone without being*
> *rude or judgemental – you most often can turn them into*
> *a supporter. He talked about what he'd do specifically to*
> *change. He also said he'd ask for feedback again in a few*
> *months to see if he'd done enough.*

That displays a different type of confidence – versions we don't give enough credence to in our current definitions. In that moment Gazder used her integrity to not only give hard feedback, but *her boss* also showed confidence. First, he asked for feedback from a junior person. Upon receiving her less than glowing appraisal, he then had two options. He could ignore her or *more confidently* he could take her comments on board and adapt his behaviour accordingly to become a *better boss*.

No doubt partially as a result of this uncomfortable, yet honest exchange, Gazder now routinely asks for feedback from her direct reports. To her, the most confident people are the ones who ask for feedback, because it's not threatening. As Gazder points out: 'Feedback is a gift and simply a way to get better.'

Let's be honest, talking about problems is vital but intimidating for anyone. In conversation with Martin Donnan he highlighted the best leaders have to take on this profoundly uncomfortable space as *it's the only way to progress*. He drew an analogy to Apollo 1 in January 1967, the fatal spaceship launch test that cost three pilots their lives. It ultimately led to the improvements necessary to make the eventual successful human-crewed flight of Apollo 7, 18 months later in October 1968.

However, getting there required authenticity and the humility to accept they'd made fatal mistakes. NASA's task-focused and utterly 'confident in their ability' approach led to errors being made along the way to that first launch. In the run up to 1967, NASA was inexperienced in human-crewed flights. However, in an effort to meet over-ambitious goals set by President Kennedy for a human moon landing before the end of the 1960s, they rushed through shoddy design and workmanship.

During those 18 intervening months after the lethal fire, the team recognised they'd erred on the side of overconfidence. Instead, they should have been focused on being 'tough and competent'. That phrase marked the beginning of their new approach.

Rather than blame the failure on a series of technical glitches, Gene Kranz, the second Chief Flight Director, looked at their overconfidence as a relatively inexperienced team. His authentic and humble perspective makes this story relatively unique. Three days after the fatal incident, but *before* the Thompson committee found the exact technical fault, Kranz gave a speech to the entire team blaming an *organisational culture he had helped foster*. With the courage of his convictions and searing honesty Kranz explained to the team:

> *I don't know what (they'll) find was the cause, but I know*
> *what I find ... We are the cause! We were not ready! We*
> *did not do our job. We were rolling the dice, hoping that*
> *things would come together by launch day ... From this*
> *day forward, Flight Control will be known by two words:*
> *'Tough' and 'Competent'. Tough means we are forever*
> *accountable for what we do or what we fail to do ...*
> *Competent means we will never take anything for granted.*
> *We will never be found short in our knowledge and in our*
> *skills ... Somewhere, somehow, we screwed up. It could*
> *have been in design, build or test. Whatever it was, we*
> *should have caught it ... Every element of the program was*
> *in trouble and so were we ... Not one of us stood up and*
> *said, 'Dammit, stop!' When you leave this meeting today ...*
> *write 'Tough and Competent' on your blackboards. It will*
> *never be erased. Each day when you enter the room these*
> *words will remind you of the price paid by Grissom, White*
> *and Chaffee. These words are the price of admission to the*
> *ranks of Mission Control.*

In interviews with Kranz's peers, this integrity and focus on competence was considered *the turning point* for the whole programme. Indeed, it was potentially the only reason the nascent NASA programme was able to continue. It's assumed had the accident happened in space, they would *never* have known what exactly failed. At that early stage, that uncertainty would likely have shut down the entire NASA programme.

Certainly, that speech shows authenticity and even anger in its delivery. However, it fundamentally recognises confidence is not the end goal, competence is. It highlights the ultimate cost confidence can extract in terms of human life. Importantly, it recognises you won't get to the end result you need without primarily focusing on competence and a *better* definition of confidence.

Three: Going against the grain

The last part of our redefinition of confidence should be a willingness to challenge the status quo. This is something many leaders *say* they do, but what's notable is how confidence comes to the fore when looking at *who* is challenging 'business as usual'. Superficially, it's easier to do when you already have seniority than if you are an outsider. This 'inner circle status' protects you from significant repercussions. This again means we need to look at the context.

By comparison, if the non-status quo speaks 'truth to power', they will often find doors closed and themselves ostracised. They are marginalised simply because they don't have insider support. Case in point, walking into a meeting ostensibly for discussion, only to find the decision's already been taken, is familiar to many of my clients. However, that's not to say they don't challenge the status quo in *other* ways.

Reem Hayati certainly is a good example of someone who challenged the status quo. She worked for an Egyptian company during the time of the political revolution in January 2011. Virtually overnight, sales visits were unofficially stopped due to safety concerns. However, Hayati explained: 'But our targets weren't any lower, so we still had to hit them.

However, I knew I couldn't ask my sales team to go out on the streets, if I wasn't prepared to go *myself*. So, I made the sales visits with my colleagues.' This was a very confident move, and not one taken by her peers in other divisions. Indeed, it wasn't even something she normally did *before* the demonstrations broke out. However, it earned her accolates from her CEO.

As we've seen, much research links female leadership on Boards to higher than average financial returns. There is, however, much less clarity as to *why* this happens. Perhaps it is related to the way some women like Hyati challenge the status quo of *what matters* when leaders make decisions.

One study suggests female Board directors use 'complex moral reasoning' much more frequently than their male counterparts in decision-making. By comparison, male Board directors were much more likely to use either 'normative' or 'personal interest' in their decision-making.[299] Simply put, the research found male Board members more likely to go with convention to secure their *individual status*.

---

299. Bart, C. and McQueen, G. 2013 Why Women Make Better Directors, *International Journal of Business Governance & Ethics* 8(1): 93–99.

That's perhaps normal for the status quo, but *not what matters* the most to some. That aforementioned study of more than 600 corporate Board directors found female business directors are more likely to consider *the rights* of others and to take a cooperative approach to decision-making.

The same research found women prioritised arriving at a fair and moral decision that benefits all parties, more frequently than their male counterparts. They did this not only to make sound decisions but also to elicit support for *their* preferred course of action.

Compromise is something the non-status quo *have to use*, simply because they can't force things through via their majority status. They've never had the majority rule. The reality is they need more support from others to get their ideas and efforts enacted. Interestingly, the study's authors observed that female directors also engaged more effectively with the complex *social issues* increasingly confronting corporations.

These findings help address the 'why' when determining why diverse teams outperform monocultural teams. They have different ways to make decisions based on the nuances of what matters to them. Based on this research, these preferences often go *against the organisational grain*. Clearly, it's not any one person's job to be the 'conscience' of any group. However, the fact women take a wider view lens, something I hear routinely from male leaders, only helps teams. This is a way they confidently challenge the status quo thinking, and that challenge has real value in the way it seems to temper *overconfidence*.

In preparation for meetings:

- **Keep a list comparing your performance in meetings; 'how you felt before' vs. 'how you felt after' for self-reflection and learning what you did went well and what needs improving.**
- **Suggest an unattributed 'Post-It Brainstorming session' to focus on potential solutions to a challenge. It helps avoid bias and generates a wider variety of ideas.**
- **Ask under-confident people to chair or take a bigger role at presentations, don't ask 'Who'd like to present?'**

A different study of over 1600 of the largest firms in the U.S between 1998 -2013 found having female board members actually *tempered overconfidence* in male CEOs[300]. It improved overall decision making for the company, particularly in male dominated fields where overconfidence was more prevalent.

In fact that same study found female board representation reduced the negative impact of the 2007 -2009 financial crisis on firm performance. The male CEO's that reported to a mixed gender board were less likely to adopt the same type of aggressive strategies that eventually made their competitors *more vulnerable* to the crisis.

By comparison, the firms without female Board membership suffered a greater drop in performance on these measures. The way board diversity can limit overconfidence in status quo leaders is compelling.

Another way confidence shines in challenging the status quo is when we decide for *whose* benefit we'll use our skills. Researchers have noted that women will concede less and negotiate harder on behalf of others *than they will for themselves.*[301]

Women downplayed their negotiation skills verbally to others, not because of an actual lack of negotiating skills, but to comply with the social norms we expect. It's not surprising this differs when they're asked to promote the accomplishments *of a colleague*. Women consistently talk up colleagues more than speak up on their own behalf.[302]

This research found the non-status quo saved their efforts in order to benefit others and even held back when asked explicitly about themselves. This is about *where and for whom people choose to put their efforts*. These choices are based on how they've been conditioned, but go against the grain of a selfish type of confidence we've come to expect from the status quo. However, here the challenge to the status quo is in the way non-status quo members often *put others above themselves*, something that seems antithetical in most organisations.

Another way to go against the grain is by violating norms and challenging 'what's expected' for your group. Violating these norms can be deeply uncomfortable, no matter your background. Let's be clear, it isn't just a challenge for non-status quo members.

---

300. Chen, J et al 2019 Why female board representation matters: The role of female directors in reducing male CEO overconfidence, *Journal of Empirical Finance*, 53: 70-90

301. Amanatullah, E. T. and Morris, M. W. 2010 Negotiating Gender Roles: Gender Differences in Assertive Negotiating Are Mediated by Women's Fear of Backlash and Attenuated when Negotiating on Behalf of Others, *Journal of Personality and Social Psychology* 98: 256–267.
302. Moss-Racusin, C. and Rudman, L. A. 2010 Disruptions in Women's Self-promotion: The Backlash Avoidance Model, *Psychology of Women Quarterly*, 34: 186–202.

For example, I've known plenty of status quo men who won't tell colleagues they don't love football or would rather be at home with their kids than going out for yet another round of drinks. We simply need to recognise more examples of what 'going against the grain' means.

For Kainaz Gazder, her experiences in Japan taught her a new lesson about confidence. Gazder explains: 'It is only recently women, and then mostly unmarried women, entered the Japanese workplace at all.' Some colleagues, particularly those from Western countries, may initially see these women as lacking obvious confidence simply because they don't openly self-promote.

However, Gazder sees her Japanese female colleagues as very confident. Instead they display confidence by going against the grain *to even work outside the home*.

For many Asian countries where Gazder has had colleagues, a woman working after marriage can be interpreted as a mark against the family she's joined. It almost suggests publicly there isn't enough money to support her at home.

This willingness to challenge strong societal conventions should count as we widen our definition of confidence. Again, as we've consistently seen, it's all about context. As uncomfortable as going against societal norms can be, getting *through that discomfort* will only grow a type of confidence we should value more.

Interestingly, one of the best ways to get through the discomfort is having *something to blame* for feeling ill at ease. In one fascinating study, female university students were asked to write an essay promoting a person's achievements. Half were asked to write about someone else and half asked to write about themselves. It was only when the women writing about their own accomplishments were distracted by a noise machine did they find it easy to write the essay.

Simply put, writing about how great they were wasn't comfortable. Oddly enough, however, the women were able to relax into the task if told there was a broken alarm in the room that emitted random noises – that also made them uncomfortable. This alarm was a distraction and not a pleasant one; it increased their heart rate, nervousness and anxiety. But it meant they subconsciously blamed any discomfort they felt in the self-promotion task, to the distracting noises they heard when penning the essay!

Amazingly, their compositions were judged much more favourably by independent assessors than those who'd had no distraction.[303] This highlights how uncomfortable self-promotion can actually be when you are socialised *against it*. It's also a reminder to not equate a lack of self-promotion as a lack of confidence. Not 'bigging' yourself up is merely a way to stay comfortable in a world where self-promotion *violates the norms* in which many non-status quo people were raised.

As evidence of the power of going against the grain and its impact on confidence, the renowned psychologist Csikszentmihalyi uncovered a related dimension. Going against the grain means you often *elude* traditional gender-role stereotyping which is a unique advantage.

He found:

> *'When tests of masculinity/femininity are given to young people, over and over, one finds that creative and talented girls are more dominant and tougher than other girls, and creative boys are more sensitive and less aggressive than their male peers ...'*

Csikszentmihalyi continued:

> *'A psychologically androgynous person in effect doubles his or her repertoire of responses and can interact with the world in terms of a much more abundant and varied spectrum of opportunities.'[304]*

This is important as it moves people past their *expectations* of certain groups. For example, we expect to see in the non-status quo 'agreeability' and 'courteousness'. It is as if any positive treatment they receieve is something they've been 'gifted'. Similarly, *we expect* amongst the status quo more selfish behaviours such as 'self-promotion' and 'willingness to speak up'. All four attributes have some value, but the latter are far more frequently rewarded than the former.

Building on this, evidence shows reframing the word 'negotiations' to simply 'asking for things for yourself' encourages women to engage in these discussions much more readily than being told they'd have to 'negotiate'.[305]

303. Smith, J. and Huntoon, M. 2014 Women's Bragging Rights: Overcoming Modesty Norms to Facilitate Women's Self-Promotion, *Psychology of Women Quarterly*, 38(4): 447–459.

304. Csikszentmihalyi, M. 1996 *Creativity: Flow and the Psychology of Discovery and Invention*, HarperCollins, New York, p. 71.

305. Small, D. A., Gelfand, M., Babcock, L. and Gettman, H. 2007 Who Goes to the Bargaining Table? The Influence of Gender and Framing on the Initiation of Negotiation, *Journal of Personality and Social Psychology* 4: 600–613.

University students played a game for which they'd be paid between $3–$10. The experimenter offered everyone just $3 as their payment. Mentioning that 'most people *negotiate* for more' wasn't enough to get women to ask for more money – though it did encourage the men to request more money.

It was only when participants were told 'most people *ask* for more' did women raise their game. That simple change in *terminology* increased women's willingness to seek more money. This simple word change may seem ridiculous, but is our incredulous reaction to the terminology change so strong partially because we assume negotiations have a clear winner and a loser?

In truth, any good negotiator knows that *both* sides need to come away feeling they've got what they need, if not more than what they expected. This is particularly vital if they want to have an *ongoing relationship*. Ongoing relationships are important as in reality, that's the way most businesses earn continued work and referrals.

I'm not advocating sound machines or a ban on the word 'negotiate'. However, these examples highlight just how uncomfortable it is for some people, most often from non-status quo groups, to self-promote – the mark of confidence as we've traditionally defined it.

It's also why we shouldn't assume someone's lack of 'selling' their skills equates to a lack of ambition or credibility. When people do go against the grain in ways that violate the social norms in which they've been raised, indeed, to work *amongst the status quo*, they are demonstrating *real* confidence.

Final words

If you value *delivery*, a lack of confidence shouldn't hold anyone back. After all, how much does boldly speaking, claiming credit or ease in politicking, really benefit *any* of us? Organisations, and society progress further when we reward competence *above* confidence. The next time you hear someone label another as 'not confident' ask: What does confidence look like to you and are those the behaviours we really need *more* of?

As we've seen, it's the ultimate con job to assume confidence is the panacea that fixes everything. It assumes the problem is with *you*, and not affected by *how* we define and reward confidence. The truth is confidence is highly contextual – something we don't talk about enough. Without taking context into account when we talk about confidence, we will forever have a system unfairly rewarding some while penalising others. We erroneously assume confidence is a zero-sum game, you either have it or you don't.

In the end, if we redefined confidence it would fundamentally shift what we value. Plus, it would equalise the playing field far more than unconscious bias training or any vanilla statements about how much an organisation 'values diversity' even when continuing to promote the status quo.

Beyond that, it would force organisations to recognise what behaviours they are *really rewarding* when they hire and promote people. It would likely also highlight which skills or insights they're missing. All in all, the biggest gains would be a truly competent workforce where actions speak louder than words and *that's* worth feeling confident about.

About the Author

Dr Suzanne Doyle-Morris has over two decades of experience advising companies on culture change around gender balance. This was inspired by her PhD from the University of Cambridge - focusing on the experiences of women working in male-dominated fields. As a sought-after event speaker, Suzanne has spoken at over 200 corporate, industry bodies and network events, in Europe, the UK and in North America via both live presentations and webinars.

Suzanne is accredited by the International Coach Federation to the Professional Certified Coach standard and has coached professionals for over 2500 hours. Suzanne has featured in both national broadcast and print media features. Before this book, Suzanne previously wrote two books based on the experiences of successful professional women: *Beyond the Boys' Club: Strategies for Achieving Career Success as a Woman Working in a Male Dominated Fields* and *Female Breadwinners: How They Make Relationships Work and Why They're the Future of the Modern Workforce.*

You can get in touch or see more at both www.inclusiq.com and her YouTube channel at Dr Suzanne Doyle-Morris, inclusiq

Lightning Source UK Ltd.
Milton Keynes UK
UKHW041553240321
380880UK00002BA/181

9 780956 268822